FIVE REPUBLICS AND ONE TRADITION

Like many countries around the world, Chile is undergoing a constitutional moment when the nature of democracy and its political and legal institutions are being challenged. Senior Chilean legal scholar Pablo Ruiz-Tagle provides an historical analysis of evolution, change and democratic crisis in the present context focused on Chilean constitutionalism. He offers a comparative analysis of the organization and function of government, the structure of rights and the main political agents that participated in each stage of Chilean constitutional history. Chile is a powerful case study of a Latin American country that has gone through several threats to its democracy, but that has once again followed a moderate path to rebuild its constitutional republican tradition. Not only the first comprehensive study of Chilean constitutional history in the English language from the nineteenth-century to the present day, this book is also a powerful defence of democratic values.

PABLO RUIZ-TAGLE is Dean and Professor of both Constitutional Law and Introduction to Law at the University of Chile. After studying at the University of Chile, and obtaining his doctorate in law at Yale University, he has lectured in Chile and abroad and published several books. He is also advisor to the Chilean Congress and other institutions on constitutional matters.

CAMBRIDGE STUDIES IN LAW AND SOCIETY

Founded in 1997, Cambridge Studies in Law and Society is a hub for leading scholarship in socio-legal studies. Located at the intersection of law, the humanities, and the social sciences, it publishes empirically innovative and theoretically sophisticated work on law's manifestations in everyday life: from discourses to practices, and from institutions to cultures. The series editors have longstanding expertise in the interdisciplinary study of law, and welcome contributions that place legal phenomena in national, comparative, or international perspective. Series authors come from a range of disciplines, including anthropology, history, law, literature, political science, and sociology.

Series Editors

Mark Fathi Massoud, *University of California, Santa Cruz*

Jens Meierhenrich, *London School of Economics and Political Science*

Rachel E. Stern, *University of California, Berkeley*

A list of books in the series can be found at the back of this book.

FIVE REPUBLICS AND ONE TRADITION

A History of Constitutionalism in Chile 1810–2020

Pablo Ruiz-Tagle

University of Chile

Translated by Ana Luisa Goldsmith

CAMBRIDGE
UNIVERSITY PRESS

University Printing House, Cambridge CB2 8BS, United Kingdom

One Liberty Plaza, 20th Floor, New York, NY 10006, USA

477 Williamstown Road, Port Melbourne, VIC 3207, Australia

314–321, 3rd Floor, Plot 3, Splendor Forum, Jasola District Centre,
New Delhi – 110025, India

103 Penang Road, #05–06/07, Visioncrest Commercial, Singapore 238467

Cambridge University Press is part of the University of Cambridge.

It furthers the University's mission by disseminating knowledge in the pursuit of
education, learning, and research at the highest international levels of excellence.

www.cambridge.org
Information on this title: www.cambridge.org/9781108835312
DOI: 10.1017/9781108883610

First published 2021

A catalogue record for this publication is available from the British Library.

Library of Congress Cataloging-in-Publication Data
Names: Ruiz-Tagle Vial, Pablo, author. | Goldsmith, Ana Luisa, translator.
Title: Five republics and one tradition : a history of constitutionalism in Chile, 1810–2020 /
Pablo Ruiz-Tagle, Professor of Constitutional Law, Universidad de Chile, Yale Law School
LLM and JSD ; Ana Luisa Goldsmith, translator.
Other titles: Cinco repúblicas y una tradición. English
Description: Cambridge, United Kingdom ; New York, NY : Cambridge University Press,
2021. | Series: Cambridge studies in law and society | Includes bibliographical references
and index.
Identifiers: LCCN 2021024594 (print) | LCCN 2021024595 (ebook) | ISBN 9781108835312
(hardback) | ISBN 9781108883610 (ebook)
Subjects: LCSH: Constitutional history – Chile. | Dictatorship – Chile – History. | BISAC:
LAW / General | LAW / General
Classification: LCC KHF2919 .R8513 2021 (print) | LCC KHF2919 (ebook) | DDC
342.8302/9–dc23
LC record available at https://lccn.loc.gov/2021024594
LC ebook record available at https://lccn.loc.gov/2021024595

ISBN 978-1-108-83531-2 Hardback

CONTENTS

TABLES

INTRODUCTION

This book does not pursue mere academic speculation. Today in Chile, many people are claiming their rights, criticizing the lack of legitimacy of governmental institutions, and demanding more political and social involvement. Popular support for both the government and the opposition has declined simultaneously. Our political environment is full of unresolved conflicts. Our institutional framework perpetuates inequality, while the economy grows modestly, in the midst of an unfavorable international climate.

In this strained environment, many people and groups encourage, on the one hand, an escalation of citizen demands and expectations, and, on the other, resistance to change, and they yearn for taking strong measures against popular demands for justice. These disturbing political realities force us to reflect deeply upon the meaning of our republican tradition. For this reason, we think it is important to direct this study towards the structure of our rights, the organization of our political institutions, and the people as agents in each historical period. If this exploration is successful, it might contribute to a better understanding of our history and also help to improve our design for the structures of our future coexistence.

This investigation draws inspiration from Alphonse de Lamartine's *History of the Girondists*, a text which many highlight as one of the most influential in nineteenth-century Chile. In this work, with unequaled eloquence, Lamartine describes the factions and transformations undergone by ideas and ways of living during moments of upheaval and change, moments of social and political revolution. While describing the parties that sat in the Assembly during that revolutionary period in France at the end of the eighteenth century, Lamartine says:

> The Assembly was made up of unequal portions of three elements; the constitutionalists, who formed the aristocratic liberty and moderate monarchy party; the Girondists, the party of the movement, sustained until the Revolution fell into their hands; the Jacobins, the party of the people, and of philosophy in action; the first arrangement and transition, the second boldness and intrigue, the third fanaticism and devotion. Of these last two parties the Jacobin was not the most hostile to the king. The aristocracy and the clergy destroyed, that party had no repugnance to the throne; it possessed in a high degree the instinct of the unity of power; it was not the Jacobins who first demanded war, and they were not the first who uttered the word republic, but it was them who uttered and often repeated the word dictatorship. The word republic appertained to Brissot and the Girondists. If the Girondists, on their coming into the Assembly, had united with the constitutional party in order to save the constitution by moderate measures, and the Revolution by not urging it into war, they would have saved their party and controlled the throne. The honesty in which their leader was deficient was also wanting in their conduct – they were all intrigue. They made themselves the agitators in an assembly of which they might have been the statesmen. They had not confidence in the republic, but feigned it. In revolutions sincere characters are the only skilful characters. It is glorious to die the victim of a faith: it is pitiful to die the dupe of one's ambition.
> (Lamartine 1847: 209, Book 6; English 221–222 book 6, rev. March 14, 2016, available at: https://archive.org/stream/history girondist01lama/historygirondist01lama_djvu.txt, accessed April 2, 2020)

In our times, the game of politics and ideas also seems to be driven by factions similar to those described by Lamartine. There seems to exist in Chile, in some groups, a spirit of rupture and a disdain for history and the past, a series of attempts to enforce by way of recasting or derogation, evoking dictatorship, of certain ideas and ways of life. These groups appear as having a monopoly on truth and morality, and tend to condemn all that is not and which should not be considered politically correct. They are the Jacobins of our days. In the face of this scenario, Lamartine's work suggests that we resist the fear and the menace generated by threatening and arrogant speeches that promote only profound changes. His work is, moreover, a good antidote against all forms of what is considered political correctness, because it shows that those who take power one day are often not able to impose their convictions for the future. The Jacobins, who held total power for a short revolutionary period, did not bequeath their ideas and their way of living upon the subsequent constitutional democracy. It was the Constitutionalists and the Girondists, inspired by liberty and gradual reformism, who, despite betrayals and resignations, defeats and, in many cases, death at the guillotine, who handed down their ideas and ways of living and showed us how to truly build a republic (Rosanvallon 2007: 178–179).

The notion of Jacobinism is also linked with the development of technocracies, in particular with violent forms of antidemocratic corporatism, sometimes self-proclaimed "modernizers" of politics, which Rosanvallon calls "Jacobinism par excellence" (Rosanvallon 2009: 89–92). These forms of Jacobinism par excellence can be found in very diverse political processes. Among them, we find coups d'état and military dictatorships, which, from the middle of the twentieth century, have taken place in Asia, and of course the experience with the so called "Chicago Boys" in Chile and other countries that fell under dictatorships in Latin America.

The foregoing insistence that Jacobinism is unable to spread its ideas in a peaceful way is one of the central assertions that inspires this book. With this statement we appeal for appreciation of the moderation that underlies the spirit of constitutionality, something which is also Girondist, liberal, republican, and (why not?) truly democratic.

In this context, I believe that it is also timely to remember the ideas of Stefan Zweig, who, in the Foreword of his famous work, *Decisive Moments in History*, said:

> Similarly, history, in which we admire the greatest poet or actor of all time, is by no means ceaselessly creative … But if a genius arises in art, he outlives his times; if such a critical moment occurs in the world, it is decisive for decades and centuries. Just as the electricity of the whole atmosphere is concentrated in the tip of the lightning rod, an immeasurable number of events then come together in the narrowest span of time. What otherwise leisurely occurs sequentially and simultaneously is condensed into a single moment that determines and decides everything: a single *Yes*, a single *No*, a *too early* or a *too late* makes that hour irrevocable for a hundred generations and determines the life of an individual, a people, and even the destiny of all mankind.
>
> (Zweig 1998: 5–6)

Our book adapts this idea of historical "moments" referred to by Zweig to understand the collective forms of republican construction which have been used to transform political and constitutional history. Inspired by this initial idea, we have tried to carry out a study of the history of constitutional law and Chilean politics, from a republican perspective, in order to identify its most important moments.

If we analyze our history from the perspective of our republican bicentenary, we have not had one, but five republics, where each one corresponds to a particular period in our history. What has indeed been constant during these five periods is the search for ways of self-government through one or more written constitutions, to use the law to limit power, to consider the Chilean people as the bearers of constituent power, and to uphold the ballot box as the preferred mechanism for representation and participation. To this list we should add the language of civic virtue that characterizes Chilean republican life. From 1810 to our days, these principles have been maintained without major variations, without ignoring the fact that political agents have held different conceptions, such as of the definition of the people and the structure of rights (Boas 1969: 167–186).

In this work, each republican period is explained through an analysis that concentrates on the legal aspects of each period, and, as such, the study might be criticized for being merely formal or institutional, or because it does not examine the social aspect of each republican experience. We acknowledge these shortcomings, but view them as inherent limitations of the methodology chosen to carry out this comparative, doctrinal, and historical analysis of Chilean law and institutions. Nor does this approach imply that we are blind to the historical limits of the republican project as the pursuit of a legal and political order free of domination. In this regard, it is very important to emphasize the two major failings in Chilean republican history, and perhaps more broadly: the domination and lack of recognition of indigenous peoples and the late incorporation of women into the political community as citizens bearing the right to vote.

Despite these very significant failings, we believe that it is useful to study the differences among the five Chilean republican periods. We can provide a richer explanation of Chilean constitutionalism. We can go beyond citing the dates of the different constitutions or emphasizing the changing, contingent character of politics, and/or the short duration of governments.

That is why, drawing on Stefan Zweig's ideas previously mentioned, and the work of Bruce Ackerman, I have adopted the idea of a "constitutional moment," as a special time that is distinct from normal constitutional politics and which is perceived by actors as different because of its foundational character (Ackerman 1991: 6, 8, 12). The concept of constitutional moment is useful to explain the development of constitutional politics in Chile. It enables us to register the most important changes and to structure the periods according to changes in the doctrinal conception of law and rights, the relationship between rulers and the ruled, and between the different government bodies, as well as the organization of political agents. All of these dimensions underwent important alterations in Chile, in at least five different eras. With these five distinct republican periods, we can appreciate that each stage in Chilean history has evolved around different constitutional moments. Thus, the first stage was marked by the moment of the Constitution of 1828; the second, by the constitutional reform of 1833; the third, by the constitutional reforms of 1871–1874; the fourth, by the reforms of 1925 which came into force at the end of 1932; the fifth, by the 1989 reforms to the existing constitutional text first enacted by the military dictatorship in 1980.

It must be noted that each of these moments in Chilean constitutional history does not necessarily fully comply with all of the requisite democratic regulations that Ackerman establishes as necessary to consider a political situation as a constitutional moment. In Ackerman's work, the constitutional moment has a marked deliberative, collective, democratic, and citizenship component. In Ackerman's words, a constitutional moment must consider that:

> Decisions by the People occur rarely, and under special constitutional conditions. Before gaining the authority to make supreme law in the name of the People, a movement's political partisans must first, convince an extraordinary number of their fellow citizens to take their proposed initiative with a seriousness that they do not normally accord to politics; second, they must allow their opponents a fair opportunity to organize their own forces; third, they must convince a majority of their fellow Americans to support their initiative as its merits are discussed, time and again, in the deliberative fora provided for "higher lawmaking." It is only then that a political movement earns the enhanced legitimacy the dualist Constitution accords to decisions made by the People.
> (Ackerman 1991: 6)

Thus, our history of constitutional law is divided into five main republican periods, which are linked, but are independent because they bear distinctive features in how they conceive of and organize the law, the bodies of the State, and the institutional participation of the main political actors.

This is expressed as follows. The First Republic, from 1810 to 1830, is initially based upon a natural law understanding of rights which, over time, gave way to a liberal conception. The First Republic suffered a loyalist interruption in 1814 that sought to return to the colonial order; in 1818 this break was reversed and the State returned to the republican constitutional path. In this first stage, there is tension to resolve between an almost dictatorial executive power and the legislative assemblies of little power, with class-based representation. This process culminates in the 1828 Constitution, whose authors, inspired by liberalism, sought to institute self-government with an emphasis on equality and the institution of Parliament.

The Second Republic, the authoritarian Republic, in place from 1830 to 1870, was conservative, restrictive of rights, and authoritarian in the form of government. A republican structure was maintained, but States of Exception were invoked continuously and fostered a tendency towards concentrating power in the Executive and ratifying the restriction of rights. This conservative involution only began to be undone politically around 1860, a process that culminated with the 1870 constitutional reforms.

The Third Republic is called the Liberal Republic because of its liberal understanding of rights and the supremacy granted to the parliamentary form of government. It held sway from 1870 to 1924.

The Fourth Republic, the Democratic Republic, began at the end of 1932, when the 1925 Constitution effectively came into force, and lasted until 1973. This period was characterized by a social and democratic understanding of rights, as well as the advancement and improvement of political participation, despite the regime's accentuated presidential character. The Fourth Republic had an abrupt and violent end in 1973. The military coup d'état destroyed the 1925 Constitution and interrupted the Chilean republican tradition from 1973 to 1990.

Finally, with the Fifth Republic, in 1990 the republican tradition recommenced in Chile, with the organization of the Neoliberal Republic, which is named for its conception of rights as barriers against State interference, and for its neo-presidentialism, concentrating all power, in an unbalanced form, in the President. In our opinion, republican ideals provide a basis for criticizing the neoliberalism and excessive presidentialism of the Fifth Republic which arose in Chile in 1990 and has characterized politics since then.

PREFACE TO THE ENGLISH TRANSLATION

This work is inspired by the bicentennial of Chilean independence (1818–2018) and explains – from a historical perspective – the creation, change of structure, and destruction of Chilean republican and democratic constitutionalism. A distinction is made between those historical moments that were de facto dictatorships and those that were influenced by democratic and republican principles. This book assumes that the historic-constitutional course of the Chilean Republic does not proceed as a single political experience which – starting in 1810 – unfolded as a continuous process, unaltered until today. Instead, Chile's constitutional history has a plural character, even though it always finds inspiration in the moment of our Independence, as again and again it seeks to attain a form of "self-government" suitable for this Latin American country.

This book seeks to contribute to our knowledge of Chile's constitutional history and to promote the promises and struggles of republican constitutionalism. The ideal type that is used in this work for the analytical comparison of Chilean constitutional law is based upon several different sources, such as history, politics, and philosophy (jurisprudence). These sources are used to formulate a comparative reconstruction of the ideological and institutional history of Chile's constitutional law. This reconstruction draws on concepts and theoretical developments originating in Western constitutional theory, history, and political philosophy, especially the French and Anglo-Saxon legal traditions.

The book consists of a Foreword, followed by eight chapters that analyze Chilean constitutional republicanism, plus an Afterword. It refers to the organization of the State, the structure of rights, and the role played by the main political agents.

Chapter 1 sets out the broad point of view adopted in this work. The idea of republicanism is analyzed, as an ideal concept and its place in the Chilean constitutional tradition. In addition, alternative visions are explored that have had great influence on Chilean political discourse. The origin and meaning of the idea of five republics is also explained, together with the tradition of republican constitutionalism.

In Chapters 2, 3, 4, and 5, the first four definitive historical experiences upon which republican constitutionalism has been built and demonstrated in Chile are examined. Their main characteristics, elements of continuity and evolution, ways of mutating, and, in some cases, abrupt endings are described.

In Chapter 6, we describe some of the main legal and political characteristics of the forced interruption to republican life in 1973 that was ushered in by the coup d'état that resulted in military dictatorship in Chile, which lasted until the return to democracy in 1990.

Chapter 7 studies the Fifth Chilean Republic, which is the present period, and considers the present organization of the State, the structure of rights, and the role played by the main political agents. The successive reforms of our present Constitution, the consolidation of executive constitutionalism, the governmental regime and its main characteristics are also issues that have been duly addressed. An analysis is included of the general conception of the law, and the theory and jurisprudence of property rights, together with a discussion of the present state of economic, social, and cultural rights, and the possible organization of a moderate and sustainable proposal for installing a Social and Democratic State, founded on law in Chile.

In Chapter 8, I offer a critical analysis of some of the main constitutional proposals that are a part of Chilean political discourse today, and of the present constitutional moment. And, by way of an appeal to the Girondists' spirit of moderation and democratic persuasion, I explore the reasons why Chile needs a new Constitution, and consider the contents and procedures that are necessary to carry out such a proposal. The book ends with an Afterword and an assessment of the most recent political events in Chile.

Unless otherwise noted in the text, quotations from Spanish-language publications, given here in English, have been translated by the translator of this work.

ACKNOWLEDGMENTS

I have presented some ideas from this book in various workshops, conferences and academic activities. The first inspiration was defined in the preliminary version of Chapter 4 by the author in *La República en Chile: teoría y práctica del constitucionalismo republicano* [*The Republic in Chile: Theory and Practice of Republican Constitutionalism*], written jointly with Renato Cristi (Cristi and Ruiz-Tagle 2006). There are also sections containing partial versions of this work in my article entitled "Una visión democrática y liberal de los derechos fundamentales para la Constitución Chilena del bicentenario" [A democratic and liberal view of fundamental rights for the Chilean Constitution of the bicentenary], published (in Ruiz-Tagle 2006) in the book coordinated by Andrés Bordalí: *Justicia constitucional y derechos fundamentales* [*Constitutional Justice and Fundamental Rights*].

The thoughts about the Chilean governmental regime presented in this work are based in part on the study carried out in 2008 by the author in the context of the project, "Viabilidad política para instaurar el sistema de gobierno parlamentario o semi-presidencial en Chile – BCN Innova" [Political feasibility of installing in Chile a parliamentary or semi-presidential government]. This research project was funded by the Biblioteca del Congreso Nacional (BCN) [National Library of Congress] and endorsed by the Ministerio de Hacienda [Treasury Department/Ministry of Finance], with funding from the Inter-American Development Bank (IDB). The first draft of this work had the collaboration of Professor Sofía Correa and the assistance of Diego Gil, Ricardo Buendía, Vicente Burgos, María Victoria Demarchi, Paz Irarrázabal, Nathaly Mancilla, Valentina Martínez, Felipe Meléndez, Pía Muñoz and Pablo Rubio from the Facultad de Derecho de la Universidad de Chile [University of Chile, Law Faculty], and also the assistance of Benjamín Alemparte.

Another preliminary version of the ideas in this book was presented at the conference of March 28, 2014, on the occasion of the inauguration of the postgraduate academic year at the Escuela de Derecho de la Universidad de Valparaíso [University of Valparaíso, Law School], and which were expressed, in part, in the article, "Dogmática sobre la propiedad constitucional y civil en Chile" [Doctrine on constitutional and civil property in Chile], published in the journal *Derecho y Humanidades* [*Law and Humanities*] (Ruiz-Tagle 2014). Part of the research which formed the basis for this article was funded by Fondecyt (Fondo Nacional de Desarrollo Científico y Tecnológico) [National Fund for Scientific and Technological Development], Regular Project 1120830.

Among the presentations of these ideas, I recall the workshop "Nueva Constitución para Chile" [A new Constitution for Chile], organized by the Ministerio Secretaría General de la Presidencia [Ministry of the General Secretariat to the Presidency], at the National Congress in Santiago, on January 23, 2015; the workshop

"Una nueva Constitución para Chile", organized by Universidad Mayor, on July 31, 2015, in Temuco, Chile; the workshop "Proceso constituyente y nueva Constitución Política" [Constituent process and a new political constitution] on August 13, 2015, at the Law Faculty, Universidad de Chile; the presentation on July 2, 2015 in celebration of 800 years of Magna Carta, at the British Embassy, Santiago, Chile. Another presentation took place in the Cátedra Global [Global Chair] on October 11, 2015, at the Universidad de San Andrés, Buenos Aires, Argentina, where I benefitted from a real opportunity for dialogue and criticism with Professors Carlos Rosenkrantz, Robert Barros, Eduardo Zimmerman, Roberto Gargarella, Sebastián Elias, and Lucas Grossman, among others, to all of whom I am most grateful.

I give special thanks to Professor Sofía Correa, for her generous suggestions for improvements to this work, and to Professors Renato Cristi, Alfredo Jocelyn-Holt, Josep Maria Castellà, Francisco Soto, Ximena Insunza, Laura Underkuffler, Rodrigo Polanco, and many other academic colleagues for their invaluable observations and comments regarding this text. In the preparation of the table of contents, bibliography and the revision of some sections, I am grateful for the special help of Joaquin Deck and Juan José López. I also thank Diego Gil, Javiera Morales, Paula Ahumada, Emilia Jocelyn-Holt, Alexis Ramírez, Pía Muñoz, and Camilo Cornejo for their valuable comments.

My thanks are also extended to the blind peer reviewers from Cambridge University Press and Editorial LOM, as well as to Professor Daniel Álvarez, coordinator of the Colección Derecho en Democracia [Law in Democracy Collection], who made critical observations on a first draft of this text, which served to improve the form and content of my work.

My thanks go also to the students and professors of the doctoral program and the courses "Introduction to Law" and "Constitutional Law" of the Law Faculty at Universidad de Chile, all of whom have contributed greatly to the airing and reviewing of these ideas, and with whom, in a trial-and-error procedure, we have revised over and over the main assumptions and arguments. I also thank everyone in the Faculty, in particular Gloria Arias, María Inés Arias, Jorge Araos, Carlos Cereceda, Ema Contreras, Nelly Cornejo, Albina Echeverría, Jeanette Palacios, Olfa Rojas, José Luis Figueroa, Marión García, Pamela González, Jovita Muñoz, Fernando Pacheco, Germán Paredes, Patricio

Pinto, Vicky López, Fernando Ríos, Mónica Veloso, Ximena Vidal, the housekeeping personnel, and so many other people who, for many years, have made a contribution to my academic work. In the translation of this work from Spanish to English, I benefit from the generous work of Ana Luisa Goldsmith and the revision of Hugh Goldsmith. I thank Mrs. Alison Tickner for her careful and dedicated work in the English edition of this book. I also thank Ms. Finola O'Sullivan, Ms. Jane Bowbrick, and the team from Cambridge University Press for their assistance.

I thank Yale Law School Professors Owen Fiss and Carol Rose for their special support in this project. Also, a special note of thanks is due to Professor Robert Barros, who recommended this book and passed away when this work was still in press. I will always admire the work of Professor Barros, which has some of the most profound insights into Chilean constitutionalism, and I will miss his good advice and generous character.

The mistakes that appear in this work are the sole responsibility of the author.

Finally, and by no means least important, I dedicate this work to my mother Magdalena, who taught me to believe in education and justice, and to my wife Isabel and our children. I hope that we can all live in peace, in one or more future republics, in our beloved Chile.

REPUBLICAN CONSTITUTIONALISM AS AN IDEAL TYPE AND TRADITION AND ITS ALTERNATIVES

It is an impossible task to resolve all the controversies that arise from the many valuable contributions that have analyzed the characteristics and form of Chilean constitutionalism. If we synthesize these observations, we might conclude following Niccola Matteucci that the development of constitutionalism and, therefore, of republicanism, is an "ideal type for reflecting about historical reality or an analytical category that highlights and reveals particular aspects of the political experience" (Matteucci 2010: 287). Thus, according to Matteucci, constitutionalism or constitutional law is not merely an academic discipline that studies the propositions of a political power of a particular State, but is also a regulatory proposal for the general political reality. And, as already mentioned, the intellectual labor of Chilean constitutionalism has had, in Matteucci's words, an interest not only in "who but also in how policies are decided and the legal procedure that makes decisions legitimate for the subjects" (ibid.: 23).

Viewed from the perspective of Matteucci's ideal type, we can see that the intellectual and political movement that we call Chilean republican constitutionalism neither begins nor ends with any particular constitution. Rather republican constitutionalism in Chile refers to a long process which originates in the deliberations of the patriots at the dawn of independence, in the writings of Camilo Henríquez, Juan Egaña, José Joaquín de Mora, and Andrés Bello, in the teachings of Jorge Huneeus, in the words of Manuel Carrasco Albano, Alcibíades Roldán, and Valentín Letelier. It is also about a more up-to-date understanding, as was developed by Gabriel Amunátegui, among many others. Most of these reflections about constitutional law emerged from the Universidad de Chile, as scholars sought to explain Chilean positive constitutional regulations, using doctrinal categories of one or more ideal types. These scholars always pursued the idea of maximizing the application of the republican principles of dignity, equality, liberty, and democracy. More recently, there has also been a reconsideration of the Christian-rooted republican tradition, largely by professors and graduates of the Pontificia Universidad Católica de Chile, such as Eduardo Frei Montalva, Raúl Silva Henríquez, or within the human rights work that was carried out by the Vicaria de la Solidaridad [Vicariate of Solidarity] during the military dictatorship of General Pinochet (Zapata 2015: 75–91).

History is written in the present to study the past and to understand all that is inherent in human beings (Bloch 2003: 70–74). From our present standpoint of knowledge, if we claim to understand the main characteristics of Chilean history, we must observe that there have been times marked by authoritarianism and dictatorship. Authoritarianism was present in Chile mainly in three different periods: (1) between 1814 and 1818, during the occupation by the Spanish army during the Spanish reconquest; (2) from 1924 to the end of 1932, in a succession of military coups and de facto governments; and finally, (3) from September 1973 to March 1990, during the military dictatorship led by Augusto Pinochet.

During these three periods, the freedom, equality, and dignity of the individual were restricted and/or ideals contrary to republicanism were expressed. In the last period, the most recent, the military dictatorship proposed a new political structure to substitute, at least in part, Chile's republican ideals and representative democracy. During these times, there was in Chile a legal system that included a version of public and administrative law, and beginning in 1980, the dictatorship orchestrated a parody of constitutional law that sought to legitimize and regulate the exercise of power and to ensure certain forms of specialized domination and submission of the people (Barros 2002: 1–116, 323–325). At the same time, from 1973 until 1990, certain contractual and property rights were recognized, though in a context which proscribed the full expression of the principles and values of republican constitutional and democratic law.

But Chilean history has not just been about authoritarianism and dictatorship. Freedom, equality, and the recognition of human dignity and democracy have been prominent in at least five main moments. In this history of the five Chilean republics, republicanism is understood to be an ideal format rather than a political alternative to monarchy. I believe that the idea of republic expresses the purpose of organizing government through laws, which are separated from the discretion or whim of certain people, however benevolent they may be. A republican government is, at minimum, one in which public authority is subject to the law in all its powers. The republican ideas also assume in their strongest form the acceptance of a division and limitation of the functions of public and private power, a concept of inclusive citizenship, and a sustained effort to avoid the concentration of power and all forms of domination between human beings (Cristi and Ruiz Tagle 2008: 12).

Thus the republic, as an ideal political type, existed in Antiquity and in the Middle Ages and has its origins prior to the development of constitutionalism and the idea of representative or constitutional democracy at the end of the eighteenth century. Constitutionalism, as a political and intellectual movement, has the purpose of limiting public and private power through the law, and of reconciling the power of government with the freedom and equality of citizens (Cristi and Ruiz-Tagle 2006: 29). The date of birth of Republican constitutionalism can perhaps be fixed at the time of the creation of representative democracy as part of the process of drafting and adopting the US Federal Constitution in 1787. From the end of the eighteenth century until today, the legal form in which republican ideals have been expressed tends to be intertwined with constitutionalism, although we can certainly identify forms of constitutionalism that are conservative, authoritarian, liberal, or even more radical or of Jacobin inspiration (Gargarella 2005: 2–3; Correa 2004: 300).

Republican constitutionalism is a set of regulatory ideals, a moral aspiration, and an ideal type that serves to model and organize politics. Amongst the political and legal characteristics of republican constitutionalism is a conception of politics as a collective citizens' activity which must be subject to the law, that values the separation of the functions of power, and is committed to certain values, such as political equality and public education, the pursuit of the general interest or common good, and a social and relational form of understanding human ontology, rights, and property which is contrary to simple individualism (Cristi and Ruiz-Tagle 2006: 12; 2014: 21). For example, in respect of the Bill of Rights, a republican government can be defined as one where citizens shall all be entitled to the same privileges and immunities; where the right of the people to be secure in their persons, houses, paper, and effects, against unreasonable searches and seizures, shall not be violated; and where no person shall be deprived of life, liberty, or property without due process of law (Amar 1998: 192). It also implies acceptance of the idea that all citizens not only bear rights, but also must fulfill certain duties, such as obligatory education, paying taxes, responding to the census, being informed about local community affairs, and participating in public affairs (Kartal 2001–2002: 124). Last but not least, the idea of constitutional republicanism implies bans on titles of nobility, the explicit guarantee of a republican form of government, the absence of property qualifications for public service, the provision that all public servants should be paid from a public treasury, the secular oath clause, the repudiation of religious tests for office-holding, as well as minimum age rules, as part of an anti-aristocratic, anti-feudal, and anti-establishment vision (Amar 2016: 23–24).

Today, in the first quarter of the twenty-first century, it is difficult to imagine a political republicanism that is not democratic, and that is not inspired by the paradigm of constitutional and representative democracy. Representative or constitutional democracy is here understood as a system in which the majority of the people govern and which simultaneously respects the rights of every citizen and promotes the inclusion and political participation of minorities (Ruiz-Tagle 2006: 69).

For the same reasons, a certain militaristic, dictatorial, or strongman tradition in Latin America, and in Chile in particular, has been criticized as being contrary to the republican model. Nevertheless, we should be aware that sophisticated ideas, including legal or constitutional ideas, have been used to justify dictatorships. Dictatorships, in any shape or form, are different from republicanism to the extent that they depart from the ideals of submitting power to the law, the division of functions, inclusive citizenship, and non-domination. Dictatorships concentrate powers and thereby depart from the contemporary struggles that are intrinsic to present-day republicanism. A dictatorship may uphold a thin idea of a legal order, but nevertheless, this thin idea of law is thin precisely because it lacks a comprehensive commitment to republican and liberal principles and values (Barros 2002: 1–9). Additionally, dictatorships often disguise themselves as republics by adopting formalistic structures similar to constitutionalism, often to seek the prestige associated with legal and political republican modalities (Loewenstein 1983: 368).

It is also important to recognize certain historical ambiguities associated with the independence struggle, in which military officers or caudillos engaged in notable courses of action that many times contradicted republican principles, when installing or consolidating new republican experiences. In this regard, consider the cases of Simón Bolívar or Bernardo O'Higgins. Both were inspired by republican principles when they fought for independence and the overthrow of the Spanish monarchy, but when it came to organizing the new political order, both acted like dictators (Vicuña Mackenna 1976: 68–122, 241–298). This ambiguity is always latent because ideas in history are not given in a pure state. For this reason, I include among the minimum republican forms the authoritarian experience associated with Diego Portales beginning in 1830 and also, despite its dictatorial characteristics, the crisis and civil war during the presidency of José Manuel Balmaceda in 1891, which is often heralded for its republican value.

One can legitimately ask whether these forms of authoritarianism effectively contributed to the consolidation of republican ideals, or whether they are merely forms of autocracy hidden behind a facade of republicanism. These legal and political parodies have restricted and falsified the fundamental rights and functions which correspond to constitutional bodies, and very often they exhibit very complex legal forms of specialization of functions, which are particularly intricate and inaccessible to the common citizen (Barros 2002: 315–322).

In this study, we must also criticize by comparison and contrast the anti-republican origins and character of neoliberalism and the authoritarian neo-presidentialism which today exists in Chile. The ideas of neoliberalism and neo-presidentialism were incubated and deepened in Chile in the period 1973 to 1990. In this context, neoliberalism emerges as a mid-twentieth-century conservative reaction, which has implied a reinterpretation of constitutional law alongside the resurgence of market economies in the USA and Europe (Purdy 2014: 195–213). On the breadth of the neoliberal position and its multiple immediate implications, Jed Purdy has written:

> There is a parallel in today's neoliberal constitutionalism, which concentrates on forms of autonomy that are more characteristic of twenty-first-century capitalism than that of a century ago: selling data, making consumption decisions, and deciding how to spend money more generally to advance one's preferences. Even as the older model of economic constitutional liberty remains largely exiled, as it has been since its rejection during the New Deal, a new set of activities has formed

a new version of economic constitutional liberty, much of it anchored in the First Amendment.

(Purdy 2014: 197–198)

Neoliberalism in no way exhausts all forms of conservatism; rather it seeks to limit action by the State to the promotion of economic freedom, which always requires a degree of inequality and which is the base for all other values. In contrast to neoliberalism, liberalism is an attitude of political and intellectual mistrust before all forms of public and private power, and involves an affirmation of people's freedom and equality. Liberalism, understood in this sense, is linked to republican ideas and republicanism's legal face, which is constitutionalism. Understood in this manner, liberalism values the power of constitutional and representative government and recognizes the function of assuring dignity, freedom, and equality to all people; this central characteristic differentiates liberalism from neoliberalism.

This anti-republican and anti-constitutional objective of neoliberalism had a foundational character during the dictatorship of Augusto Pinochet, following the coup d'état of 1973. Of course, as Roberto Castillo has explained, the dictatorship presented itself as "savior and protector" over the exercise and title to power (Castillo Sandoval 2007).

This idea differentiates Pinochet's dictatorship, particularly from the conservative traditional conception, which was more pragmatic, and sometimes even hedonistic, and distinguishes other Chilean authoritarian politicians, such as Diego Portales. And even if there might have been more deaths in the 1891 civil war battles of Concón and Placilla than disappearances in the period 1973–1990, the difference between 1891 and 1973 is that President Balmaceda's failed project involved using violence to attempt to impose a definitive resolution to an existing constitutional controversy. President Balmaceda did not try to found a new anti-republican order through violent means, nor to institute a new political economic model, as occurred after the coup d'état in 1973, a project whose partial influence continues to the present.

In the cold war scenario such as that which existed before the 1973 coup d'état, the dictatorship did not restrict itself to taking over the public apparatus. It also sought to impose a project that went beyond control of the forces and powers of the State that would persist once the military withdrew from power, as well as to introduce its own mechanisms of power, whether these be the financial market, neoliberalism (in this case, it was a pioneering experiment), or the (paradoxical) introduction of moral elements to the institutional framework which had been "eclipsed" under previous republics. These elements in the military junta's project gave the regime depth and resilience, much more so than the violence in itself – which is not to minimize or justify in any way even the smallest violation of people's human rights and liberties. This process involved a highly technical and sophisticated project that was an effective and dangerous alternative to republican ideals.

The dictatorship expressed a violent discourse set against the republican order, coupled with a militarized version of State terrorism, and organized a regime that sought to found a new authoritarian political order. The supporters of the dictatorship at first presented themselves as guardians of the 1925 Constitution, a fundamental charter which in fact they had destroyed. This political posture was used mainly for propaganda purposes, and to grant legitimacy to the dictatorship and the new authoritarian regime that emerged after September 1973; one recurring effect has been that many Chilean citizens still believe themselves to be the inhabitants of an alien country.

Chilean republican liberalism prior to 1973 had many faults and suffered a democratic deficit; and it is true that the inspiration underlying the tradition had been predominantly anti-revolutionary, with moments akin to Bonapartist experiences. This tradition also assumed a political form that evokes Alexis de Tocqueville's ideas, particularly his often nostalgic views regarding the decline of aristocratic privilege and suspicions concerning the consequences of equality (Tocqueville 1981: 556–568).

The fact of a civilian-military alliance between authoritarian presidentialism and deliberating armed forces further complicates Chilean political history. This other tradition can be traced back to at least 1810–1870, to be revived between 1924 and 1938, and again between 1952 and 1958. This alliance was consolidated after 1973 and continues up to our time. The military's influence on the shaping and functioning of the Fourth Republic, and on the imposition of a doctrine of national security in the Chilean Fifth Republic, has affected notions of citizen rights and has validated hyper-presidentialist constitutional institutions. On too many occasions during the twentieth century one notes the influence of Generals Ibáñez and Pinochet, and other champions of this civilian-military alliance in Chile.

Despite this anti-republican civilian-military alliance, from the point of view of society and the identification of the historical individual characteristic of Chilean politics, it should be noted that the republican ideas have been inclusive by definition and admitted the possibility of a mixed society, in which the elite, with all its privileged structures, lives together with the popular expression of the citizens. The diversity of identities and ways of life, which include the elite and the ordinary people, are mutually legitimized and intercommunicating in the public and private spheres. It is true that the five republics which have existed in Chile so far have been a series of projects which have benefitted mainly the elite, but there have been moments which have allowed the expression and acceptance of several different popular identities in their most variable forms. This mutual tolerance and coexistence is derived not only from the values and norms of society, but also from the principles, practices, cultural forms, and symbols of the most diverse groups, even from the marginal sectors of Chilean society. The assertion of the exclusive leadership of the elite, or of one or more of the popular identities in terms of the historical avant-garde, implies a reduced valuation of the republican experience and denial of the validity of the law and of the legal and political system developed in our country. This interpretation is a radical statement of the precariousness of the law and politics, and its integrating character, and also constitutes a mistaken and excessive expression of mistrust. The republics, and the law of the State which has sustained them, have been collective projects, greater and more valuable than the elites that have led them, and they have had more strength to secure a manner of pacific coexistence than that which the man in the street would be willing to provide. The five Chilean republics have allowed the peaceful coexistence of an ever-growing population, and have been political and legal structures that have guaranteed a civilized way of life to people and groups with very diverse outlooks on life.

It is true that Chilean constitutionalism and law are not a "solid" social construction if compared to the values that they should embody. Our legal system is not organized according to logical parameters, and at all times it has been influenced by the elite's conceptions about political ideas, religion, the economy, and so on. But from there, to think that the privileged elite entity has been able to add any value, by its own and singular judgment, to all the regulations and principles of the legal system, and that it was able to change our history in a way of its own choosing, is asking a lot in principle. If one accepts the notion that the elite, according to its whim, defines the forms of our law and politics, the persuasive value of the republican ideals loses all its sense. The same conclusion follows when thinking that only the people's actors make history – that is, to think that all forms of cultural expression are transformed into mere exercises in cynicism, in facades of domination. Such an extreme idea seems mistaken and is not founded in the reality of our political history, because the elites and the popular actors share their power and the benefits of our society with other institutions, and are intermingled among themselves from very early in our history; and among them are craftsmen, civil servants, teachers, rural landowners, and so on, who constitute the basis of the Chilean middle class (González 2011: 365–370).

Republicanism has not been able to validate as always just, the decision which is imposed in the name of the majority, because it requires the participation and the rights of minorities to be respected, being the rights of the elite or of one or more of the marginal groups of people's entities which may be excluded arbitrarily and unfairly from society. The law, from this republican perspective, is considered to be linked to philosophical, historical, sociological, economic, and cultural reasoning. The law is part of culture and it cannot be reduced to a mere system of a positive technical character for controlling power, with mechanical and automatic characteristics. The law always has to respond to certain values, protect certain beliefs and promote certain attitudes that society cares about, and among the most valuable are the republican forms. Therefore, constitutionalism supposedly gives an answer to the relationship between the law, politics, and its institutions. In the first place, the concept of "politics" can be understood in a broader way than the "law," in the sense that it includes aspirations that cannot be imposed by coercion. A decision based on a political criterion takes into account interests not represented before the entity that decides on behalf of none of the parties involved in the case, and could even give such interests preference. In this light, the concept of law is more restricted than the concept of politics, because it considers basically the interests of individuals or groups in conflict among themselves or that are distinct from the community. On the other hand, and apparently contrary to the previous statement, politics is concerned with questions common to all and with a peaceful form of resolving conflicts. The law expresses primarily the idea of private interests. The word "law" implies the resolution of disputes and conflicts between individuals or between groups and individual people with different purposes, preferences, or interests. However, it is also possible to understand the law as policy sanctioned or approved publicly. And a given policy needs to be expressed in the form of law in order to be consolidated. However, the rules of law and politics interact, shaping one another. In this way, some policies cannot be implemented when certain provisions or forms of the law exist, and some parts of the law cannot be fulfilled due to the existence of policies that block their application (Ruiz-Tagle 2001b: 55–57).

Moreover, it is pertinent to consider that there are important comparative differences in the way that the law and politics are perceived in Europe, and certainly in Latin America, the United Kingdom and the USA. In the latter, the law is not perceived as much as a body of doctrine (as in Europe, or even in the UK), but as an instrument of economic and social policies. The way in which politics is incorporated into the law varies according to the characteristics of each legal system. To illustrate this unstable relationship between the law and politics, let us imagine them as two spheres that touch each other at their margins, while each one of them tries to include or incorporate the other completely. Politics and the law are linked to each other in a way that gives rise to a fixed set of institutions, and it is in this context that the regulatory ideal of republican constitutionalism arises, or its imitations and mimicries, which are expressed in the form of authoritarian constitutionalism.

While recognizing the precariousness of the Chilean constitutional experience, it is important to consider that our constitutionalism is not an isolated phenomenon because it is exposed to a continuous process of reciprocal influence. Firstly, the origins of constitutional law are common to America and Europe. This simultaneous development of constitutional law can be explained by the influence of the North American experience that is recognized by European constitutionalism. However, neither in Europe nor in the USA is the influence of Latin American constitutionalism recognized. In this respect, in the USA and in Europe it is only the constitutionalism that comes from the Querétaro Constitution, adopted in Mexico in 1917, that seems relevant and distinctive. Instead, in the countries of Latin America, the influence of Europe, the UK, and the USA in constitutional matters is widely recognized.

1.1 A SAMPLE OF DIFFERENT CONCEPTIONS ABOUT CHILEAN CONSTITUTIONAL LAW

In the past, there have been many distinguished writers and historians who have dedicated their work to studying the relationship between the law, the institutions, and the political actors in their historical context, among them: Miguel Luis Gregorio, Domingo and Gabriel Amunátegui, Diego Barros Arana, José Victorino Lastarria, Benjamín Vicuña Mackenna, Manuel Carrasco Albano, Alcibíades Roldán, Jorge Huneeus, José Guillermo Guerra, Alberto Edwards, Jaime Eyzaguirre, Mario Góngora, Fernando Campos Harriet, and Ricardo Donoso. In fact, Donoso, at the beginning of his famous work, *Las ideas políticas en Chile* [*Political Ideas in Chile*], quotes Eduardo de Hinojosa, who, in 1890, clearly suggests: "Of all the issues which most strongly appeal to and attract those who study the development of country history and law, very few could be as interesting as the study of the tie, sometimes ostensible, at other times veiled and hidden, that joins the history of ideas with the history of institutions" (Donoso 1967: 7).

Without intending to be exhaustive, in this section I will analyze some ideas regarding the way in which the timing of the different periods of Chilean history has been arranged. Its purpose is to analyze the criteria on which these divisions are based, and then to propose some conditions for a new classification of Chilean constitutional law that is consistent with the evolution of republican principles from a comparative viewpoint.

1.2   THE DECADENCE OF REPUBLICANISM IN THE WORKS OF ALBERTO EDWARDS AND JAIME EYZAGUIRRE

Alberto Edwards is influenced by the ideas of Oswald Spengler and is interested in explaining what he calls "Chilean political decadence," which is really the loss of power by the aristocracy during the republican period in which he lived. His explanation for all evils is centered on the parliamentary system and liberalism (Cristi and Ruiz 2015: 41). The theme of his thought is the need to preserve a strong authority that could take Chile back to a period like that of the conservative republic and where it would be possible to guarantee order and freedom. That is why Edwards saw in the authoritarian figure of Diego Portales, and later of General Ibáñez, in whose first dictatorial government he was a minister, a possibility of expressing his political ideals. Renato Cristi summarizes the conservative ideas of Alberto Edwards as follows:

> During the course of the parliamentary regime, Edwards was in favor of a strong executive power, but framed within the parliamentary

republican system. It is only from 1924, when the military entered the political scene and later on the basis of his personal and political commitment to the Ibáñez dictatorship that the revolutionary change of direction in his conservative posture is consolidated.

(Cristi and Ruiz 2015: 38)

However, the way of thinking of Alberto Edwards is changeable and he adapts his ideas to the prevailing political regime. His earliest writings combine some acute observations about the relationship between social structure and the conduct of politics in Chilean history. According to Cristi, the change in Edwards' thinking could show that there are two predominant positions in his work, and that they can be summarized by their main characteristics, as follows:

During his earlier period Edwards does not realize the extent of the aristocracy's compromise with liberalism. His error in consequence was to think that they treasured pure spiritual values, that they were the standard bearers of honor, loyalty to traditions and respect for authority. A deep change in his perception of the aristocratic as such, is a determining factor in the second phase of his ideas. The idealization of the upper class gives way to a realistic and resigned vision.

(Cristi and Ruiz 2015: 44)

Alberto Edwards, in his influential book *La fronda aristocrática en Chile* [*The Aristocratic Frond in Chile*] published initially, during 1927, as essays in the *El Mercurio* newspaper, displays a skeptical, authoritarian, and conservative posture, foreseeing a very negative view of constitutionalism, liberalism, democracy, and the Chilean parliamentary system as a whole.

What I have called the aristocratic frond, that is to say, the almost constant pacific fight of our bourgeois and feudal oligarchy against the power of presidents, a fight that started in 1849 and had its final outcome in 1891, is an identical phenomenon to that which transformed in Europe, above all from 1848, the old monarchies of divine right into parliamentary governments, dominated by the bourgeois plutocracy. In history, as in all sciences, it is essential to name things by their right name. The nineteenth-century revolutions were not democratic, neither by their origin, nor by their tendencies, nor by the spirit and methods of the social and political regimes that resulted from them.

(Edwards 1993: 282)

Edwards invents a regulatory concept and an ideal type of presidential leadership, of strong authority that is opposed to the frond, that is

committed to disorder, revolution, and democracy, which he alternatively demonizes and idealizes. By following the failure of the dictatorship of General Ibáñez, a political regime he supported, he assumes
a skeptical conservative way of thinking. Perhaps he was disillusioned
with the failure of the authoritarian experiment that he had decided to
support and thus became a political skeptic.

Edwards' criticism of representative democracy undervalues the
strengths of the republican element in Chile; neither does he give
any value to the gradual and collective building of freedom and equality, which constitutes the basis of Chilean liberal constitutionalism. His
ideas greatly influenced later historians, like Francisco Antonio Encina,
Jaime Eyzaguirre, and Mario Góngora (Cristi and Ruiz 2015: 13).

Carlos Ruiz has summarized the tendencies which play a key role in
the thinking of Jaime Eyzaguirre, another very influential conservative
writer inspired by Alberto Edwards, noting:

> there are three basic semantic tendencies around which are consolidated
> and articulated the different themes of Eyzaguirre: a conservative and
> traditional interpretation of the Catholic doctrine, a political option in
> favor of corporativism and in third place, an interpretation of the feeling
> of Spanishness together with traditionalism, based on which,
> a conservative vision of the history of America and Chile will later on
> be built.
>
> (Cristi and Ruiz 2015: 70)

It is important to note the significance that Jaime Eyzaguirre gives in
his thinking to a reinterpretation of the Catholic social doctrine that
he combines with millenarianism. Millenarianism is defined as the
belief in the proximity of the second coming of Christ to reign on
earth before the final judgment, and Eyzaguirre, and other Chilean
conservatives, are announcing it around the end of the 1930s (Cristi
and Ruiz 2015: 70–77). Furthermore, with an outlook related to that of
Edwards, Jaime Eyzaguirre, in his work *Historia constitucional de Chile*
[*Constitutional History of Chile*], proposed a breakdown into periods of
Chilean history that has been very influential and which attributes too
high a value to the colonial period and to the conservative republic,
distinguishing the following stages:

> In the history of Chile we can distinguish two main periods: a pre-
> constitutional period and a constitutional period. (a) The pre-
> constitutional period includes the Chilean Kingdom or Spanish
> administration period, where national history starts. It begins legally

with the taking possession of Chile by the Castilian crown, carried out in Copiapo by Pedro de Valdivia, in the final months of 1540, and with the foundation in 1541 of the Santiago Chapter, the first sowing of Chilean institutionality. This period closes on September 18, 1810, with the installation of the First Chilean Government Body. During this long period, Chile was a province or kingdom of the vast monarchy of the Indies, tied to Spain by the personal link of the common king. During this period, two stages can be distinguished: the period of the House of Austria and the period of the House of Bourbon. (b) The constitutional period includes: (1) The liberating revolution, beginning on September 18, 1810 until the battle of Chacabuco, February 12, 1817, which put an end to the Spanish administration in the country; (2) the formation of the Republic, which lasts from February 12, 1817 to the battle of Lircay, April 17, 1830, ending the period of anarchy and governmental experiments; (3) the organized Republic, beginning with the triumph of the conservative group [bigwigs] in Lircay and statutorially with the 1833 Constitution, which continues to the present day. During this period we have to distinguish the following stages: (i) Conservative or bigwig period, from 1830 to 1860; (ii) Liberal period, from 1861 to 1891; (iii) Parliamentary period, from 1891 to 1924; (iv) Presidential period, from 1925 onwards.

(Eyzaguirre 1962: 9–10)

In Eyzaguirre's periodic structure, we can challenge the idea that the formation of the Republic only begins after the battle of Chacabuco, and the excessive prominence that he gives to the conservative period beginning in 1833 which he believes continues until his present day, calling it *organized republic* or *republic in structure*. This conservative form of organizing the understanding of Chilean republican history has been very influential and has generated alternative explanations, such as the proposal of Fernando Campos Harriet, which we examine below.

1.3 THE ANTI-PARLIAMENTARIAN PRESIDENTIALISM OF FERNANDO CAMPOS HARRIET

The influence of Jaime Eyzaguirre and Alberto Edwards can be seen in the work *Historia Constitucional de Chile* [*Constitutional History of Chile*], written by Fernando Campos Harriet. His work gathers together a mass of data and information and is based on the distinction between general or external history, and internal or exclusively legal history (Campos Harriet 1956: 14). The body of precedents on which the work is based is enormous, sometimes with too much detail, and the conception of which is colored by an unbalanced prejudice in favor of presidentialism.

Campos Harriet's understanding of Chilean constitutional history does not distinguish between republican and constitutional periods, and is based on the dates of assuming and relinquishing power of each of the governments (or rather, their presidents), irrespective of their political affiliation or whether it was a de facto or a republican democratic government. Furthermore, he considers the 1891 revolution as a break between the liberal republic and the emergence of a new parliamentary republic, which does not seem entirely justified. The more general periodic structure of our history, as proposed by Campos Harriet, is as follows: I. Hispanic period, 1541–1810; II. Struggle for independence, 1811–1823; III. Struggle for organization, 1823–1830; IV. The organization, 1830–1924. In this last period, with respect to general or political history, he distinguishes between an extended conservative or bigwig period, from 1830 to 1891 (in the index of his work, he says that it lasts until 1924), and a liberal parliamentary period, from 1891 to 1924 (Campos Harriet 1956: 15, 595–598).

These periods, in their turn, are composed of successive governments, identified by those who preside over them. As for the legal or internal history, Campos Harriet reconstructs its Chilean evolution around the ideas of constitutional bodies of law, electoral codes, economic and financial laws, substantive and procedural law, and administrative codes of law, which encompass the date and contents of all kinds of legal regulations, of whatever sort, which without doubt denote, from our point of view, a very objectionable and incomplete form of explaining the different stages of our republican history, despite its erudition, documentary value, and archival research (ibid.: 461–581).

Excessive admiration for presidentialism leads Campos Harriet to establish, in effect, a sinister history opposed to a parliamentary system (ibid.: 377–380). He criticizes the Chilean parliamentary system for the rotation of ministers; he accuses the governments of not having long-term plans; he complains because different political groups negotiate and come to power one after the other; and he blames the rulers for all the resentment and social bitterness. Then, in a slanted and grudging way, in an insignificant footnote to his work *Historia constitucional de Chile*, Campos Harriet, contradicting what he himself has stated, recognizes certain merits of the Chilean parliamentary system: "To tell the truth, we should record that there was administrative continuity permitting the overall plan for public works to be carried out under such headings as school premises, roads, railways, drinking water, sewage" (Campos Harriet 1956: 380).

1.4 THE LIBERAL REPUBLICANISM OF GABRIEL AMUNÁTEGUI, RICARDO DONOSO, AND FEDERICO GIL

At the outset of his work, Amunátegui gives us a clear and concise definition of a political regime: "A political regime ... is a system of government, that is, the relationships between the ruled and the rulers" (Amunátegui 1951: 13). He recognizes, at the same time, several factors which would explain our democratic regime and the alleged Chilean political stability that stands out compared with other countries in America. According to Amunátegui, these factors would be an alleged social homogeneity (an idea that is controversial in comparative terms), and external security and relative domestic peace in Chile. To these he adds intellectual factors, such as the significant number of intellectuals contributed by the 1842 generation, and legal institutional factors, such as the duration of the 1833 Constitution and of the statutes that brought order to the Chilean legal system (ibid.: 189–190). The idea that there has been great stability in the history of Chile is controversial. In this respect, and in a series of observations that I share, Sofía Correa has explained that in Chile there has not been such a period of institutional stability.

> To start, let us clear away the idea of 150 years of democracy. Taking only institutional continuity into account, we have never achieved a period of even fifty years' stability. In the nineteenth century: civil wars in the post-independence period, as well as in 1829, 1851, 1859, and 1891. From this last milestone up to the military intervention in 1924, there were thirty-three years; afterwards, we had a period of institutional disruptions, including a period of dictatorship until December 1932. From 1933 to 1973, we had forty years of institutional stability. A good record for Latin America, but only that far.
>
> (Correa 2000: 117)

Despite the controversial aspects surrounding this idea of institutional stability in our country, I think that the way in which Amunátegui divides the constitutional history of Chile in relation to its political regime is useful. He differentiates between three main periods: first period, or experimental period, beginning in 1810 and ending in 1833; second period, or Autocratic Republic, from 1833 to 1874; and finally, third period, or Democratic Republic, starting in 1874 and continuing to the beginning of the 1950s, which is precisely the period in which Amunátegui writes his work (Amunátegui 1951: 191).

As critical observations on Amunátegui's conception of the republican history of Chile, I can say: (1) I do not agree with labeling the period from 1810 to 1833 as "experimental," when it seems the 1828 Constitution institutionalized in Chile a consolidated republican structure. (2) The third period proposed by Amunátegui, from 1874 to 1950, is too long and does not take into account the interruptions of the civil war of 1891 and the coups d'état and de facto governments in Chile from 1924 to 1932.

This is why the periodic division by Ricardo Donoso, who arranged, in his work *Las ideas políticas en Chile* [*Political Ideas in Chile*], the different issues related to independence and the republic, seems better tuned. Donoso considers as particularly relevant and successful among these issues the transition from monarchy to republic, the organization of politics, the struggle against the aristocracy and the Church, the organization of education, freedom of the press, electoral freedom, and democratic organization (Donoso 1967: 9). Using these criteria, Donoso tries, in addition, to highlight the features of constitutional law in each of the different stages of our republican life.

Furthermore, the explanation offered by Federico Gil, whose work *El sistema político de Chile* [*The Chilean Political System*] has two sections, is also provocative. The first section of his work, relating to the process of political development, takes account of the autocratic republic (1830–1871), the liberal republic (1871–1891), the parliamentary republic (1891–1925), the uprising of the electorate, the Frente Popular (Popular Front; 1938–1941), the politics of coalition (1941–1958), and evolution through suffrage (1958–1964). In the second section of his work, called "Government institutions and political processes," Gil considers the separate description of the Chilean Fundamental Charters (Gil 1969: 9). Despite its qualities, Gil's proposal is inconclusive because he does not develop through to the end the structure of republican periods, which distinguishes three different stages from 1830 to 1925.

Federico Gil's proposal blends, in his classification, political elements or characteristics from each period, such as the Frente Popular or the revolution through suffrage, and he does not classify the period after 1925, despite the fact that his work was published in 1969. Furthermore, Gil, like Simon Collier (1977: 299–300), overrates the conservative republican development, and that is why he fixes 1830 as the beginning of his periodic structure, which, together with making it seem partial to Chilean presidentialism, diminishes the value of his proposal.

1.5 THE AUTHORITARIAN REPUBLIC IN THE WORKS OF BERNARDINO BRAVO

Republicanism and Chilean republican constitutionalism have been questioned many times in their foundations, in their definition of time and in their periodification. The Chilean democratic and liberal constitutionalism was a product of the contribution of many people, belonging to several generations, and this process of intellectual and political construction was interrupted from the second half of the twentieth century.

In Chile there have been several works that have given an ideological basis and support to dictatorships and authoritarian governments, and that have justified the interruptions that have taken place in our republican constitutionalism. Among them, perhaps the most influential is the work of Professor Bernardino Bravo, who, in 1978, during the military dictatorship, published his work *Régimen de gobierno y partidos políticos en Chile, 1924–1973* [*Chilean Government Regime and Political Parties, 1924–1973*], in which he expresses sharp criticism of the influence of political parties on Chilean democracy, based on the distinction between those political parties more inclined to agreement and negotiation, and those more ideological parties in respect of which agreement and political transaction are more difficult (Bravo 1978: 55–162). In the above-mentioned work, Professor Bravo proposes nothing less than the overturning of constitutionalism and the codifying and construction of a new society built on the basis of the associative movement. About these controversial ideas, which contradict democratic principles, Professor Bravo says:

> the decline of classical constitutionalism is inseparable from the decline of written law. What is extinguished is the basic aspiration that served them both as support: uniform legislation for the whole population. In one sentence, the dominating aspirations are shifted from affirmation of

generic guarantees, somehow idealistic in the face of the power of the State, such as life, property and free initiative, towards the attainment, in collaboration with the power of the State, of individual material rights such as personal security, a proper job and decent living conditions.

(Bravo 1978: 165)

Even more, Professor Bravo's inspiration comes from the ideas that the Nazi jurist Carl Schmitt presents in *La defensa de la constitución. Estudio acerca de las diversas especies y posibilidades de salvaguardia* [*The Guardian of the Constitution: A Study of Different Forms and Means of Safeguarding*] of 1929, to say that Chile needs a new government regime and a new type of State:

Chile would have achieved permanent separation from the cycle that drags the majority of Western States, from the absolute State of the seventeenth and eighteenth centuries, through the intercession of the liberal neutral State of the nineteenth century, towards the total State that identifies State and Society. The fundamental conditions for designing a government regime in accordance with the Chilean character and present requirements have been available since 1973. What is missing is knowing how to recognize them and take advantage of them.

(Bravo 1978: 168)

These same ideas supporting an authoritarian stance are reiterated by Bernardino Bravo in his more recent work, published in 2016 with the thought-provoking title, *Una historia jamás contada. Chile 1811–2011. Cómo salió dos veces adelante. De la modernización desde arriba al despegue desde abajo* [An Untold History. Chile, 1811–2011. How it Came Through Twice. From Top-Down Modernization to Take-Off from Below]. In this work, Professor Bravo sets forth as the political ideal of a government regime for Chile what he calls an enlightened republic, which maintains the main political forms of monarchy and, in his words, is based on the following components:

[Bello and Portales] are thinking of a viable substitute for modernizing monarchy, based on its own constituent components, as is the case of the dual supreme powers [civil and ecclesiastical], strong government, a network of departments depending on it, and also the participation of an enlightened minority, used to cluster around a modernizing government. In this context, we see set forth no longer an enlightened monarchy, but for the first time an enlightened republic.

(Bravo 2016: 129; names in square brackets added)

The authoritarian model of an enlightened republic, as described by Bernardino Bravo, contradicts the ideals of constitutionalism because it is defined differently, as follows:

> Briefly, the enlightened republic is everything but a bookish construction, conceived in the nineteenth-century style, by a few so-called constitutionalists. Rather, those who succeeded in shaping it did not hide their contempt for paper constitutions because they had a well-defined and different way of acting, but above all, very effective: to consolidate the actual institutions of the country, instead of hiding behind papers as argued over, as they are ephemeral.
>
> (Bravo 2016: 141)

Inspired by this controversial ideal of an enlightened republic, Professor Bravo proposes a new ordering and period division of Chilean history, which is shaped by three main eras, as follows: (a) first period of modernization or enlightening, in which Chile moves from the Bourbon monarchy towards an enlightened republic, beginning in 1750 and extending to 1925; (b) second period, called eternal crisis and decadentism of the enlightened republic, from 1925 to 1973; and finally, (c) a third period, called the launching, or the moment when the true Constitution replaces the paper one, beginning in 1973 and/or established from 1980 onwards (Bravo 2016: 496ff.).

The concepts presented by Professor Bravo seek to build an ideal type of "enlightened republic," in which he assigns a privileged role to a modernizing elite which gathers around the President of the Republic, the Universidad de Chile, and the training colleges, the armed forces and the judicial authorities; and which is above and independent of the Constitution, and where political parties and Parliament are criticized for their relevance. He understands the main periods in our history as those in which authoritarianism has been strongest, or plainly dictatorship. These notions are incompatible with a republican and democratic understanding of our constitutional history because they do not recognize the fundamentally egalitarian and democratic drive that was consolidating in Chile around the presidential institution, public education, the armed forces, and the Judiciary.

Professor Bravo, as well as wanting to credit extraordinary activity to certain political ideals of absolutism and to depreciate the true republican ideals which are contrary to it, assigns an excessive importance to the foundational conservative moment around 1830 and to the right-wing military dictatorship, beginning in 1973. In the case of Professor Bravo, it means the setting out and expansion of a series of ideas that were first anticipated by the conservative notions of Jaime Eyzaguirre and Alberto Edwards.

1.6 CHILEAN CONSTITUTIONAL ORIGINALISM AND THE EXPANSION OF ADMINISTRATIVE LAW

Constitutional "originalism" sought to ground the values, principles, and rules of the Chilean charter in the light of the statements made by those commissioned by General Pinochet to write a constitutional text in the Comisión Ortúzar [Ortúzar Commission] during the military dictatorship. These ideas were linked together by their disdain for liberal constitutionalism, and were also tied to the expansion of administrative law, which in authoritarian periods was used to replace constitutional law. All these are issues that must be considered in Chilean constitutional history and, in relation to them, it is appropriate to understand that often they have served as sophisticated and sometimes very clever ways to justify constitutional authoritarianism.

From 1973, Chilean constitutional authoritarian originalism proposed to limit the analysis of the Chilean constitutional system to the opinion (not always clear and distinct) of the members of the Comisión Ortúzar, a group of lawyers with constituent aspirations, appointed by the military (Evans 1999; Verdugo, Pfeffer, and Nogueira 1994: 75–88). In today's Chile, the work of the originalists has lost most of its influence, but still persists. This way of understanding constitutional principles and rules transformed constitutional law, once the 1925 Constitution was destroyed, into a pure and simple commentary of the opinions held by Pinochet's advisors.

In addition, the originalism of the commissioners fails to mention the important enactments of democratic and liberal constitutionalism before 1973, and it could not justify its statements in the context of comparative law. In this way, our republican understanding of public law has been impoverished, and therefore it is not strange that alternative ideas have risen up that reject the power of the State and of the law, and seek an alternative way to build forms of coexistence that distance themselves from the more traditional principles of constitutional democracy.

Furthermore, from 1973 in Chile, in a way similar to the Fascist and Nazi experience in Europe, republican constitutional law becomes invalid and is replaced by a scholastic, legalistic, formal, and apparently technified version of administrative law (Soto Kloss 1996: 11–19; Stolleis 1998: 87–126). Constitutional law loses conceptual mass and is no longer the guiding thread of public law in our country.

1.7 THE ALTERNATIVE, MARGINAL, SOCIAL, AND ECONOMIC ORDER OF GABRIEL SALAZAR

In today's Chile, from the perspective of the left in politics, the criticism of Gabriel Salazar stands out. Professor Salazar has addressed, with great skepticism, the topics of republican constitutionalism, and has questioned all the traditional periodic structures in the history of our country, from both the political and the economic point of view, because according to Salazar, they are based on an incomplete understanding of our reality. Salazar proposes an alternative to order our history into three periods, which are: (a) discovery and conquest (1541–1598); (b) colonization (1598–1810); and (c) independent republic (1810 until the second independence, which for some was 1938, and for others 1973). Regarding the traditional periodic breakdown of Chilean history, Gabriel Salazar says:

> This breakdown into periods is based on the recognition of *archetypical heroic feats* and fundamental situations (conquest and independence), and also in the supremacy given to the political-state function over social, economic, and cultural aspects. As such, it is a useful framework to accommodate the (static) past in terms of the cult to pomp and emblems of "the origins," but not for the (dynamic) projects entwined in the historical conscience of its inhabitants ... If what is needed is to study the history of Chile in order to resolve its economic and social crisis, then it is possible and even necessary to cast aside this periodic breakdown, without too much regret. It is for this reason that development economists (mainly) and sociologists have improvised an alternative breakdown into periods, based on the major changes registered in the evolution of *Chilean foreign trade*.
>
> (Salazar 2003: 27)

To give viability to his left-wing proposal, Gabriel Salazar argues that it is necessary to build an alternative breakdown into periods that does not give such importance to the political factor and to the State. He hopes that this new form of historical breakdown, which has a more economic and social orientation – and, according to him, a better grip on the more up-to-date documental and statistical sources – could help to solve the crisis in Chile. This thinking means taking up a regulatory point of view that emphasizes the history of social, economic, and cultural aspects in Chile; and in Salazar's view, the new breakdown of Chilean history in its main stages should consider the following:

> (1) Gestation of the methods of colonial production and accumulation in Chile (1541–1580 approximately) ... (2) Second phase of the methods of colonial production and accumulation in Chile (1580–1690), normalization of the market (setting up of the intercolonial viceroyal market) ... (3) Third phase (peak) of the methods of colonial production and accumulation (1690–1873) (subordination of the vice-royal market and progressive opening towards world market) ... (4) Fourth and last phase of the methods of colonial production and accumulation: the crisis (1860–1878 and afterwards) ... (5) First phase of the transition from the colonial economy to a capitalist industrial economy (1870–1930) ... (6) Second transition towards industrial capitalism (1930–1973). The trade crisis of 1930 displaced the dominant foreign trade conglomerate, resulting in a great strategic vacuum in leadership of the economy. (7) Third stage of the long transition towards modern capitalism (1973 to date: the recession).
>
> (Salazar 2003: 29–30)

As can be seen, Salazar's breakdown into periods coincides, at least in part, with that proposed in this work, which differentiates five republics. However, Professor Salazar criticizes giving predominance to the political workings of the State and to republican constitutional law. In truth, his breakdown seeks to establish a substantial difference from his regulatory social, economic, and cultural point of view. Also, Salazar's mistrust and criticism does not only fall on the State and the predominance of politics, but extends to the law, the political parties, and republican institutions, and in this skepticism also his point of view seems excessive and mistaken. Salazar defends a version of corporativism which gives predominance to certain popular agents and their organizational forms as alternatives to constitutional democracy, and that is why he also criticizes political parties: "[The political parties] more than forming citizens and political actors aware of their sovereignty, form disciplined militants within a functional charter, which, from the generic point of view, is conformist. This could be an important input to politics, but, more often than not, a deficient contribution to policy" (Salazar 2009: 17–18).

The problem is that Salazar's proposal connects with a model that does not accept the basic tenets of constitutional democracy, and in this sense his project is truly a utopian alternative that does not recognize the value of social, cultural, and economic integration, which has been provided in our history by the multiplicity of political and social structures in which the republican project of the State has taken shape in Chile.

1.8 THE GREAT LATIN AMERICAN CONSTITUTIONAL COMPARISON OF ROBERTO GARGARELLA

In contrast, the comparative proposal of Professor Roberto Gargarella, expressed in *Los fundamentos legales de la desigualdad* [*Legal Foundations of Inequality*], a leading role is attributed to the political parties, and he tries to characterize the main political actors of Latin American constitutionalism, extrapolating the categories used in US academia. These groups described by Gargarella are also related to and evoke the ideas of constitutional parties, Girondists and Jacobins, which Lamartine recognizes in his work, *History of the Girondists*. Thus, Professor Gargarella has arrived at the identification of three ideal types, which are very similar to the main denominations of the Chilean political parties. Gargarella distinguishes between conservative, liberal, and radical or revolutionary actors. The richness of these categories is best transcribed in full:

in the models that I will denominate conservatives, it is usual to concentrate power and strengthen, in particular, the authority of the executive function, at the same time that the laws are transformed into dependants of property, such as that connected to the Catholic religion (that is, conditioning freedom of the press out of respect for Christianity). However, in the radical projects they managed to strengthen (instead of destroying or replacing) the authority of the citizens (essentially, conferring a more central position on the legislature), at the same time that respect for rights was adjusted, in this case to the complaints and needs of the majorities. In liberal constitutions, on the other hand, they sought to avoid what were considered the defects of the previous ones: so it was proposed to limit and balance the attributes of the different government functions, avoiding both the risks of tyranny as well as anarchy, while at the same time a special accent was placed on protecting the rights of the individual, which in earlier versions appeared neglected: the rights are considered in this case inviolable and not dependent on someone's convenience or on the notion of good asserted by some group. All the actors mentioned (conservatives, liberals, and radicals) tend to differ significantly about the citizens' capabilities in their approach to the debate raised above. The conservatives are accustomed to appear skeptical about the proposition that the life of society should be left to rest on the initiatives of each individual. They considered that there were adequate models that, independently of what the individual thought about them, should be defended and promoted through the powers that be. On the other hand, the liberals tended to defend a very strong individualistic position, assuming that each person's life, and by definition the life of the whole community, should depend only on the will of the individuals themselves. The radicals, for their part, started from assumptions similar to the liberals, but admitted the right of the majorities in society to impose their authority even in the face of the most basic protests by particular individuals.

(Gargarella 2005: 2–3)

Together with the characterization of the main political actors, and the ideas that can be attributed to each of them, and which have had protagonists in our Latin American continent, Roberto Gargarella, in his work, *La sala de máquinas de la Constitución. Dos siglos de constitucionalismo en America Latina (1810–2010)* [*The Engine Room: Two Centuries of Latin American Constitutionalism (1810–2010)*], has proposed a new periodic breakdown of constitutional history. This breakdown will cover the whole of the Latin American continent and describes five main historical periods, as follows:

The first period refers to the first Latin American constitutionalism, which we would place between 1810 and 1850, that is to say, from the date of the declaration of independence to the middle of the nineteenth century ... The second period starts from the middle of the nineteenth century and lasts to the beginning of the twentieth century. Let us call this moment that of fusion constitutionalism, because it is here that a crucial constitutional pact between conservatives and liberals takes place ... The third period will be the period of crisis of that post-colonial model, and we place it between the end of the nineteenth century and the beginning of the twentieth century. The fourth period will be social constitutionalism. This interval begins with the crisis of 1930 and has its peak in the middle of the twentieth century ... The fifth and last period that will be examined begins towards the end of the twentieth century and continues up to the turn of the twenty-first century. Here we will talk about the new Latin American constitutionalism and we will explore the latest and important constitutional reforms, dedicated in general to expand significantly social commitments in terms of rights:

even though normally as modest as their predecessors in terms of democratization of political organization and the restraints of political
power.

(Gargarella 2014: 10)

It is difficult to think that Professor Gargarella's period breakdown
will be applied equally in all Latin American countries. Gargarella has
proposed that after a liberal conservative period, or *fusion constitutionalism*, also called the post-colonial model, this period is substituted, in
his scheme, for a fourth period that imposes a *social constitutionalism*,
from 1930 to the middle of the twentieth century. However,
Gargarella, in the proposed periodic structure, has not considered the
re-emergence of the kinds of authoritarian constitutionalism which are
proper to the twentieth century, and in his work, the identification of
a marked authoritarianism, with the constitutionalism of fusion, liberal
conservatism of the nineteenth century, seems anachronistic in his
thinking and therefore exaggerated. Furthermore, once Gargarella
establishes his position regarding the present policies of the republican,
democratic, and constitutional model, which he calls *new Latin
American constitutionalism*, he says the following:

> The criticism of presidentialism formulated here does not imply
> a defense of the parliamentary system, as if it were the only alternative
> to presidentialism. The parliamentary system does not appear as
> a viable option in the light of the principles that we have defended
> here (least of all in the light of the present situation in Latin
> American congresses). At the same time, our criticism does not
> represent a way of supporting the new role of the judicial power in
> recent decades, as the fundamental deciding entity in new democracies
> (least of all, in the light of the elitism that continues to distinguish
> Latin American judicial powers).

(Gargarella 2014: 297)

In the paragraph cited above, Professor Gargarella criticizes all the
fundamental institutions of constitutional democracy and, while
describing his *engine room* model, to which he aspires, concludes with
the rather worrying observation: "The two most important social
events this century, that is, the incorporation of the working class
into politics and the outbreak of multicultural policies, had only
a limited impact on constitutionalism. Its vibrant presence was
reflected in the charter of rights, but not in changes related to the
organization of power" (Gargarella 2014: 360).

In relation to the most recent period, which he calls *new Latin American constitutionalism*, it is true that Professor Gargarella has been particularly critical, and with good reason. However, in some paragraphs in his work *La sala de máquinas*, such as the one just quoted, he seems to express the idea of appealing to a utopian political form, maybe of Jacobinistic origins, which seeks to give special political representation or participation to the workers and make them become political actors or privileged public powers. In his work *Los fundamentos legales de la desigualdad*, he discusses authoritarian constitutionalism and links it preferably to conservative constitutionalism and does not recognize that authoritarianism can also be linked to some manifestations of social constitutionalism.

Additionally, Roberto Gargarella wants the political system to give more recognition to marginalized people and the working class, and to reinforce, in particular, the guarantee of their rights, and perhaps that is why he has mentioned the possibility of also giving organic expression to these groups, without dismissing the suggestion that they should be incorporated in the "engine room" of the Constitution. It is at this point that I differ from Professor Gargarella, because I can see a difficulty of reconciliation, and a potential tension with the notion of equal citizenship which is the basis of representative constitutional democracy, including in its most participative current aspect.

Roberto Gargarella, with great generosity, had a private exchange on this point with the author and declared that he does not believe he has a substantial difference with my critical observations of his work, because in his proposal to incorporate these groups in the engine room where constitutional power is exercised, he does not mean to incorporate them as workers, but as citizens. His idea is that society continues to have difficulties accessing power, which does not get more democratic, and argues: How does it get incorporated? At the given time, with universal suffrage, then with women's suffrage, later – it could be – with measures of reverse discrimination. On this point, Professor Gargarella says that he is postulating ideas on representation similar to those in New Zealand, where there are permanent "positive" policies to indemnify and integrate the indigenous people, excluded for centuries from all positions of power (for example, with a special tribunal that takes care of claims; or such as those in Norway, where there is a special forum to deal with the complaints of the Sami people).

My own feeling is that, if it is about adopting these measures of exceptional representation of excluded groups through forms of positive discrimination, in principle, these, although exceptional, seem compatible with constitutional democracy. However, doubt continues over the way in which to incorporate workers or other entities into the constitutional engine room, without generating a kind of popular democracy which is distant from the democratic and liberal republican model.

On this subject of the weaknesses in representation of constitutional democracy, Robert Post has recently reflected and has shown how citizens, at the moment of being elected to a public position, identify themselves excessively with their political parties and distance themselves from the electorate and from the general interest that they should serve. The political parties attend to the interests of the businesses and the rich who have financed them, and efforts to use the media and public opinion to limit this disproportionate influence of money in politics have failed (Post 2014: 62).

That is why, despite recognizing that these criticisms can justify the adoption of special forms of representation and recognition, such as quotas, special rights, tribunals, or institutions that embrace the problems of some marginal groups, I do not believe that this justifies the substitution of the system of democratic representation, nor the swapping of *the engine room*, where decisions are taken, for a functional or corporate form of representation, be this made up of workers or other disadvantaged groups (Young 1989: 250–251, 258, 261, 271; Kartal 2001–2002: 101–130).

Incidentally, as has been noted before, the periodic breakdowns of Latin American history proposed by Gargarella, at least with regard to their application to the Chilean reality, show their limitations. The major flaw is that Professor Gargarella does not appear to clearly take into account the powerful anti-republican movement, opposed to constitutional democracy and anti-liberal, which began in the twentieth century and which also has its roots, in part, in *social constitutionalism*. This movement has been explained by Sofía Correa in her work *El pensamiento en Chile en el siglo XX bajo la sombra de Portales* [*Twentieth-Century Philosophy in Chile under the Shadow of Portales*], and on this matter she concludes:

> Despite several doctrinal interpretations that can be differentiated, philosophical thought in Chile during the twentieth century has in common its distancing from and its rejection of liberalism, despite the fact that this had constituted the doctrinal basis in the nineteenth

century, enabling the building of a solid public institutionality and an increase of economic wealth ... the rejection of liberalism among twentieth-century intellectuals expresses itself in different ways: nationalism, State or social corporativism, structural reformism, socialism, and neoliberalism. Despite their diversity, they share several common characteristics.

(Correa 2004: 300)

1.9 THE IDEA OF THE FIVE REPUBLICS AND CHILEAN CONSTITUTIONAL TRADITION

In this work I have been inspired by some researchers into French history and public law, who have explained the succession of political experiences which characterize their country, beginning from the idea of a multiplicity of republics. Of course, all these attempts at ordering and taxonomy could be controversial, in particular when assessing the period of the French Revolution and its republican, democratic, and constitutional characteristics (Duverger 1970: 505–606; Furet 1983: 173–211; and, among others, Favoreau et al. 1998: 289–321). Despite the controversies that surround these various explanations of French history, it has been useful to draw inspiration from them to better understand the shapes of our Chilean history. These ideas serve to analyze and help us to understand our constitutional history, both for the structure of its political institutions and for the rights of the citizens. Using these ideas, moreover, one can distinguish between the sources of inspiration for our political experiences, and illustrate their most significant similarities and differences. That is why I have been influenced by this research and have used this taxonomy and the plurality of historical periods of which it is composed.

I believe that despite our democratic deficit in terms of politics, in Latin America, and particularly in Chile, the republican option is not substituted in a permanent way by any other form of government. For example, the period of the Spanish reconquest, from 1814 to 1818, even though it affects the optimism of patriots, does not change the course taken in Chile in 1810, which is finally consolidated in the First Chilean Republic. The revolts which began against the government and the established order in the middle of the nineteenth century – some promoted by the ideology of the *Sociedad de la igualdad* [*Egalitarian Society*], as can be appreciated in the letter written from prison in 1852 by Santiago Arcos to Francisco Bilbao (Arcos 1989: 57–114), and even the civil war of 1891 – may have interrupted the normal life of politics, but did not give rise to a new form of republic substantially different in terms of the laws and the structure of constitutional power.

There are anti-republican interruptions of much longer duration between 1924 and 1932, and later, between 1973 and 1990. In these two periods there is such an interruption to the normal constitutional republican politics that in both cases, at the end of the period, a new republican period was generated which is characterized by the form of the laws and the way the State was organized.

It is already known that from the end of 1932 there arises in Chile a way of understanding the law which emphasizes its social aspect, and that it was proposed to broaden the right to vote in order to have a democratically based organization of political power, which is combined with great pre-eminence of the presidency. This is the Democratic Republic that existed in Chile from 1932 to 1973. From 1990 to date, in Chile the influence of neoliberalism is accepted, which establishes rights to block State interference and which concentrates public power still more in the President of the Republic. The anti-State concept of rights and the neo-presidentialist or hyper-presidentialist form is the structure of the distribution of power which characterizes the Neoliberal Republic in which we have lived since 1990.

Ultimately, in Chile, liberal, democratic, and republican constitutionalism is the most substantial of our collective efforts in terms of the law, despite not being a set of deeply rooted and historically conditioned ideas regarding the nature and function of the law in society and the form of government, the operation of a legal system, and the way of creating, applying, studying, teaching, and improving the law (Merryman 1971: 15). Many times, our constitutionalism has been reduced to an individual, fragmentary, and sporadic effort which is not organized as a systematic transfer of ideas between generations, a characteristic that is inherent in academic or political traditions which succeed in establishing themselves as such (MacIntyre 1990: 158–169). Sporadic and circumstantial though Chilean constitutionalism may be, its most important and lasting ideas have been based on republican, democratic, and liberal principles.

The fact of having had five republics in Chile does not mean abandoning the possibility of accepting some of these historical experiences with more sympathy and of rejecting others. The wealth and diversity occurring during each one of these republics up to the present day, to the contemporary Fifth Republic, is an object of admiration and also of criticism. The taxonomy and historical break-down into periods that is proposed here seem to be closer to the broader character we find under Chilean republicanism, which shows a certain unity at the most basic level, but in no case homogeneity or continuity in the incidental. Its unity is marked by interruptions and breaks, and its taxonomy and periodic structure merely reflect its phases, its main characteristics, and advances and setbacks. It could be argued that the period under Minister Diego Portales is not republican because of its authoritarianism, or that some forms of the State and revolutionary socialism of the Unidad Popular Government are difficult to reconcile with republicanism. However, during the Portales era, the elections were carried out and the law was respected, which implies the existence of a republic in its minimal form of expression. For their part, during the Unidad Popular Government (1970–1973), some forms of participative democracy and social advances appeared, which sought to expand equality of opportunities, basically republican aspirations.

It is possible also to explain the characteristics of the five Chilean republican periods, by the counterpoint they represent with the de facto governments which take place during the years 1814 to 1818, 1924 to 1932, and 1973 to 1990. For example, between 1814 and 1818, the Spanish reconquest restored the monarchic principle in the territory of Chile, the idea of self-government was abolished, and the notion of the Chilean people and of Chilean citizens independent of the Spanish metropolis was restricted. Between 1924 and 1932, there were several military coups, which closed Congress, restricted citizens' rights, and imposed the autocratic will of the military in the public sphere. Between 1973 and 1990, a right-wing dictatorship was installed, which closed Congress, gave the constituent power to the representatives of the armed forces, and governed with a state-of-exception regime, giving rise to severe violations of human rights.

The objective of this study is not to concentrate on the examination of dictatorships or de facto governments which have existed in Chile, nor to equate their methods of political parody with republican governments – quite the contrary. An attempt has been made to describe the individual characteristics of each one of the republican political experiences which we have had in Chile, some more democratic than others, by their most distinctive way of organizing the State and of recognizing the rights of its citizens, and by the characterization of its main political actors. These will be the topics treated in the following six chapters.

The method of comparative law will be used as a way of analysis which describes and explains the differences and/or the similarities between a principle, a regulation, or a legal institution and its expression in one or more legal systems (Ruiz-Tagle 2008: 92–93). Also, the idea of Mirjan Damaska will be taken into account, which considers the forms of authority as especially indicative of what should be the object of comparative law, and particularly the structure and function of State authority (Damaska 2000: 9–32). The comparison seeks a better understanding of our forms of government, our rights, and the main political agents who participate in each historical period. The comparison is focused on the characteristics of our republican forms, as expressed in the different eras of Chilean history, particularly in that which has been broken into periods with the name of five republics. At the same time, references to principles, regulations, and institutions of other countries have been used with the object of comparing them to our legal and political reality, and a foreign solution is considered as a model, or to contrast it with our reality, in order to better understand the republican experiences which have taken place in our country, and to find in the future some solutions which could be reasonable for Chile (Schlesinger 1980: 1–45).

CHAPTER TWO

FIRST REPUBLIC: THE INDEPENDENT
REPUBLIC, 1810–1830

From a comparative point of view, there are common factors between the Latin American and the North American independence processes. In both situations it was a case of cutting links with a metropolis which imposed economic restrictions on its colonies; additionally, both processes were movements of the elite influenced by the ideas of the Enlightenment (Keen and Wasserman 1984: 146–147; Wood 1969: 3–10).

Chilean independence, and in particular the ensuing period of the civil war among the patriots, is explained by the strength of the Spanish reconquest and the less tolerant character of the Latin American people, which is similar in its brusqueness to the turmoil during the French Revolution (Irisarri 1946: 27). Compared with other Latin American emancipation processes, Chilean independence has its own original characteristics because Chile would seem to have been a colony less prepared to achieve independence, due to its poverty, backwardness, and the lack of attention from the mother country (Barros Arana 1962: 384). In its origin, the Chilean case, as in the rest of Latin America, is triggered in part by an external cause – that is, the lack of leadership in the mother country caused by the Napoleonic invasion. From that moment of breaking away, the argument progressively takes over to justify independence due to the social inequality between those from the Spanish peninsula and those born locally, as perceived through the new ideas imported from the USA and France (Estévez 1949: 17–18; Blanco White 1810, quoted in Goytisolo 2010: 104–105).

Gabriel Amunátegui calls the First Chilean Republic the period of constitutional "tests." The republican ideals of submitting to the law, separation of the attributes of power, majority rule, respect for the rights of individuals, and political inclusion were not yet present in a mature form. Amunátegui detects this initial lack of clear definition of republicanism in Chile and notes: "The Chilean institutional evolution is directed towards the realization of its democratic government, and within this evolution manifests the determined intention of trying to harmonize the revolutionary movement with the legitimist principle" (Amunátegui 1951: 188).

The First Chilean Republic, as a constitutional political project, began with the meeting stated in the minutes of the *Acta del Cabildo Abierto* [Open Cabildo Act] of September 18, 1810. At that moment, the colonial link with Spain was revised, and even though independence was not proclaimed, nor a form of republic adopted, the first lines of a kind of self-government in Chile were drawn up. Our independence was declared formally much later, with the *Proclamación de la Independencia de Chile* [Chilean Proclamation of Independence] of February 12, 1818, where it is explicitly declared as such and where a new political unity was created. The truly republican format was perfected and consolidated only later, with the enactment of the 1828 Constitution.

The First Republic, in this way, goes through three phases: the initial phase, which actually constitutes the intent to organize self-government, between 1810 and 1814; the second phase or middle phase, which declares specifically our political independence, but whose institutions show an autocratic spirit which includes attempts to combine with legitimistic proto-monarchic forms, between 1818 and 1823; and the third or final phase, which assumes more decidedly the republican form of government, from 1823 to 1830.

The first *Junta de Gobierno* [Government Council] uses as its model the decision of the *Junta de Cádiz* [Cadiz Council]. The *Acta del Cabildo Abierto* mentions that just as the Governor of Cadiz "bestowed all his authority on the people that they might agree on the form of government most worthy of their trust" (Diario Oficial 2005: 35), the Chilean *Conde de la Conquista* [Count of the Conquest] and all the neighbors who attended the *Junta de Gobierno* meeting proceeded in the same way. In no way can it be said that in 1810 the people had taken over the constituent power. The *Acta* declares formally that the *Junta de Gobierno* elected by the people swears loyalty to Ferdinand VII. It is,

45

therefore, a provisional government which recognizes and affirms monarchic legitimacy and seeks a new way of organizing power. It is true that in the *Acta* there is a republican discourse mixed with a scholastic and legitimist rhetoric. However, that confusion must not make us reject this period as the beginning of the First Republic because, as Alfredo Jocelyn-Holt points out, it is a declaration of political autonomy (Jocelyn-Holt 1999: 164–165).

As a consequence of such autonomy, on July 4, 1811 the first *Congreso Nacional* [National Congress] met for its first session. In the *Sermón* written by Friar Camilo Henríquez for this occasion, it was determined that this Congress was set up as a constituent assembly with the purpose of establishing a Constitution. Henríquez maintained that, from the dissolution of the Spanish monarchy, its colonies had to assume the defense of the nation, religion, honor, and property. According to Henríquez, in the absence of a king, only a Constitution can ensure the safekeeping of these assets:

> But as such great benefits cannot be realized without setting up through our representatives an appropriate constitution for the present circum-stances of our times, that is to say, a fundamental regulation which will determine the way in which public authority is exercised ... we might reveal to the world the following propositions: First proposition: the principles of the Catholic faith, where concerned with politics, authorize the *Congreso Nacional de Chile* to set up a Constitution. Second propos-ition: the Chilean nation has inherent rights by virtue of which its representative body can establish a Constitution.
>
> (Diario Oficial 2005: 40–41)

Henríquez affirmed the Catholic doctrine that all authority comes from God, and quoted Saint Paul, Romans 13:1: *Non est potestas nisi a Deo*. His argument set out to demonstrate that the destruction of the Spanish monarchy meant that this authority had been transferred to the people. Henríquez merely confirmed what was explicitly recognized in the *Acta del Cabildo Abierto*. However, when Henríquez inaugurated the *Congreso Nacional*, the political circumstances were very different to those of the *Junta de Gobierno* in 1810. In 1810 the intention was to organize a new government that was loyal to the overthrown king. In 1811, on the other hand, a Congress was formed as an independent entity from Spain, representative of the Chileans in character; and furthermore, the formation of a new Constitution able to govern Chile was sought. It was the first republican government body constituted in Chile, expressing a concept of citizenship – and maybe also of the Chilean nation.

2.1 THE DEVELOPMENT OF CITIZENSHIP AND REPUBLICAN INSTITUTIONS

Since the French Revolution, citizenship is seen as a new idea that displays the public expression of a kind of idealized family. It is a stereotyped concept developed to inter-relate people of different gender, and different social and economic positions, which is supposedly shared as an indivisible characteristic, a common identity. Citizenship is understood as a sublime reciprocity between the individual and a presumed general will that links people, despite their differences, as equal bodies, for the purposes of being represented in assemblies, in imitation of the collegiate bodies of ancient times, in particular those of the Romans (Schama 1989: xv, 354, 359). When explaining the origins of Chilean constitutionalism, and in particular when referring to the background before independence, some authors have argued that in the Spanish colonies, before independence, there were some legal and political features which anticipated this process. The declarations of rights that are typical of constitutionalism in the colonial period would have been organized, to some extent, with certain resources and guarantees which enable legal instruments to take effect. The thesis underlying this proposition is that constitutionalism cannot work in a vacuum, and that its declarations, regulations, and principles were grafted onto a previous legal structure which already contained a fragmented conception of resources and actions, and certain substantive rights which could be traced back to Spanish jurisdiction and to Indian law (Eyzaguirre 1948: 86–92; 1962: 7–9; Figueroa 1967: 33–37).

This same idea is useful for understanding the way in which the configuration of constitutional rights could have been influenced by the way they were shaped among the indigenous people before the arrival of the Spaniards. For example, as far as concerns the main characteristics of indigenous property law, in place at the time of independence, it can be said that these were affected by the Spanish conquest and colonial period, with very significant changes. In relation to this point, Ricardo Latcham has pointed out:

> in all the documents of the sixteenth century we were convinced that the kind of totemism present at that time corresponded to the system of

maternal affiliation and that in certain parts of the country, inheritance still came down from the mother and the feminine line. On the other hand, we had the emphatic declarations of chroniclers and many documents that at the same time, the father was the head of the family, that the women were acquired by purchase, that polygamy existed and that the recognition of parental authority and the succession of children to the property of the father were deep-rooted traditions among the Araucanians. How to reconcile these two series of events?

(Latcham 1924: 57)

Latcham's explanation of the previous situation and the change or transition which took place among the indigenous Araucanians or Mapuches with the arrival of the Spaniards is the following:

There was no kind of communism among the Araucanians, not even nominal as in Peru, and each person was sole owner of the property that he was able to assemble. They did not even pay tribute to anyone for anything, except a voluntary wartime payment which generally meant providing food, weapons, and other supplies for the troops. Before 1550, military organization among the *Araucanos* had not had the importance that it acquired later with the constant wars against the Spaniards and it seems to have been subordinated to civil organization. This, despite the little obedience given to the family heads, existed within conditions relatively well-defined; the true power was found in the heads of the totemic groups.

(Latcham 1924: 155)

Under the assumption that there were certain people who were heads of the social organization of the indigenous people, and according to whether the system were of maternal or paternal affiliation, in the indigenous groups there was an extended family structure, very flexible and dispersed, which in turn gave shape to the structure of ownership. This system, according to Latcham, had the following characteristics:

In the area north of Cautín, neither common ownership of property nor the hoarding of all property in the hands of the father existed. Each one was the owner of the goods that they managed to acquire, although the individual exclusive ownership of land was not recognized. Any Indian person could cultivate as much land as he liked and he could pocket the products; but he could not dispose of the land as his property, neither sell it, nor rent it. Ultimately the land belonged to the community, but the benefit deriving from its exploitation was individual. What has led some to believe that there was a community of property was that some tasks were communal, but this community of labor did not establish common ownership of what was produced. It was carried out on the basis of mutual help – if you help me, I will help you – and the individual rarely had to seek help from others than his own relatives, whom he in turn helped. As these collective tasks were always occasions for parties and drunkenness, there was never a lack of cooperation.

(Latcham 1924: 171)

José Bengoa, in more recent studies, confirms this social structure which gives form to property in some of the main pre-Hispanic indigenous populations, and he identifies it with a feudal system. The feudal system is a system for social organization and therefore for ownership; it is not a State organization and its leadership is not temporary, but becomes permanent over time, even hereditary (Bengoa 2003: 163). Bengoa adds that this feudal form could have been established among the Chilean indigenous people from their pre-Hispanic contact with the Quechua Incaic culture: "The presence of a feudal system such as the Quechua Incaic, which they were obliged to face in the century before the arrival of the Spaniards, must have occasioned tension and a process of increasing concentration" (Bengoa 2003: 163).

It is a form of social and ownership organization difficult to define because it was very adaptable and was in constant change, as Bengoa tells us:

they had a basic unit similar to the extended family. They were big families for the simple reason that the father, the central core, lived with his wives, his children and their wives, the young and the children. Every so often one of the children separated from the family core to a nearby place or migrated to a different place, which was very common until recently, and there would start a new nucleus or *lov*. These enormous families in very large houses, with several of these gathered together, constituted the central groupings. The alliances between these units were multiple and complex, depending on the reason for their formation.

(Bengoa 2003: 169–170)

To substitute in part the social and ownership context of the feudal structure existing among the indigenous people, the Spaniards imposed their colonial system. This process gave origin to many legal disquisitions, one of the most famous among them being the lawsuit for fair titles that at the beginning of the sixteenth century was expressed in the famous text written in 1512 by the court lawyer don Juan López de Palacios Rubio, called *Requerimiento* [Requirement]. This document was read and explained to the main chiefs or chieftains among the indigenous people, and implied a legal justification for the transfer of the titles of their properties to the Spanish crown:

> We require that you understand well what we have said to you, and that you take the necessary time to understand it and deliberate over it, and that you recognize the Church as lord and master of the world and the Holy Father, called the Pope, in its name and the King and Queen Juana, our lords, in their place, as masters and kings of these islands and mainland . . . and if you do not do this or should you maliciously delay it, we assure you that with God's help we will mightily attack you and we will fight a war against you everywhere and in every way that we can, and we will subject you to the yoke and obedience to the Church and to their Majesties, and we shall take your persons and those of your wives and children and we shall make them slaves and as such we shall sell them and dispose of them as their Majesties may command, and we shall seize your goods and we shall do to them all evil and damage that we may, as to vassals that do not obey nor wish to receive their lord and resist him and contradict him; and we declare that the deaths and damage that might follow, that will be your fault and not their Majesties, nor ours, nor of these gentlemen that come with us.
>
> (Zavala 1971: 215–217)

Some indigenous people agreed to this forced transference of dominium and property, and others resisted firmly, as happened in Chile with the Araucanians or Mapuches. At the imposition of the Spanish colonial regime, a mixed and diverse system of the structure of ownership was established, in which more importance was given to private property than that existing among the indigenous people, but which implied the coexistence of forms of exclusive ownership, with all kinds of special regimes, such as primogenitures, land grants, mining rights, the property of the religious orders, and so on (Ruiz-Tagle 2001c: 133).

This organization of property in the first years of our country has been described by Alessandri and Somarriva as a complex process that has several origins and that is organized around certain particular legal forms, among which the most important are the following:

> The estates, mostly vast in extent, were divided into farms, and these, in turn, were subdivided into smaller plots. However, some estates were maintained undivided due to the system of primogeniture, which began at the end of the seventeenth century and remained in effect until the middle of the nineteenth century. The concession of land grants lost importance during the eighteenth century, during which time an

attempt was being made to introduce managed colonization, by giving land to soldiers, graduates, or people who promised to produce wheat, flax, and hemp. All this contributed to bring order to property in the Chilean territory between Copiapo and the Bio-Bio River. In short, the origin of private territorial property in Chile has been the allocation of plots, the land grants, the auctions of public land, and easement by prescription in cases of possession without concession of the authorities with an arrangement in accordance with the law. Therefore, occupation by itself has not brought about a constituent title of landownership.
(Alessandri, Somarriva, and Vodanovic 1993: 49)

Thus, in the period that we have called the First Chilean Republic, marked by the idea of self-government, which corresponds to the new Chilean State, whose construction was sought from 1810 until 1830, there arises a form of protection of property at a constitutional level, which is expressed in the 1812 *Reglamento Provisorio* [Provisional Ruling]. This regulation, in generic terms, is a guarantee of due legal process because it creates a judicial guarantee linked to the rights of people and things in the recently independent territory, and it refers to property as follows: "Art. 16. The right of citizens to the security of their persons, their homes, personal effects and documents will be respected; and no orders will be given without probable causes supported by a judicial oath and without a clear designation of the places or things that are to be examined or confiscated" (Valencia Avaria 1951: 48).

In the Provisional Ruling of 1812 the truth is that the more abstract concept of property is not used, but protection is given to rights regarding homes, effects, and documents, and "places or chattels," which implies a guarantee of the title of people to their goods, from the point of view of the common citizen (Ackerman 1977: 10–20).

Gabriel Salazar recognizes the existence of a supposed connection between the configuration and organization of power in the colonial regime with later constitutionalism. Salazar explains how, in America, the old European idea of popular sovereignty reappears under other forms: in the comradeship of the conquest in the new towns and cities, and, of course, in their new councils and chapters. In this way, according to Salazar, rejuvenated and modernized, under some of the local forms of Indian law, a right of the people reappears (Salazar 2005a: 67). This right of the people coexisted with the imperial claims of the Spanish crown and started a permanent conflict with the monarchic authority.

These pre-republican legal forms, to the extent that they were locally constituted, created tension with the organization of the 1810 *Junta de Gobierno*, with Carrera's militarism expressed in the constitutional regulations of 1811, and with the first republican and patriotic ideals, and their influence even survives until a later period and the formal declaration of Chilean independence in 1818 (Salazar 2005a: 136–137).

It is debatable whether an understanding of republican-based rights or of certain forms of institutional organization could have been anticipated prior to our independence. In this regard, it has to be recognized, in any case, that with the installation of the constitutional government in Chile we could find a more modern notion of rights corresponding to a period post-French Revolution, and which is already inherent to republican constitutionalism. The constitutional texts of 1811, 1818, 1822, 1823, and 1828 include several explicit recognitions of the rights of the Chilean people (Diario Oficial 2005: 46, 69, 98, 123, 199), and also, in a most particular way, of the right of property. Later, and at the moment of the definitive installation of the First Republican Government in Chile, the whole colonial system becomes subjected to revision and, step by step, its change is proposed. This change is expressed in the *Declaración de Independencia de Chile* [Chilean Declaration of Independence], a document that asserts the idea of republican self-government, imposes a new transfer of ownership in favor of the new government, and seeks to end colonial domination and its abuses. In the Declaration of Independence, the patriots are recognized as citizens who agree to found authority on consent and on suffrage, at least exercised tacitly; and who recognize the impossibility of issuing a summons to Congress, which is, by definition, a republican institution. All the above is secured by dignity and life, and fortune – that is, with the property of the citizens who concur in this founding moment.

The strength of the republican political idea expressed in the Declaration of Independence was consolidated gradually in our country, and on that basis it was intended to secure the new form of political legal organization. The effect of republican principles on the law is a matter of controversy among the scholars of our history. When referring to pro-independent and modernizing revolutions of the nineteenth century in Latin America, Octavio Paz says:

> The many countries ... continued to be the old colonies: the social conditions did not change; the reality was just covered up by liberal and

democratic rhetoric. The republican institutions, like facades, hid the same horrors and the same miseries. The groups that rose against the Spanish power used the revolutionary ideas of the time, but were not able and did not want to reform society.

(Paz 1994: 132–133)

In our country, the historian Alfredo Jocelyn-Holt views our independence process with more optimism, and perceives it as an evolution towards the modernity which had been dragging itself along since the eighteenth century, and which is supported by two pillars: the State and the elite. Independence did more than just confirm the changes, reinforcing the new republican political institutions and the influence of the local elite, and giving them both a new legitimacy. He claims "a sustained change, but not audacious; evolutionary, not revolutionary; utopic and ideological, not always real and immediate; rather measured even though inevitable; partial, never global; above all institutional, rarely social; in brief, a change preferably more public than private (everyday life continued virtually unchanged from the colonial times)" (Jocelyn-Holt 1992: 286).

Regarding the insecurity of constitutional rights with a liberal base, it is important to remember the problems that Camilo Henríquez had with his liberal and federalistic opinions, not only with conservative sectors in Chile, but also during the actual government of José Miguel Carrera, who wanted to censor him. For example, Henríquez published the famous discourse of John Milton, in which the author defends the freedom of expression, in the same edition of *La Aurora* in which he was forced to publish the decree that obliged him to show his newspaper first to a government censorship commission, and then to the censorship of the *Tribunal de Apelaciones* [Appeals Court]. His problems became worse with the fall of José Miguel Carrera's government.

In the process of building the autonomy of the State and republican citizenship in Chile, the liberalism that the Spaniards developed from 1808 to 1812 had a decisive influence and became an inspiration for American creoles (Heise 1996: 9, 16). North American political literature also has influence in Chile, as expressed in the work of Hamilton, Madison, and Jay (1961), published in *The Federalist*, and the political ideas of Story, Kent, and Jefferson (Heise 1996: 20). Among these authors there was a revolutionary conscience, which is revealed, for example, in Jefferson, who already, in 1816, was asserting that the idea of a representative democracy rendered useless everything that had been written (and thought) about the government until that date (Wood 1969: 563). Rousseau was also very influential, specifically on Camilo Henríquez (Eyzaguirre 1957: 126–129).

This same revolutionary feeling, and the language of civil virtue and public good inherent in the republican spirit was present in independent Chile, and it emerges in the work of Camilo Henríquez and Juan Egaña (Castillo 2003: 19, 35, 50). After José Miguel Carrera's rise to power, this ideology served to give a more independent character to the patriotic cause, even though it was still not altogether inclined to declare total separation between Chile and the Spanish crown. However, it is important to recall that in 1814 the catastrophe of the reconquest occurred without warning, and with that political setback, the enthusiasm, innocence, and impulsiveness which characterize the early period of the initial revolutionary patriotism were weakened. This new way of thinking is more conservative about rights, authoritarian in institutional aspects, and moderate in political, which has an impact on the republican possibilities of Chile and is reflected in the modification of the thinking of Camilo Henríquez and Egaña after 1814 (Ruiz Schneider and Castillo Rojas 2001: 1063, 1082). However, more recent studies have demonstrated that these authoritarian republican forms, which were developed in the shadow of the influence and power of military leaders, were present in Chile before 1814 and at least from 1812, because they are manifest, for example, in the rivalry between O'Higgins and Carrera (Recabal 2015: 88–89, 139–140).

2.2 THE DECLARATION OF INDEPENDENCE AND THE CONSTITUTIONAL EXPERIMENTS OF 1818, 1822, 1823, AND 1826

Once power was recovered, the patriots proclaimed the independence of Chile on February 12, 1818. Through this action, Chile was able, in due course, to become a member of the society of nations, as a State among States, even though its independence was only later recognized in formal terms (Donoso 1967: 39). For example, the United States of America only recognized Chile's independence in 1822.

The Chilean independence process did not include a revolution against the prevailing legal system; rather it was limited to exchanging metropolitan centralization and the colonial system of control by the Spanish crown for a locally derived system. Even though the text of the Declaration of Independence does not clearly establish a republican government, it reiterates the September 18, 1810 idea of political autonomy, because it considers our country as a free State, independent and sovereign, and notes that:

> By the extraordinary powers with which the people have authorized us for this particular case, we solemnly declare in their name in the presence of the Almighty and make known to all mankind, that the continental territory of Chile and its adjacent islands de facto and by the law constitute a free, independent, and sovereign State, and will be always kept separate from the Spanish monarchy, with full competency to adopt the form which is most convenient for their interests.
>
> (Diario Oficial 2005: 68)

After the Declaration of Independence, the Constitution of 1818 was enacted; this recognized that the people and their representatives had the right of approval of the fundamental charter. This Constitution assigned sovereignty to the *Director Supremo* [Supreme Director] and a Senate appointed by him. It defined the fundamental political unit as independent and self-governed, and it identified this with the *Estado de Chile* [State of Chile] and used republican discourse to legitimize the military dictatorship of O'Higgins (Salazar 2005a: 157). This ambiguity in terms of republican principles is explained because an important group of Chileans regarded the new ideals with skepticism and even considered the idea of installing a monarchy (Donoso 1967: 39–49; Alemparte 1963: 248). However, the monarchic project did not prosper.

Whatever the judgment on the effect produced by these changes, the truth is that property was at the center of the matters that the new republican governments wanted to regulate. Thus, the 1818 Constitution, in several articles, contains provisions that are more specific when referring to the protection of property. These regulations authorize the expropriation of property in urgent cases, as determined by the Senate, in order to defend the country and in case the titleholder had committed an offense. The 1818 Ruling orders the following:

CHAPTER ONE. *About the rights of the person in society*
Art. 1: Human beings by nature enjoy the inviolable and inalienable right of individual security, dignity, property, freedom, and civil equality . . .
Art. 5: Every person's home and documents are sacred, and this law can only be suspended in urgent cases accorded by the Senate . . .

Art. 9: The State cannot deprive any person of ownership and free use of their goods, unless it is required for the defense of the country, and even in this case, with the indispensable condition of a rate assessment proportionate to the capacity of each individual and never with violence and insults . . .

CHAPTER THREE. *About the Appeals Chamber*
Art. 23: Neither may more goods be confiscated than the precise amount to answer for the offense, and if it be of quality, let some financial fine be demanded.

(Valencia Avaria 1951: 54, 55, 68)

In 1822 a new Constitution replaced the authoritarian text of 1818 and was influenced by the 1812 Spanish Constitution of Cádiz. It declared that sovereignty was vested in the nation, which was the union of all Chileans and provided for a representative government made out of three independent powers: Executive, Legislative, and Judiciary. It extended citizenship to all males older than twenty-five years who could read and write and who had economic means (Estévez 1949: 27–29). A confirmation of the principles of republican constitutionalism is seen here in its minimum aspect, and features of democratic republicanism can barely be recognized in this initial historical moment.

The 1822 Constitution recognized as constitutional bodies a Congress which was formed by a Senate elected from among the government authorities and a Chamber of Deputies elected by the councils of the people. The executive power was exercised by a Director Supremo who was elected by Congress and who remained in power for six years. The Fundamental Charter subjugated the councils to the Director Supremo, which caused the rebellion of the Concepción council and, later, of other councils against the central government in Santiago (Salazar 2005a: 171). In the 1822 Constitution were enunciated the first concepts of the separation of powers and of suffrage as an expression of sovereignty.

Furthermore, the 1822 Constitution included sections that referred to rights, with three articles referring directly to property; and it reiterated the idea expressed in 1818, in accordance with the principle of expropriation of property for the defense of the country, and set up a compensation procedure, as recorded in Title V, Chapter II, referring to the limitations of the executive power. In these regulations, property was guaranteed indirectly, in relation to taxes, and these regulations were complemented by Title VI, Chapter II, referring to the administration of justice. These provisions are:

> Title V, Chapter II. *Limitations of the executive power*
>
> Art. 115: No one will be deprived of their possessions and properties; and when a rare case of the common utility or need demands it, the value will be compensated at a fair valuation of honest men ...
>
> Art. 116: The common use and need will be qualified by the two Supreme Powers: Legislative and Executive, and by the *Tribunal Supremo de Justicia* [*Supreme Court of Justice*] ...
>
> Title VI, Chapter II. *On the administration of justice*
>
> Art. 222: Every citizen has the free disposition of his property, income, work, and industry; thus, taxes may not be levied except in very urgent cases, to save the country, lives, and the remainder of each one's fortune.
>
> (Valencia Avaria 1951: 83, 92)

On the other hand, the 1823 Constitution represents a frustrated effort in the development of Chilean constitutionalism. It was inspired by the ideas of Juan Egaña, who, in turn, was inspired in his readings and observation of the English experience. In his words:

> A constitution is really as the English people name it, a big charter or written document executed between the rulers and the people. The first have the duty to govern and protect, acting always according to the conditions of that document, and having no authority to act in a different way. On the other hand, the people have an obligation to obey as many laws and administrative measures as may be enacted and applied. To make this obedience effective, they hold in their hands the armed forces, the money from the tax payments, the influence given by the granting of employments, the splendor and authority of the magistrates and all the illusions of opinion and senses. Therefore, it is essential that the people retain in their favor some kind of guarantee that ensures that the rulers will not abuse such great resources, in order to violate the constitutional covenants and satisfy their ambition and whims.
>
> (Egaña 1830: 135–136)

The 1823 Constitution was not a success, despite taking its inspiration from these accurate doctrinal definitions of English public law. The reason for this unsuccessful experience is that the constitutional thinking of Juan Egaña, in a confusing way, mixed enlightened and conservative ideas, which hindered the consolidation of a truly republican government in Chile. Salazar characterizes Egaña's ideas as follows:

> The political philosophy of Juan Egaña (*Presidente de la Asamblea* [President of the Assembly] and of the *Comisión Constituyente* [Constitutional Commission]) diverges from the historic line of action adopted by those "people," because, ultimately, a centralistic, enlightened and aristocratic political system was chosen, which coincided with the propositions defended by the people (oligarchy) of Santiago, (who scorned the lack of enlightenment of the people in the provinces), and entailed, even, subscribing to the same concept of sovereignty as that supported by the César-like governments before 1823 (O'Higgins rejected the sovereignty of the people, alleging their "ignorance"). This would generate ... a confused internal contradiction, both in the revolutionary as well as in the constitutional process.
>
> (Salazar 2005a: 213)

Alfredo Jocelyn-Holt has set forth the constitutional ideas of Juan Egaña and has highlighted his encyclopedic enlightened inspiration, which does not seem to him to be conservative, recognizing Chilean independence as a matter of fact derived from the French occupation of Spain, adopting those republican ideals which favor the notions of virtue and public interest, and which introduce collegial and moralistic entities to the ruling group, so that they serve as a counterbalance to self-orientated authoritarianism and as a model for their new concept of public affairs (Jocelyn-Holt 1999: 111, 161, 216, 266). Egaña's basic objective was "to transform the laws into customs, and customs into civil and moral behavior because ... a rigid constitutional control is insisted on so as to finish with a self-orientated control that has in fact already failed" (ibid.: 267, 268). According to Jocelyn-Holt, the Constitution failed not because it was unrealistic, but because it did not take into account the traditional elite already established in Chile, and because it thought of the Chilean ruling group as a bureaucracy of mandarins and did not present a constitutional proposition compatible with the degree of political maturity and moderation already achieved (ibid.: 269).

Ultimately, the 1823 Constitution was resisted for being unclear and for creating contrived institutions: a class of distinguished citizens, a moral code which regulated their awards, a celebration of public morals, and a cumbersome system of administration and bureaucracy.

This official system of morality imposed by 1823 seems characteristically alien to republican constitutionalism, but it fits the classical idea of founding a republican government on the virtue of its citizens. Moreover, there were other constitutional plans in Latin America in which it was proposed to organize, at constitutional level, a moral power. The famous Angostura speech made by Simón Bolívar on February 15, 1819, with its proposal of constitutional government for Venezuela, contains a similar proposition (Battista 1990: 37–68). It is possible to argue that this constitutional high-mindedness is a common strategy among the Latin American elites at this early stage, whose end objective is to create a more homogeneous political community (Rojas 2009: 12–14).

In any case, Jorge Huneeus describes Juan Egaña's Constitution, adopted in 1823, as vague, legalistic, and impracticable, and thereon declares:

> There was promulgated on December 29, 1823, the Political Constitution known as the 1823 Constitution. A work, in great part, of Mr. Juan Egaña, that Constitution, which has been the law, in judicial affairs, until March 1, 1876, was in all other ways extremely complicated, vague, legalistic, and so impracticable, that a simple law enacted on January 10, 1825, declared it without substance in all its parts.
>
> (Huneeus 1890: 51)

Like the 1822 Charter, in the moralistic Constitution of 1823 property is guaranteed, and it is mentioned in Title XII concerning the judicial power as a matter linked to individual rights, defined mainly by its relation to, or as part of, the jurisdictional powers. The precepts of the 1823 Constitution state the following in relation to property:

Title XII. *Regarding judicial power*
Art. 116: Judicial power protects the rights of individuals according to the following principles.
Art. 117: Nobody can be deprived of their property, except for public necessity, qualified as extremely serious by the Senate, and with previous compensation.

(Valencia Avaria 1951: 119)

At this same time, a segment of the Chilean liberal movement voiced their sympathies for the ideas of federalism. José Miguel Infante, who was in charge of the government by delegation of power, in the moments when General Freire was trying to free the southern islands of Chiloé from Spanish domination, proposed a series of federal laws following the model of the United States Constitution. Infante thought that from this political structure, order and prosperity should arise. According to Collier, "Federalism meant more than the decisive affirmation of the recognition of the provinces. It expressed in a profound way and with force, the liberal aversion for dynamic executive power" (Collier 1977: 290).

2.3 CONSOLIDATION OF THE FIRST REPUBLIC IN THE 1828 CONSTITUTION

The First Republic is not clearly defined in relation to its governmental propositions. A concept of the collegial executive is suggested, and at the same time, several one-person formats; the legislative and executive functions are mixed up; both autocratic and liberal governments are proposed; a federal regime is introduced and some even dream of some kind of monarchy (Amunátegui 1951: 193). Amunátegui is right to emphasize the "trial-and-error" character of this First Republic. However, he is wrong when he defines the period from 1826 to 1830 as "political anarchy." It is precisely during this period that some of the truly republican features of Chilean constitutionalism are established. This republican regime is consolidated in one of its best manifestations in the 1828 Constitution. Thus, Francisco Antonio Pinto can say in his Preface: "Chileans: The solemn day of the consolidation of our liberty has arrived. It cannot exist and has never existed without fundamental laws" (Diario Oficial 2005: 199). Pinto explicitly expresses the republicanism that inspires the new Constitution, and he contrasts it with monarchical legitimism: "We will, therefore, witness the disappearance of that monstrous disparity observed between the requirements of a republic and the antiquated laws of a monarchy" (Diario Oficial 2005: 200).

The 1828 Constitution originates in a Congress that assumes constituent powers and which, after consulting the provinces, opts for a new political form. Its rhetoric does not reject the setting up of provincial assemblies, but its form is unitary and liberal, and its inspirational ideas are the following:

> The 1828 Constitution of 134 articles, recognizes as sources the 1791 and 1793 French Constitutions, the 1812 Spanish Constitution and the 1826 Chilean Federal Experiment . . . It declares expressly that the form of a popular representative Republic is adopted . . . and the separation of

powers ... the Executive's authority being reduced with the aim of establishing a balance of powers.

(Carrasco 2002: 97)

José Joaquín de Mora drafted this Constitution. A Spaniard, Mora arrived in Chile on February 10, 1828, to be banished by Portales in February 1831 (Amunátegui Solar 1933: 63). Mora had escaped from Spain at the moment of the re-establishment of absolutism with Fernando VII and traveled to Chile, where he dictated one of the first courses in public law in republican Chile. He set forth, as one of his fundamental ideas, that society is founded on an agreement from which are derived authority and the three fundamental rights: equality, liberty, and property. An original idea of Mora's is the affirmation that security is not a fundamental value of civil society, because within that which has to be a Constitution, this value is already included in the three fundamental rights. The *Curso de Leyes del Liceo de Chile* [Law Course for the Chilean Secondary School], which contains Mora's teachings, was published in 1830 and is the first text on constitutional law in our country. According to Mora, security cannot be differentiated from equality and cannot be established without freedom. For this reason, he criticizes the idea of including security as an independent constitutional value:

> In most of the treatises on political legislation, and in many modern constitutions, security is included in the catalog of basic rights that society concedes and sets up. I have believed this new element to be useless and the reason seems clear to me. Security does not appear to me to be a separate right from the others that I have mentioned, but an indispensable quality in each one of them.
>
> (Mora 1830: 115)

For Mora, security exists to the extent that there is freedom and equality. In this regard, Mora distances himself from Hobbes, who thinks that the basis for civil society is the need to survive – that is, the need to overcome the permanent state of insecurity. In this respect he writes:

> We can conclude by deducing that from everything said, equality must be one of the first laws of nature; that every positive law which is in contradiction with it is repulsive to nature itself; that everything contributing to stimulate work, to increase the means of industry, to provide human beings with new instruments of wealth and power, essentially and directly contributes to establish, widen, and consolidate equality.
>
> (Mora 1830: 15)

In this way, he assigns to equality an important position in his version of republican liberalism. This principle must be recognized because that way reciprocity can develop between human beings, which constitutes the wisest and most celebrated law on which is founded the pact that is the basis of civil society (ibid.: 14). Equality is based on the common sense shared by human beings of having been created equal, able to reason, subject to the same social rights, and the imperative that the strong shall not oppress the weak (ibid.: 14–15). According to Mora, equality and freedom are strengthened and perfected as civilization advances and the jobs created by it multiply. Equality is opposed to violence; it broadens and strengthens through industry, employment, and the new resources of wealth.

Mora's political views influenced the drafting of the 1828 Constitution, which contains a catalog of rights, where the emphasis is on the principles of equality, freedom, and property, the right to petition and to publish opinions, and the confidentiality of correspondence, and where the supremacy of legislative power is secured (Carrasco 2002: 97–98).

Unlike the previous constitutional regulations and with its own proposed legislation, the 1828 Constitution contains, in its preamble, a direct reference to property that is signed and adopted by Francisco Antonio Pinto. There, property is understood as part of a system of rights and as one of the main guarantees that the new Fundamental Charter proposes to establish. The preamble of the 1828 Charter states that the Constitution "establishes the most formidable guarantees against abuses by any kind of authority, by any excess of power. Freedom, equality, and property, the power to publish your opinions, the right to present your demands and complaints to the different entities of national sovereignty, are protected from any attack" (Valencia Avaria 1951: 139).

The new way of understanding property in the 1828 Constitution is set out directly and fully developed in relation to other individual rights, such as respect for freedom of opinion. At the same time, in the 1828 Charter, property is regulated in relation to a bundle of individual faculties and entitlements that can operate as limits to the action of authority, among which stands out the right to be indemnified, should one be required to surrender property for reasons of public interest. The 1828 constitutional precepts state the following:

Chapter III. *Individual rights*

Art. 10: The Nation guarantees to each person imprescriptible and inviolable rights: freedom, security, property, and the right to petition and to publish their opinions ...

Art. 16: No home may be broken into, unless it is a case of resistance to the legitimate authority and by virtue of a written mandate of such authority.

Art. 17: No citizen may be deprived of their property or of property over which the person has legitimate right or of any part of it, however small, except by virtue of a judicial order. When the public service demands someone's property, the owner will be paid its exact value, and compensated for damages in the case of the property being retained.

(Valencia Avaria 1951: 143)

Additionally, the 1828 Constitution, true to its liberal inspiration, in several provisions tried to remove the class structure of the Spanish colonial regime. These regulations discriminated in the access to and exercise of public posts, and also imposed charges or linked property arbitrarily to certain personal qualities, such as the case of the primogenitures. The regulations of the 1828 Constitution that sought to modify these discriminatory forms stated:

Chapter XII. *General provisions*

Art. 125: All men are equal before the law.

Art. 126: All Chileans can take up employment. Everyone must contribute to the burden of the State according to their means. There is no privileged class. Primogenitures are abolished for ever and all encumbrances that prevent the free transfer of farms. The present owners may freely dispose of them, except for a third of the value that is reserved for the immediate successors who may dispose of it with the same freedom.

(Valencia Avaria 1951: 158)

In this same founding period of Chilean constitutional law, Mora introduces a law of the press with panels of jurors, which Ricardo Donoso describes as doing honor to Chilean law, which is justified because freedom of the press is the best guarantee of the other laws and of maintaining the republican regime (Donoso 1967: 256). Mora also includes in the 1828 Constitution the procedure of constitutional charges which inaugurates a legal and political innovation based on a republican concept giving effective life to the principle of constitutional equality (Ruiz-Tagle 2000a). It is important to note that in the 1828 Constitution, the constitutional impeachment coexists with the colonial institution of an inquiry into a person's performance in public office, which is recognized in Article 128 of the Fundamental Charter. The inquiry into a person's performance in public office could be initiated against any civil servant, and the aforementioned Article 128 indicates that a special law will regulate its procedure. The coexistence of these institutions shows how constitutional change does not assume in Chile the total abolition of institutions inherited from Spain. In any case, the incorporation of the constitutional charge in the 1828 Fundamental Charter is a reflection of the main idea of republicanism: control of the exercise and abuse of power. Additionally, in matters of religious tolerance, one of the fundamental issues in every republic, the 1828 Constitution was the first decisive step in that direction, because as Ricardo Donoso has said:

> It was the 1828 Constitution, drafted by the restless and courageous Mora, that took an important step on this issue because while Article 3 recognized that the religion of the country was the Catholic, Apostolic, Roman, with exclusion of public practice of any other, in the following article it established the principle that no one will be persecuted or pestered for their private opinions.
>
> (Donoso 1967: 141)

In any case, with the enactment of the 1828 Constitution the organization of the First Republic was achieved in Chile because this fundamental law interprets with great accuracy the historic-cultural reality of the time. It is necessary to note that the great majority of its provisions were incorporated in the 1833 authoritarian reform, which, despite being inspired by opposite ideas, cannot undo what was already established (Heise 1996: 37).

Among its critics, José Victorino Lastarria recognizes that the 1828 Constitution was difficult to apply given the characteristics of the government of the time, and points to a series of problems and political-contingent reasons for this: the incomplete reform of the Army, the exhausted treasury, a series of religious conflicts, shortcomings in respect of the law, demagogy, problems of public unrest, and so on (Lastarria 1865: 202–203). According to Lastarria, it was not the 1828 Constitution that failed, but the political reality on which it rested, because the liberal government lost its drive. Thus, the authoritarian opposition in Chile was reorganized on the pretext of reforming the 1828 Constitution.

A more complete and up-to-date vision is found in the work of Alfredo Jocelyn-Holt, *La Independencia de Chile* [*Chilean Independence*], where he argues that despite the approval and initial prestige enjoyed by the 1828 Constitution:

> Indeed, where it failed was in what we have identified as the root problem which needed to be solved: to bring about legally a relatively successful governmental process, in which political mediation fell back on the executive-military power. In this, the 1828 Constitution erred in not being very pragmatic. It continued to trust in simple legal arbitrariness as sufficiently corrective in extreme situations. It did not contemplate constitutional mechanisms of safeguard and protection for facing situations in which the constitutional system itself could be in the balance. It only strengthened the Executive in its legislative role, and not in its political driver's role. It did not grant it extraordinary rights and neither did it foresee exceptional situations. It only put itself in the theoretical situation in which everyone will pay attention to the permitted legal structures. In other words, it ignored the prevailing political regime. It maximized liberal prejudice against the Executive without providing the government with moderating legal instruments of an authoritarian-constitutional style, as the 1833 Constitution would do ... To the intrinsic inadequacy of the Constitution was added a paralyzing lack of political will on the part of those who should have interceded once again. The Constitution failed for lack of foresight; the regime until now proven, eliminated itself by the apathy of its leaders.
> (Jocelyn-Holt 1999: 273–274)

This explanation takes into account the lack of political will of the leading liberal group, which coincides with the idea that in the Chile of 1828, republican political principles, despite being recognized as the basis of legality, were still not sufficiently established in terms of political practice (Collier 1977: 299–300).

It is important to make clear that in the Chilean constitutional documents of 1812, 1818, 1822, 1823, and 1828, the state of siege was not considered, but the exercise of extraordinary powers and the suspension of some articles of the Constitution were foreseen. For example, the text of the 1828 Charter disposed that the executive power could, in some extreme cases of external attack or internal commotion, or of serious or unexpected events, provide for prompt security measures, informing Congress immediately (see Article 84 No. 12). Some of these extraordinary powers could also be justified by the need to mount military actions against Spain, and other conflicts that followed the installation of new governments in Chile.

Despite these exceptional regulations, what most scholars accept is that the 1828 Constitution is a document that introduces a new way of republican life in Chile. This fundamental Charter prevailed at least until May 25, 1833 (Carrasco 2002: 101). The Constitution lasted even longer, if the times and constitutional changes of 1833 and 1925 are treated as its reforms. In that case, the validity of the 1828 Constitution would have lasted for approximately 150 years of the republican life to which it gave origin (Salvat 1982: 223).

Among the political agents who stand out in the First Republic, the military have an important role throughout this period. From the wars of independence, which early on have a military appearance with the Carrera dictatorship, the military become protagonists of the First Republic. In any case, it should be taken into account that at the time there was no professional military body. To serve in the military did not imply a different category to that of a civilian, notwithstanding that the distinction appeared gradually as the Republic was established. Its political presence was expressed in the role of guarantors and referees of proven status, which explains its constant presence in the Republic's highest positions (Supreme Director and President of the Republic) during the decade of 1820 (Ramón Freire, Manuel Blanco Encalada, and Francisco Antonio Pinto, among others).

On the other hand, the Church seems to be divided during the First Republic, between those who supported the independent process (Camilo Henríquez is the most obvious example) and those who were openly opposed to the ideal of republican self-government and, later, to independence. Despite this, both groups actively participate in politics, mainly by taking positions in the National Congress.

That is why, when distinguishing the period of settlement, colonial emancipation and consolidation of independence, from the later stage which saw the organization of the First Republic, we note that from the 1828 Constitution an early form of republicanism is partially achieved in Chile. This consists of the submission of the main public powers to legal regulations, its liberal understanding of the law, and a certain tension over predominance between Congress and the Assemblies and the Executive, in terms of the organization of government during its consolidation, from 1828 to 1830.

2.4 THE RISE OF NEW POLITICAL AGENTS AND THE END OF THE FIRST REPUBLIC

This First Republic, which, in its complete expression, emerged with the 1828 Constitution, was liberal and republican. For example, it suggested finishing with institutions that restricted equality and free movement of goods, and with those which could be considered as forms of domination, such as primogenitures and certain ecclesiastical privileges. There was active participation and discussion on public affairs by the main political actors of the day. This participation and discussion was restricted mainly to the elite, because in Chile, as recent historical studies show, "the word people in its modern meaning of political community associated with a certain territory (does not include) the members of what were then known as plebs or lower classes. Except for the instrumental mobilization of some of them" (Pinto and Valdivia 2009: 333–334). However, it seems true that citizenship and the vote were exercised by political actors who did not belong solely to the aristocracy and elite, but were small property owners or craftsmen, and therefore it can be said that the limits of citizenship were broadening during this period (Ramírez 2014: 133–157). In this initial period of our political system, the notion of citizenship and representation was built by trial and error, step by step, and was mixed with forms of the colonial cabildo, and with the principles and regulations of republicanism. In this respect, Pablo Recabal has said:

> to characterize society in the first half of the nineteenth century to determine which individuals will be citizens at the time, has an appearance of accelerated change. The electoral regulations provide us with a series of requirements for citizenship; however, they are economic criteria (of property, income, activity), age-related, of education (knowing how to read and write), abstracts, which do not tell us anything about the social group of the citizens, if it includes only the elite or allows participation of craftsmen, middle-class groups, small traders, peasants, farm laborers, medium or small farm owners, and so on.
>
> (Recabal 2015: 46)

It should also be noted that the structuring of citizenship in the republic was linked to the administrative political division of Chile, and to the union between the State and the Church. Pablo Recabal's conclusions from the study of this political and administrative division and its link to the notion of citizenship are as follows:

Summarizing, we could say that at the beginning of our republic the country was divided administratively into two provinces or intendancies (Santiago and Concepción), and in 1811 Coquimbo was added. Each one was divided into departments under a sub-delegate and headed by a principal city. Each city was led by the respective town council, controlled by the elite of each city because the positions were publicly auctioned, and had its respective rural areas, called districts or deputations, under a delegate magistrate. In each city there was a parish, and in the rural areas, vice-parishes under parish priests. That is how representation and citizenship towards 1810 and during the independence process would emerge from the cities, and in particular from the council, as shown by the actions of the prominent residents of each department's principal city. Socially, the country in its first years of independence was divided into different groups, the large property owners, owners, merchants, miners, and traders (the country's elite), and the middle and lower groups respectively from the countryside and the city, whose income varied considerably according to the geographical area. Also, there were a large number of tenants and laborers whom we could call the lower class. At the beginning (until 1823) it was exclusively the elite who participated in the electoral process (the civil and military elite), including the middle and low groups, but not the lower class. Representation in the period studied always stems from the diversity of local power concentrations (formed by the local elites in the big cities, and by medium and small property owners, traders, miners, and craftsmen in the towns that were smallest and most remote from the main urban centers) and from the pre-eminence of the provincial elite (Santiago, Concepción, La Serena), in pursuit of the building of an organism representative of such diversity (National Congress and, occasionally, executive juntas), and therefore the political conflicts of the period will be aired among the different conceptions of the structure of the State (centralist-federalist) arising from such diversity.

(Recabal 2015: 88–89)

Furthermore, the symbiotic form of the political military elite in the studied period is an object of analysis in the thesis of Pablo Recabal, who, in very clear words, expresses the following regarding the composition and education of the military and its relationship with the civil political elite:

During the time of O'Higgins, the Military Academy was the main institution for training officers, coming from "good families," under the direction of the Spaniard Santiago Arcos and his assistant Beauchef. The Legion of Merit was another system of creating an elite among the officers because, as well as their military privileges, they were given land, so that "the majority of them would divide their time between the strictly military and their landownership activities." At the same time, the foreigners that did not receive land "speedily made connections with the local landowner aristocracy. The cases of the Frenchman Benjamin Viel and his fellow countryman Beauchef are typical." Consequently, it is wrong to pretend that the military elite were different from the civilian, and many officers, such as Colonel de la Lastra, were not even in charge of men, but had a title that gave them only prestige. Beneath these high ranks were the troops who earned a monthly salary that was less than that of a farm laborer, which was a cause of frequent army revolts. As studies of social historiography have shown, the bulk of its members were from the lower class, through a system of pressed recruitment and also from among the craftsmen, whose relevance was essentially greater to the militia than to the army.

(Recabal 2015: 83)

The modes of dissent are not always solved peacefully during this early historical stage. From the triumph of the conservatives in the Battle of Lircay in 1829, a set of authoritarian political reforms emphasizing presidentialism was generated. They were profound reforms, which almost led to an anti-republican government in Chile, as we will try to explain in the following chapter. From 1830, the supremacy of the legislative power was replaced by the supremacy of the executive power, which announced an authoritarian hyper-presidentialism during the first part of this period. Furthermore, people's rights were subjected to limitations by intensive use of the State of Exception.

CHAPTER THREE

SECOND REPUBLIC: THE AUTHORITARIAN REPUBLIC, 1830–1870

The supporters of the 1833 authoritarian reform used the 1828 Constitution for more than three years and governed under a facade of republican legality until they managed to impose their own constitutional conception. The 1833 constitutional reform, of conservative inspiration, reproduced the complete catalog of rights of the 1828 Constitution, but it was limited in its application by the states of emergency, in particular by the introduction and repeated application of the state of siege. This new conception generated ambivalence and confusion among the supporters of republicanism. On one hand, they blamed this period for bringing the silence of terror and dictatorship to Chile, by asserting the almost absolute form of presidential power. At the same time, they recognized that this same absolute power assumed a moderate form of authority, and that, when stabilized, it maintained the forms of legality and was adapted to republican principles (Lastarria 2001: 63). That is how Barros Arana recognizes the progress achieved by the 1833 reform, but at the same time criticizes its terms:

> That regime, republican and democratic before the written law, was in reality an oligarchy founded on an effective authoritarianism. The 1828 Constitution, re-formed or remade in 1833, which had harmoniously organized the public powers, creating an administrative mechanism easy and practical to manage, and creating as well a central government sufficiently strong to gain respect and to suppress anarchy, nevertheless gave sufficient guarantees for the enjoyment of freedoms from which the country might benefit. The functioning of the Constitution, dressed always in legal forms and ordered in its progress, was in fact the exercise

of a strong and, to a certain extent, discretionary power, artificial in its proceedings, or frankly authoritarian, by the use of the extraordinary faculties with which the President of the Republic was easily endowed each time that he thought them necessary to maintain public peace.

(Barros Arana 1987: 412)

In these observations, Barros Arana draws our attention to his idea that this Fundamental Charter consigned the freedoms from which the country might benefit. This reveals a resignation or political realism, leading to an accommodation with the new constitutional regime. A pre-eminent position is given to the person occupying the executive function, placing them almost above the law. In this way, it weakens the separation of powers in favor of the presidential figure, and the people's constitutional rights are restricted, by using extraordinary faculties which are demanded by the incumbent government. The concept of citizenship and of political representation is excessively restricted. It amounts to a regime that is extremely authoritarian in the application of laws, and hyper-presidentialist in the definition of its constitutional legality.

The debates of the 1833 constituents did not adhere to the theoretical line of democratic republicanism, but echoed the practice of the traditionalist bourgeois group, which required a political organization that would enable order, and their dominance, to be secured (Heise 1996: 48). According to Heise, during the period known as the *República Pelucona* [Bigwig Republic] (1830–1861), the final and most beautiful chapter of Spanish colonial history was written (ibid.: 56). Ricardo Donoso expresses something similar, even though he credits the 1833 Constitution with the merit of having given legal form to the Chilean social reality. For ourselves, we disagree with Heise's thesis, according to which this period is a resurrection of the colonial period. We consider, on the contrary, that the 1833 authoritarian reform creates an imperfect form of republic because it allows a political practice that excludes the participation of the liberals, even though among them there were heroes of the independence (Donoso 1967: 86; Irisarri 1946: 30–31). More recent authors have denominated this period as oligarchic or conservative, but in no case have they deprived it of the name republic (Keen and Wasserman 1984: 187, 320–321).

Portales was the great instigator of the overthrowing of the First Republic, and he brought about, with his conspiratorial political actions, the emergence of the Second Republic: the Authoritarian

71

Republic. Portales' authoritarianism was founded on an omnipotent executive power, by which the springs of the representative popular machinery were broken and a new principle of authority was installed. The authority imposed in 1830 was not impersonal, as Alberto Edwards proposes (Edwards 1993: 64). On the contrary, as Mario Góngora explains, the basis of Portales' power was to distinguish between friends and enemies, good and bad, supporters and opponents. This idea recalls the simplistic and erroneous understanding of Carl Schmitt regarding politics (Góngora 1986: 42–44; also Schmitt 1991: 62–66).

3.1 THE DOMINANCE OF THE EXECUTIVE FUNCTION AND THE USE OF STATES OF EXCEPTION

In the Second Republic, the President is the Head of State, chief holder of national sovereignty, and the figure alone who defines all the coordinates of the political system (monocratic). The President determines the budget and the salaries of the administration; and appoints and promotes military officers and officials of the Supreme Court. The intendants, governors, and prefects, who maintain the work of local government, depend directly on the President. Parliamentary candidates on the government list have their triumph assured, given the Executive's control; in many cases, they are even nominated by the President, and are civil servants. Chile acquires a very centralized, unitary, and hierarchical political system, a State in which, at the same time, property is guaranteed, equality before the law as well as freedom of movement are declared, and the constitutional text proclaims that there is no privileged class (Zeitlin 1984: 33).

Government was based on a system of census and majority representation, according to which the members of the Senate and the President of the Republic were elected indirectly. The members of the Senate were elected by a unique and national electoral college; the Senators comprise twenty full members and the same number of substitutes, who are elected for a period of nine years. The Senate was ordinarily in session for three months every year, and was replaced during its recess by a commission of its members, called the *Comisión Conservadora* [Conservative Commission]. The President was elected for five years, with the possibility of being re-elected for a second term. The President's powers were similar to those of a temporary, absolute, and unaccountable monarch, who has a veto over all the laws, can call Congress, and can use extraordinary faculties. He appointed his collaborators, among whom the main ones were the ministers, and at the same time he was advised by a *Consejo de Estado* [Council of State], made up of ministers appointed by him. He also oversaw the prompt administration of justice.

In this context, it is important to take into account that at the time, the State was weak and limited (Jocelyn-Holt 1997: 23–29). This weakness allowed the elite to exercise a moderating influence over the Executive, which in the end gave way to the development of a parliamentary system.

During almost the entire period of the Authoritarian Republic, constitutional states of emergency were enacted. Furthermore, the approval of new constitutional reform projects became more difficult from 1833, because their approval required a majority in both Chambers (Amunátegui 1951: 194–195) of two successive legislatures, in addition to the power of suspensive veto also held by the President.

In short, the regime that began in 1830 was republican in form and authoritarian in practice; therefore it has been called the Authoritarian Republic (Loveman 1988: 111). Amunátegui points out that the 1833 Constitution cannot be classified as presidentialist or parliamentarian, but was more of an aristocratic and autocratic government, founded on some rulings of the 1823 Constitution and on a reform to the 1828 Constitution (Amunátegui 1951: 193–194). According to Brian Loveman (1988: 135), the regime that began in 1830 favored the economic interest of the higher classes and met the demands of the foreign capitalists, and in order to do that, it imposed internal order. The restoration of Hispanic centralism maintained the social stratification of the colony, but at the same time protected property and freed up trade, and would last for many decades well into the next century (Véliz 1980: 238–239).

However, as Sofía Correa has suggested, this characterization by Loveman could be questioned, because the problem addressed by the 1833 constitutional reform is about control of the internal political order, and not about a conflict between economic models contested by different social classes. Additionally, there is no apparent foreign intervention in the 1833 Constitution. Finally, it does not seem correct to talk about restoration of Hispanic centralism, because in the previous period the political control of Santiago was never profoundly disputed, and the inherited social stratification was never questioned during the Chilean nineteenth century, except in the works of Francisco Bilbao (Carrillo 2014: 93–112).

The Constituent Commission which brought about the 1833 reform, and in which Andrés Bello participated, was observed closely by Portales because he feared a limitation of his powers. Therein were two groups: the first led by Manuel José Gandarillas, who supported the reform to the 1828 Constitution; and the second, led by Mariano Egaña, who sought to impose a quasi-monarchic kind of authoritarianism with parliamentary structures, which was designated Egaña's personal vote (Villalobos et al. 2000: 531). Ricardo Donoso (1967: 81), while explaining Egaña's personal vote in 1831, notes that under republican outward appearances, he aspired to strengthen the social and political power of the landowner oligarchy, and to introduce organizational structures inspired by the English monarchy. In relation to this, Donoso notes:

> In this project the President of the Republic was given all-embracing power to appoint and dismiss civil servants from the administration, complete control over the courts of justice, the armed forces and the Church, whose leading dignitaries he appointed; a Council of State was created, whose members were appointed by the President with illusory powers of decision; a completely oligarchic Senate was established and the dissolution of the Chambers by simple decree; the President of the Republic was given absolute veto over the making of laws; suffrage was restricted; a Conservative Commission was created, formed by seven Senators elected from among themselves; provision was made for the suspension of constitutional guarantees with the agreement of the Council of State alone, the non-accountability of the President and his re-election for an indefinite time.
>
> (Donoso 1967: 81–82)

3.2   THE DEBATE ABOUT THE AUTHORITARIANISM OF LATIN AMERICA IN BELLO AND LASTARRIA

Some of the causes of this authoritarian relapse in Chile from 1830 are also explained by Andrés Bello, who compares the Chilean political reality with that of the USA. Bello recognizes that in Chile, property is concentrated in a very few hands, that in practice, respect for constitutional rights is weak and that there is a very powerful group whose interests clash with liberal principles. In 1830, Bello, in his work *Las Repúblicas Hispanoamericanas* [*Hispanoamerican Republics*], says:

Others, on the contrary, have denied us even the possibility of acquiring our own existence in the shadow of free institutions which they believed to be totally opposed to all the elements that could constitute Hispanoamerican governments. According to them, the representative principles that have been so well applied in the USA and that have made from the English enactments a great nation that daily increases its power in industry, trade, and population, could not have the same result in Spanish America. The situation of one and the other peoples, at the time of getting independence, was essentially different: some had properties that were split up, it could be said with equality, others saw property concentrated in a few hands. Some were used to the exercise of great political rights, while others did not enjoy them and still had no idea of their importance. Some could raise liberal principles up to the heights that they enjoy today, and others, even though emancipated from Spain, had at their heart a large and influential class with whose interests such principles collided. These have been the main reasons why the enemies of our independence have caused despair about the consolidation of our governments.

(Bello 1979: 126)

In relation to the emerging Chilean constitutionalism, Bello proposes that two main parties existed from the beginnings of the Republic. On one hand, he recognizes the party of those opposed to independence because it threatens their interests, which collide with the changes required in the country. On the other hand is a party that fights for the ideals of constitutionalism that still survives. This can also explain why Bello, in his work *Constituciones* [Constitutions], published in 1848, shows skepticism about the possibility that a written constitution could be used entirely for the organization of government, because he declares:

A political Constitution is born from the heart of a party or from the head of a man; and if it is built with some skill, and has not been inspired by false theories, if it consults the interests of the community, then it could have complete influence over it, modify its feelings, its customs and eventually truly represent it ... We have said, and we repeat, that written political constitutions very often are not truly emanations from the heart of society because they tend either to be dictated by a dominant faction or to be created in the solitude of the study of one man who does not even represent a party ... and it causes us no little surprise that in this year 1848, after so many abortive constitutional experiments, there are people who consider written constitutions as essential and invariably emanating from the heart of society. We say

75

essential and invariably because that, and no other, is the opinion that we deny.

(Bello 1979: 49, 51)

At this point it is appropriate to remember that Bello, while staying in England, observed the working of the jurisprudential and customary system of Anglo-Saxon common law. Therefore, he appreciates with a kind of skepticism the capacity of texts, documents, and written legal regulations to shape social reality. His proposal is conciliatory and moderate and is based on different sources, such as Roman law, Spanish law, modern codes, and a very attentive and pragmatic consideration (sometimes utilitarian) which derives from eclecticism regarding the actual social conditions in which the legislation will have to take effect (Jaksic 2001: 215). His vision emphasizes the effectiveness of the Constitution, the practice of constitutional law, and not only its declarations and texts that very often have no relationship with social identity. Bello's proposition is that constitutions must reflect the idiosyncrasy of the society in which they are applied, therefore, Chilean constitutionalism should be adapted to the reality of the country. In his explanations, Bello quotes Lastarria as an inherently Chilean liberal constitutionalist, and he shares with him some of his ideals arising from the French Revolution.

This link of Bello with French revolutionary ideals is partially identified with the idea of giving more publicity to the law (Bello 1979: 128, 129). Additionally, in *Las Repúblicas Hispanoamericanas*, Bello criticizes the fact that Chile has had constitutions that do not reflect the social and political reality of our country. He is of the opinion that the Constitution requires certain practices on which it should be based, particularly in consideration of South American historical evolution; and maintains that it is difficult to establish with certainty which is the origin of each idea or political institution, saying:

> Nobody conceived at that time [1811] that the unity and energy of action so necessary for the revolutionary government, could not be achieved by a governing body composed of men who represented different interests and principles; but it was necessary to imitate, and the only model available was a distorted copy of the French Revolution which became blurred in the proceedings of that of Buenos Aires; this is what the *Bosquejo Histórico* [Historical Outline] says. A Chilean form of government which copies that of Buenos Aires, which itself is a copy of the French Revolution, from whose heart has it emanated?

(Bello 1979: 55)

In Andrés Bello's work we can find a form of conservative and republican constitutionalism which sees itself as committed, firstly, to the legal organization of freedom. Iván Jaksic quotes the referenced work on the publication of judgments to illustrate how Bello has made his own the basic principle of republicanism, by saying: "freedom is nothing other than the rule of law" (Jaksic 2001: 214).

For Bello, another basic principle of a republican government is the principle of accountability, a criterion from which – as he puts it in his article, "Necesidad de fundar las sentencias" ["The need to give grounds for sentencing"], published in *El Araucano* [*The Araucanian*] in 1834 and 1839 – springs the obligation to explain the reasons for legal sentences or decisions, and to interpret the law in accordance with reason (Bello 1979: 108). In this same text, we also find in Bello a vision closer to French constitutionalism. Admittedly, his Frenchification is perceived in his declared intention of trying to limit the power of the judges, who, in his eyes, represent the most contemptible face of Spanish despotism, which needs to be literally eradicated by means of demolition and an ax. Bello uses this strong language to illustrate how the colonial judicial system must be destroyed in order to lay down a new judicial structure, based on Chilean republican ideals (ibid.: 107–109).

That is why, in relation to the structure of government of the Chilean Second Republic, he says in his work *Independencia del Poder Judicial* [*Independence of the Judiciary*] that he recognizes two powers in the form that the newly born Chilean national State should adopt: the power to enact the laws (Legislative), and the power to exercise the laws (Executive and Judiciary) as a branch of this (ibid.: 85–88). Indeed, Bello criticizes the 1811 constitutional text because he is against the total concentration of power in only one entity:

> While recognizing the need to adapt the ways of government to the organic constitutional laws, national traditions, and character, we should not for this believe that it is denied to us to live under the protection of free institutions and to enshrine in our land the salutary guarantees that ensure freedom, heritage of every human society worthy of the name.
>
> (ibid.: 128)

Ultimately, Bello's constitutionalism proposes that the law serves us in a finite way to regulate power, because for everything to be controlled by written legislation is an impossibility, and in this sense, his republican ideals are rather skeptical. Additionally, he makes his own kind of moderate liberalism (Jocelyn-Holt 1998: 439–485), which considers that more freedom can be achieved with gradual changes that are able to maintain order, and that traditions and constitutional practice should be respected in order to make progress towards a true liberal constitution.

In this regard, Bello, when declaring the importance of constitutional practices and postulating an undeniable influence of the executive power over the Judiciary, becomes a defender of the hyper-presidentialism that many have highlighted as the main characteristic of the Chilean constitutional political structure. It must be remembered that Bello had full knowledge of the authoritarian nature of hyper-presidentialism, but thought that with the control mechanisms, typical of the republican system, the necessary civil liberty to secure the new order could be achieved (Rojas 2009: 193–194).

A disciple of Bello, but with a philosophy sometimes contrary to his, José Victorino Lastarria is considered the first native-born lawyer of Chilean constitutionalism, and the first professor of constitutional law in our country. Lastarria's proposal is democratic and republican, like that of Mora, but unlike him, Lastarria's work is focused on the Chilean reality. Lastarria compares the two points of view about the existing Constitution: the conservative view expressed in the 1833 Constitution, and the liberal view expressed in the 1828 Constitution (Lastarria 1865: 204).

Lastarria's critical and doctrinaire conception of the 1833 Constitution was framed by the discussion of how to achieve fuller development for Chile. This Constitution, according to Lastarria, is distinguished by centralizing power, reinforcing executive power, restricting freedom of the press, dismantling the electoral system of the previous Constitution, and installing a system of government based on states of emergency. This new Constitution is more imperfect than that of 1828, but according to Lastarria, there is more political will to enforce it. Lastarria argues that the Constitution achieves order sufficient to allow economic development, but he criticizes it for being abusive and retrograde. In his work he seeks to annul its authoritarian regulations, with the intention of a liberal reinterpretation of it. With this objective, he actively engages, from within Parliament, in the generation of practices that finally consolidate the liberal reinterpretation of the Constitution. Lastarria's proposal is to make it compatible with a less authoritarian regime, which some have called parliamentarian and others, government by assembly (Heise 1974: 11; Barros 2000: 89–98). As Ricardo Donoso indicates, after the 1833 constitutional reform, the supporters of liberalism, led by Lastarria, adopt the following strategy:

> Considering itself the inheritor of the ideals of the liberating revolution, it will from now on direct its efforts towards modifying the social, political, and spiritual structure of the nation to open the way for a regime with democratic roots. The battle lines would be drawn up between the Executive and Congress, to seize from the former the mass of powers with which it had been armed and to conquer the independence of the latter. Whereas the path chosen was not that of military uprising or coups d'état, but rather that of disseminating information to the public and the promotion of culture.
>
> (Donoso 1971: 41)

José Victorino Lastarria, professor, Member of Parliament, and publicist, despite having chosen the path of persuasion and education to drive the change that authoritarianism required, does not spare criticism, and puts forward with exceptional force his liberal and republican ideas. For example, he criticizes with special attention the attitude and ideas expressed by Vice Chancellor Andrés Bello in the *Discurso inaugural de la Universidad de Chile* [Inaugural speech at the Universidad de Chile] in 1843, and dares to say:

> The old regime had powerful representatives, who even though, as we have said before, had not destroyed the liberating movement at its beginning, subsequently, little by little, they take control of it and steer it into pathways very opposed to those that its supporters had laid out for it. The government promoted public education; but just as the law that created the University had laid down the basis that allowed the Vice Chancellor to declare confessional one education, one science, one literature, and even one morality denomination, it also encouraged all the institutions that the clergy and its supporters founded, not only to educate the youth in accordance with the course set by the university, but according to the plan by which the Jesuits had managed to create a certain order of interests and doctrines which were contrary to the interests and principles of modern civilization and of democratic regime.
>
> (Lastarria 2001: 194–195)

Bello is seen as a conservative by Lastarria, in particular in the exercise of his educational duties, because he gives priority to order over freedom. The idea of Bello's education is seen as part of conservative ideology and therefore, even though Lastarria was considered an outstanding student by the Vice Chancellor, he seriously disagreed on this aspect and in his views regarding authoritarianism. Carlos Ruiz refers to this important question:

> For Bello and his disciples, education is an institution whose main objective is the preservation of order against revolutionary threats. This means, in his thinking, that even if all individuals must get an education, not all must receive the same education. Education must be adapted to differences in social class, with secondary and university courses concentrated on the elite of active citizens, and a primary course for passive citizens, in which the most important courses are reading and writing, mathematics, religion and ethics.
>
> (Cristi and Ruiz 2015: 178)

The liberal and parliamentarian project begun by Lastarria was carried on in the work of Manuel Carrasco Albano and Jorge Huneeus, who represented the highest peak of Chilean constitutionalism in the nineteenth century.

3.3 THE FIRST CHILEAN CONSTITUTIONALISM COMPARED IN CARRASCO ALBANO AND HUNEEUS

It is precisely in this context that the figure of Manuel Carrasco Albano stands out, sharing the liberal strategy of Lastarria and his group. In his critical comments on the dispositions of the 1833 Constitution, Carrasco Albano develops an impeccable legal elucidation and compares our institutions with those of Europe and North America at the time. Despite his youth, he puts forward ideas very well-founded in Chilean constitutional history. Regarding the 1828 Constitution, he says that despite establishing a unitary State, it basically created an organization of federal character, and from a historical perspective he prefers unitarianism for the Chilean State (Carrasco Albano 1874: 5). His concept of sovereignty is mainly influenced by the ideas of Hobbes, and he distinguishes in this regard between the law and the exercise of sovereignty:

> Applying these ideas to civil society, we will agree with Hobbes that it is necessary to have a common will that dominates the individual will, a superior and general power that may oblige all citizens to respect their reciprocal rights and to live in peace with one another. This

cannot be achieved unless each individual submits his own will to that of a superior power, whose opinion on all matters is followed absolutely and held by all those composing society. This supreme power that cannot be annulled or paralyzed by any human will, and whose acts are independent of any other superior power, is what is called national sovereignty.

(Carrasco Albano 1874: 10)

Regarding the discussion concerning the relationship between State and Church, Carrasco Albano maintains the great need for religious freedom, anticipating the debate that will culminate with the civil laws of religious tolerance at the end of the nineteenth century. His arguments in favor of religious freedom invoke the need for immigration to enrich the diversity of the Chilean population with new members, mainly of Protestant denomination, and in that way prevent the totalitarian threat that underlies the exclusive cult that could arise in our country. He also maintains that the admission of other cults would be in the interests of the Church itself, because competition would inspire the purification of its traditions, and the arrival of a big group of migrants would open up a great opportunity for evangelization and, therefore, new conversions: "religious freedom is needed in the country and it is convenient for the Church itself. Chile needs immigration and especially, Protestant immigration. The European nations providing us with a mass of industrious, moral, and entrepreneurial settlers are Germany, Scandinavian countries: Sweden, Norway and Denmark, Switzerland and Great Britain" (ibid.: 22).

Carrasco Albano also develops, like Mora, a concept of the principle of constitutional equality that assumes an explicit criticism of the old Chilean colonial regime. He identifies this principle with the broader exercise of suffrage, with the same possibility, for all citizens, to participate in the formation of the law and with equality between Chileans and foreigners confirmed by civil legislation, as effective ways of expressing this principle. He points out, as causes of Chilean colonial inequality, the existence of slavery, the privileges of the nobility and the Church, and the caste divisions recorded in the *Código de Indias* [Law of the Indies], which distinguishes between indigenous, black people, mulatto, zambo, mixed race, Spaniards, and other colonial settlers (ibid.: 88). His criticism, inspired by liberalism, also refers to the continued existence of ecclesiastical and military privileges, which seem to him excessive and an unlawful exception to republican principles (Donoso 1967: 322).

When comparing the constitutional conception of Carrasco Albano with Mora's ideas, the virtues of the latter stand out, in terms of his ability to anticipate what will be the relevant constitutional issues half a century later. Mora not only was right in his diagnosis of the Chilean situation and shares republican principles with Carrasco Albano, but also, and as a consequence of his vision of constitutional equality, he assigns a leading place to it. The most complete constitutional concept that we had in Chile during the nineteenth century is expressed in the 1828 text and survives the conservative reform of 1833, because in Article 12, in the part of the constitutional text referring to constitutional rights, is included: "1. Equality before the law; 2. Admission to public employment and office; 3. Equal sharing of taxes, contributions, and other public levies (Diario Oficial 2005: 224).

The same liberal stance of Lastarria and Carrasco Albano is also present in the work of Jorge Huneeus, who deliberates about the constitutional period of 1828–1833, from his Chair of Constitutional Law at the Universidad de Chile and in his parliamentary duties. In his work *La Constitución ante el Congreso* [*The Constitution before Congress*] Huneeus analyzes article by article the 1833 Constitution. Compared with Lastarria's political perspective, Huneeus offers a profound legal reading of the 1833 authoritarian reform. In relation to suffrage, he maintains that this must be understood as a public obligation and not as a right. Additionally, he accepts the majoritarian ideas of his time, and understands that a universal system of suffrage can never be absolute because it will always have some kind of limitation – for example, a minimum age. Huneeus warns that the important issue regarding suffrage is that the limitations imposed on it must not be arbitrary or discriminatory:

> From the previous presentation it can be deduced that universal suffrage, understanding this to demand solely a minimum age condition, without any other, be it to know how to read and write (as in Chile and Brazil), be it to pay taxes or equivalent (as in Great Britain and Spain), is in effect in the USA, Switzerland, and France. This is an issue that has occupied us in another book where we have declared ourselves supporters of Stuart Mill's theory, who considers suffrage a public obligation and not a right. The great majority of established States have considered it in this way, even though they have not expressly said so, by the sole act of limiting the vote to a more or less restricted number of people, establishing that to be able to vote, conditions of ability, intelligence, and independence are imposed. The same nations, who have adopted the theory of universal suffrage, do

not make it universal, because they limit it to those over twenty-one years of age, as in the USA and France, or twenty years of age, as in Switzerland. Nobody has dared to embrace the full consequences that logically follow from the theory itself.

(Huneeus 1890: 29–30)

Consequent on the foregoing, Huneeus proposes a system of registration to exercise the role of elector. By this proposal he encapsulates what will form the discussion of electoral reform during the nineteenth century. "It can be deduced also that the old English system of voting without being previously registered has given way, and rightly, to the system that demands that the citizen must previously be listed in the corresponding electoral rolls or registers to be able to exercise the role of voter" (ibid.: 29).

Huneeus recognizes the importance of equality in relation to the elimination of privileges, in the distribution of public offices, and in access to public positions and functions (ibid.: 34, 35). According to the doctrine of the time, the protection of the rights of the individual would depend basically on the legislative power. Huneeus suggests that the legislative power should be the principal power of the State, and Congress the essential institution:

We do not want all-powerful heads of the Executive; neither do we want all-powerful Parliaments. If the Executive should not legislate, Parliament should not govern, much less administrate. The objective of Parliament is twofold: scrutinize the actions of the Executive and, within certain limits, those of the superior judges. That is its main purpose and its primordial duty. The other one is to legislate. The scrutinizing role assumes superiority over the scrutinized power, as is assumed also of the legislative role, given that the executive and judiciary powers have, in general, the obligation to execute and fulfill the law. Within the representative system, whose foundation is the division of public power into at least three branches – Legislative, Executive, and Judiciary – we consider that the dominance of the Legislative is a key condition for good organization. The difficulty is to avoid exaggeration; but we think that in terms of the principle itself, Parliament should be the first of the authorities in every nation properly constituted, there should be no place for uncertainty, unless the cult of personality is preferred, or in other terms, the Caesarism of the Roman Empire, that of Louis XIV or that of the Napoleons. We consider, then, that it is an indispensable condition of any good political organization that there is a Parliament invested with the necessary powers of scrutiny and legislation, and whose will, in cases of conflict, prevails over that of the Executive,

> without this making it lawful to encroach upon the peculiar powers of the latter. If that is the way a parliamentary system is understood, it is clear that it would be inseparable from the representative system.
>
> (ibid.: 17, 18)

Huneeus sees the 1833 Constitution as an obstacle to achieving the parliamentary system, and, from this observation, his intellectual work focuses on creating a new conception of Chilean public law. He defends a legal interpretation of the provisions of the Constitution, where liberal convictions and the democratic practice of Congress are in disagreement with the constitutional text. Huneeus concludes that in terms of religion, the only rational system is the separation of the Catholic Church from the State. The reform which allows an approach towards religious freedom is the means by which a modification of the concept "public cult" is achieved, which can be interpreted as meaning that the private celebration of all religions is authorized, without any prohibition. This reinterpretation amounts to a waiver of the constitutional precept related to the restriction of religious cults other than the Catholic, which does not stop being the official religion.

> It is true that the *Ley Interpretativa* [Interpretative Law] of July 27, 1865 has defined in Chile what is understood as public cult; but it must be said truly that such interpretation was really an indirect waiver of the constitutional precept to which it refers, and that it is high time resolutely to eliminate from our Fundamental Charter the stain that spoils and discredits it, and which presents us to the foreigner in a state of backwardness scarcely conceivable even in colonial times, and which not even the 1886 Colombian Constitution has accommodated.
>
> (ibid.: 21–23)

Regarding this, one must take into account the mistrust that existed, in the first years of the Republic, about judges and their independence. This idea of Huneeus is shared by Andrés Bello, together with the desire of some liberal intellectuals to transform the regime stemming from the 1833 Constitution into one less autocratic and inspired by parliamentarianism in style. In regard to this aspect, Huneeus' contribution is fundamental. Huneeus does not assess the Constitution in the light of its original text, but by taking into account the parliamentary reforms introduced in the 1870s and 1880s. During this time, the mutation takes place from the centralized presidentialist political system to another, more parliamentarian in style. For Huneeus, the reforms show how a Constitution can be gradually achieving its regulatory identity:

the Constitution that still rules us today, with the reforms carried out in strict accordance with the rules it prescribes, by the law of August 8, 1871; that of September 25, 1873; those two of August 13, 1874; that of October 24 of the same year; and finally, that of January 12, 1882, which changed substantially the system previously established in order to adopt the reform of the Fundamental Code itself. If this, from the beginning, suffered from an evident vice, it must be confessed that the passing of half a century has purged it to excess ... The constitutional regime has put down in our land such deep roots that the meagre and feeble plant of 1833 has become an overarching and gigantic tree under whose dense foliage take shelter all the good citizens that live in the fertile and enjoyable land of Chile.

(ibid.: 54, 55)

3.4 THE STRUCTURE OF RIGHTS AND OF CONSTITUTIONAL PROPERTY LAW

During the Chilean Second Republic, which corresponds to the period beginning in 1830 up to approximately 1860, which we have called the Authoritarian Republic, the regulations of the 1833 Constitution broadly recognized the protection of property. This sweeping recognition of constitutional property had the purpose of taking back the validity of the regulations that eliminated the primogenitures and other traditional forms of entailing property, and it expressed a constitutional concept of "properties" that understood the institution of multiple ownership, an idea that the text of the 1833 Fundamental Charter also linked to the recognition of the property of communities:

Chapter V. *Public law in Chile*
Art. 12: The Constitution ensures all inhabitants of the Republic ...
5. The sanctity of all properties, without distinction of whether they belong to individuals or communities, and without possibility of anybody being deprived of its ownership, nor of a part of it, however small it might be, nor of the right that they may have to it, other than by virtue of a legal decision; unless there is a case in which the requirement of the State, qualified by law, demands its use or disposal; which will take place once the owner has received the corresponding compensation to be agreed with him, or as valued by the assessment of honest men.

(Valencia Avaria 1951: 163–164)

Finally, in the 1833 Constitution, as though announcing the muta-tion of its validity, into what will be the liberal Third Republic, begin-ning with the constitutional reforms of around 1860 and ending in 1924, a special section was added, dedicated to property guarantees with several references to this right. These regulations are:

Chapter X. *On guarantees for security and property*

Art. 146: The house of every person who inhabits Chilean territory is an inviolable refuge and it can only be broken into for a special reason determined by law and by virtue of competent authority.

Art. 147: Only Congress can impose direct or indirect taxes, and without its special authorization it is forbidden to any authority in the State and to any individual to exact them, even if the pretext is insecurity, voluntary or of any other kind ...

Art. 150: No armed body can make requisitions, nor demand any kind of help unless it is through the civil authorities and by their decree ...

Art. 152: Every author or inventor will have exclusive ownership of their discovery or production, for the time allowed by law; and if this demands publication, the inventor will receive the appropriate indemnification.

(Valencia Avaria 1951: 182)

Until now we have seen how, in the nineteenth century, in the first republican experiences taking place in Chile, very different constitu-tional forms were adopted in order to recognize and guarantee property or properties.

The constitutional regulations mentioned were the object of a first attempt at classification and doctrinal standardization during the republican period in Chile, which begins in the nineteenth century and continues to the beginning of the twentieth century. In our legal system, even at a constitutional level, property is expressed in a fragmented way. This right is incorporated in the Chilean legal system in a series of constitutional clauses that repeat certain com-mon elements. Among these, we find that in the Chilean constitu-tional regulations referring to property, its guarantee and way of expropriation is linked to matters of general interest, like national defense or public service. At the same time, in every case of expro-priation of property, compensation is given to the titleholder. Also, property is understood to place a limit on executive and legislative powers, and for its protection and guarantee it requires recognition as one of the roles of judiciary power. Many of these regulations at constitutional level coexist in the Republic of Chile with the Spanish colonial substantive and procedural law, without prejudice to the extension and strengthening of private property in independent Chile, which took place, in particular, from the taking effect of the *Código Civil* [Civil Code] in 1857.

It is remarkable that despite the novelty and multi-form character of the recognition and guarantee of property rights in Chilean constitutions, there was not a great development of the dogma concerning it during the nineteenth century. There are early references of doctrinal character to property in the work of José Joaquín de Mora: *Curso de Leyes del Liceo de Chile*, which we have already mentioned in part, and which includes the treatment of property in the context of government's intentions and as an object of the social contract. Mora follows the thesis of Rousseau's social contract and, as we have mentioned before, he develops an original idea of property related to security, equality, and freedom:

> I do not believe that security is a separate right from others that I have mentioned, but an indispensable quality for each one of them. How does this apply in practice? To the person? This is called freedom. To assets? This is called property. To rights? This is called equality. There is no security unless it is related to one of those three benefits. We want and demand that they are secured, but this call indicates one property and not one essence. *Non sunt multiplicandae sine necessitate.* The three rights specified in the course are enough to respond to all the aims of society. It is indispensable that they are clear and yet not for that will we define clarity as a right. Rights must be long-lasting, and yet duration is not a right. What is violated when security is lacking? One of the three issues referred to by the faculty of being free, the faculty of being equal, and the faculty of being owners. There is nothing outside this circle. It is therefore a wrong and senseless denomination.
>
> (Mora 1830: 115–116)

Andrés Bello also lectured on important issues regarding property in his famous work *Principios de derecho internacional* [*Principles of International Law*], where he addresses this right, with great profundity and erudition, from a doctrinal point of view, as a natural right, and also in its relationship with the ways of acquisition (occupation, accession, tradition, and the law) in relation to the territory of the State (including water), and in relation to the domain, rule, and jurisdiction of the sovereign power (Bello 1864: 34–89). Bello also explains the doctrine regulating the situation of assets, such as properties and ships, in the cases of the South American wars of independence:

notwithstanding the support of some of the old European governments for the Spanish cause, none of them disputed the right of the new nations to capture the ships and properties of their enemy on the high seas ... The Supreme Court of the United States declared in 1818 that when civil war starts in a nation, separating part of it from the old government and setting up a different one, the Union's tribunals should regard the new government as it was regarded by the legislative and executive authorities of the United States, while these maintain neutrality recognizing the existence of a civil war, the Union's tribunals may not consider as criminal those hostile acts which war permits and which the new government commits against their adversary. According to the doctrine of that Court, the same testimony that would have been sufficient to prove that a person or ship was serving a recognized power, would have been sufficient to prove that they were in the service of one of the newly created governments [of the new South American Republics].

(Bello 1864: 321)

The most successful work in terms of the doctrine on property inspired in natural law is that published originally in 1888, which emerges from the theoretical treatment that Rafael Fernández Concha gives to the right to property as an acquired right (Fernández Concha 1966: 53–99). To this work are added the comments of Manuel Carrasco Albano on the 1833 Constitution, of Jorge Huneeus, and the works of José Victorino Lastarria and of Valentín Letelier. However, strictly speaking, except in the case of Jorge Huneeus, I do not find that these works, despite their quality, can be considered works of Chilean constitutional doctrine about property because their occasional references to the regulations regarding property are very general, not based on legal doctrine, and sometimes lack a strictly defined analytical or conceptual point of view about the issue.

Therefore, despite the importance of José Joaquin de Mora's ideas, and due to the extended validity of the 1833 Constitution, it is the comments of Manuel Carrasco Albano and the work of Jorge Huneeus that give continuity to constitutionalism rooted in liberalism in relation to property law during the nineteenth century. For example, Carrasco Albano, in his famous thesis, notes that the 1833 constitutional reform does not include, in the article ruling on property, a broader concept ensuring freedom that was formerly incorporated in the same disposition in the 1828 Constitution. "The paragraph that we examined ensures us only the freedom of the individual, or according to

Mr. Dupin, freedom of the body: precious guarantee, in truth, that we do not know how to appreciate unless it is suspended in states of emergency, just as we do not appreciate health until we are ill" (Carrasco Albano 1874: 50).

In relation to property, Carrasco Albano's comment seems accurate, because the 1833 constitutional regulation dealing with property says:

> *Inviolability of Property.* The guarantee contained in this article regarding inviolability of property is one of the fundamental conditions of any civil society and it has not introduced any innovation in the dispositions of the former Spanish laws. It was always a principle of common law that property is sacred, whatever on the other hand might have been the burdens and the unjust duty that weighed on it. Its inclusion among the guarantees of public law has rather more importance relative to community properties than the article ascribes to private property. With this specification, it was hoped to avoid the confiscation of ecclesiastic properties or those belonging to religious orders which, since the sixteenth century, had been victims of the reaction against the wealth and pomp of the religious orders.
>
> (ibid.: 50)

In this rather brief explanation, Carrasco Albano gives support to three main ideas: (1) the relationship between property and civil society; (2) the similarity and link between property regulations in the 1833 reform and the Spanish colonial legislation; and (3) the justification of the constitutional clause that protects community property, including the property of religious orders. A similar situation can be found in the origin of the first constitutional recognition of property law in the USA, based on the idea of preventing the arbitrariness of the government and protecting all property, even that of the supporters of the British monarchy, once independence was achieved (Ruiz-Tagle and Martí 2014: 82–83; Ely 2008: 34–35).

Meanwhile, the exception that I have made regarding the work of Jorge Huneeus, in terms of the quality of his constitutional doctrine, is based on his rational and well-argued examination of the regulations of Article 12, No. 5 of the 1833 Constitution above-mentioned, presented in his work *La Constitución ante el Congreso* [*The Constitution before Congress*]. Huneeus confirms the idea that constitutional regulations hold property inviolable and protect the assets of legal agents, among them the religious communities and convents (Huneeus 1890: 108). However, Huneeus distances himself from Carrasco Albano's explanation of this important issue, because it takes inspiration from doctrines of natural law:

One has fallen into the error of believing that the Constitution also ensures the inviolability of the properties of corporations. This is how Mr. Carrasco Albano expresses it in his comments. But this is a mistake, because the right of corporations to acquire and hold assets is governed by the Civil Code, and that of public limited companies is governed by the *Código de Comercio* [*Commercial Code*]. These are not natural persons and therefore cannot have natural rights. Their existence is due to the law, and this has sovereignty over all the conditions of their development and extinction, which does not happen with man, whose physical, intellectual, and moral organization is something that the legislator must necessarily respect, as we have already said.

(ibid.: 109)

Huneeus analyzes in great detail the limits to property, which he summarizes as those coming from legal decisions and those that have their basis in expropriation by reason of public use. He deals in detail with six issues: (1) if the expropriation can only be of benefit to the State, or also to another public entity, like a municipality or city, accepting this second possibility; (2) if the expropriation requires a general or special law, concluding that a general law is sufficient; (3) if the rights of way on farms (property) in favor of the State are constitutional, denouncing their unconstitutionality; (4) if the expropriation of work or intellectual property without remuneration is proper, concluding that it is inadmissible; (5) regarding the payment of fees to experts (called honest men) who set the value of the expropriation, and concluding that this falls on the expropriating tax office or municipality; and finally, (6) if the indemnification of the object expropriated makes obligatory the payment of its highest valuation, Huneeus opting in this case also for the affirmative (ibid.: 109–116).

3.5 THE MAIN POLITICAL AGENTS AND THE MUTATION OF THE SECOND REPUBLIC

Regarding the fundamental part of the Constitution, that is to say, the organization of the State, Juan Bautista Alberdi, when comparing the Chilean Fundamental Charter with the Peruvian and Argentinian constitutions, concludes that the 1833 reform, whose author was Mariano Egaña, concentrated power in the executive branch, which to him seems suitable for the early part of our republic. However, he criticizes Chile and Peru for the restrictions placed on obtaining nationality, which do not have the republican spirit of inclusion and which limit the access of foreigners to public positions; and because their constitutions give privileged status to the Catholic religion (Alberdi 1998: 133–140).

The predominance of Catholicism throughout the period of validity of the 1833 Constitution had great importance because it drew strength from the law of ecclesiastical patronage, as can be appreciated in the dispute with the Vatican for the appointment of bishops, and the extensive clerical influence in terms of education, cemeteries, weddings, and other issues of civil legislation (Carrasco 2002: 132).

We have noted that the Second Republic implied an authoritarian shift in relation to the First Republic. A conservative conception of rights was imposed and prevalence was given to the executive function in the government organization, based on extraordinary powers. The Second Republic centralized all authority in Santiago and among those holding the executive branch of government.

The Second Republic promoted the coexistence of the traditional social order, with some limited republican principles. It sought to revalidate ways of immobilizing property and to have an impact on the circulation of assets, which can be considered types of domination linked to primogenitures and some ecclesiastical privileges. The participation and deliberation of the governed in public affairs and the right to dissent are considerably restricted.

Respect for the law is erratic and unstable, and political participation and the fight against excessive power concentration are limited until the middle of the nineteenth century. From that moment, there gradually starts developing a constitutional conception which is of a broadly republican and liberal base in terms of the law, and parliamentarian in terms of its notions of political organization.

Parliamentarianism reaches its best expression in the 1860s and 1870s, in a series of reforms that installs this form of government through a process of mutation. According to Loewenstein, a constitutional mutation is produced through a transformation of the configuration of political power, of the social structure, or of the balance of interests, without such a transformation being updated in the constitutional document, because that remains intact (substantially) (Loewenstein 1983: 165). Additionally, such process of mutation is accompanied by the gradual giving way of the military to the civil power, which in this way progressively breaks down the political influence that the former had exercised over the First Republic.

During the government of José Joaquín Perez came the first constitutional changes that announced the arrival of the Third Republic in Chile: the Liberal Republic, so-called for its conception of rights and because it assumes a parliamentary form of government. Among the first measures announced by the Third Republic we find the political amnesty statute, the statute decreeing private religious freedom in 1865, and the statutory constitutional reforms of 1871, 1873, and 1874. These reforms give birth to the Third Republic in Chile through mutation of the Constitution reformed in 1833.

CHAPTER FOUR

THIRD REPUBLIC: THE LIBERAL REPUBLIC, 1870–1924

The Third Republic coincides with the period described by Heise in his work about the parliamentary system in Chile, even though he places its beginning ten years earlier. To justify his bringing it forward, Heise maintains that Jorge Huneeus proclaims that from 1861, at the political and intellectual level, there is already a parliamentarian regime. In Heise's opinion, the supporters of a series of reforms and parliamentarian practices that began in the 1860s managed to change the nature of the authoritarian regime by modifying certain political practices, which brought about a constitutional mutation (Heise 1974: 33, 35). Unlike Heise, in this work we have positioned the third republican moment in Chile around 1870, because Chilean historiography recognizes the existence of a constituent generation of parliamentarian and liberal base, which finds expression in the famous work of the brothers Justo and Domingo Arteaga Alemparte, *Los Constituyentes de 1870* [*The Constituents of 1870*] (Arteaga Alemparte and Arteaga Alemparte 1910: 2–7).

Additionally, this political and intellectual generation expresses itself in a characteristic way by the constitutional conception emerging in the reforms of 1871, 1873, and 1874 that regain a leading position for the titleholder of the legislative function, which, incidentally, inaugurates a political practice that submits more intensively to the rule of law all the constitutional bodies. The division of powers in favor of Congress is reinforced and the authoritarian presidential figure enters into a state of tension with Parliament, in a way that continues unresolved until the 1891 civil war. During the Third Republic, the constitutional rights of individuals are broadened through legislative interpretation, by means of which the text of the Constitution is reformed and altered, and the use of extraordinary powers being given to the government of the day comes to an end. It means the consolidation of a republican form, liberal in its dogma and in the exercise of rights, and parliamentarian in terms of its constitutional fundamental structure. The Third Republic is interrupted during the 1891 civil war, but it stretches from 1870 to 1924, when a coup d'état interrupts the constitutional government.

4.1 THE EXPANSION OF THE RIGHT TO VOTE AND THE NEW LIBERAL POLITICAL ATMOSPHERE

This Third Republic disowns the previous authoritarian legacy and Chile identifies itself spiritually with France, and under the influence of its liberal philosophy, a secular tendency is strengthened (Heise 1996: 71). According to Heise, this new Chilean liberal spirit reflects the revolutionary romanticism that inspired all the Chilean political movements from the second half of the nineteenth century. This influence emerges from Alfred Lamartine and his work *The Girondists*, published in 1847, and from the revolutionary movements of 1848 (ibid.: 65).

As for the doctrinal aspect, concerning constitutional principles and rights, in the period which begins in the middle of the nineteenth century and is consolidated in 1871, political democracy is deepened. Public opinion is strengthened, a press law is enacted, and a republican culture is more strongly secured. A system of political parties arises, some of which will last until the middle of the twentieth century, as in the cases of the *Partido Conservador* [Conservative Party], *Partido Liberal* [Liberal Party], and *Partido Radical* [Radical Party]. In 1874, while legislating to fix the amounts of the census-based suffrage, Congress approves the assumption that any person able to read and write would have enough income to vote. This way, through legislative intervention and without having to change the Constitution, which would involve two legislatures, census-based suffrage is eliminated. Thus, the concept of citizenship and of representation or political inclusion is also expanded in such a way that census-based suffrage could all but be done away with. At the same time, the cumulative vote is introduced, which enables parliamentary representation of minorities, to which is added the already mentioned presumption of right according to which anyone who reads and writes has the minimum requirements to be a citizen, thereby eliminating census-based suffrage. The constitutional reforms and the use of interpretative laws tend to a democratization of the government regime and to the reduction of presidential power (Amunátegui 1951: 196).

Among the changes that occur during this period, the following stand out: the expansion of suffrage, the election of the Senate by provinces, and the reduction of the duration of parliamentary positions to six years. The Conservative Commission is composed of members of both Chambers and it is given the power to require the President to call for extraordinary sessions of Congress. The Council of State is composed of members of each Chamber, and the Ministers of State have the right only to be heard in those sessions. The extraordinary faculties of the President are restricted, in respect of the rights that he can exceptionally infringe, and the places and forms of detention. At the same time, the President's powers in legal issues are restricted and parliamentary legal incapacities are increased to avoid presidential influence over these. The legislative quorum is reduced, impeachment is regulated, parliamentary audit is increased, and the limiting of electoral intervention is sought. In terms of individual rights, the new rights of assembly, association, and freedom of education are incorporated, and the acquisition of Chilean nationality is made easier, as are the procedures for constitutional reform (ibid.: 197–198).

Among the merits that should be noted in the period from 1870 to 1924, a decline in the influence of militarism in Chilean politics stands out (Heise 1996: 93). Among the causes of this decline, it is said that from 1861 the extraordinary powers of the President and the states of emergency begin to be discredited, added to which, in the session of October 31, 1873, the constitutional reform is approved that declares these extraordinary powers rendered to Congress (Donoso 1967: 339).

The parliamentary practice and the legislative work in Congress made Chile the first country in South America to reform the Spanish legislation in force since the colonial period. The Civil, Commerce, Mining, and Penal Codes and the *Ley Orgánica* [Organizing Statute] of our tribunals and the procedural legislation are enacted and sanctioned between 1857 and 1907 (Heise 1996: 111–112). The parliamentary incompatibilities are revised and the number of political parties increased to six, which implies a greater variety of political representation. This greater representation is significant from the political point of view, because until 1860, Congress was formed in its majority by public administration employees, and even the judges who occupied these positions obeyed the Executive (Donoso 1967: 342).

4.2   THE SUPREMACY OF THE LEGISLATIVE FUNCTION AND THE 1891 CIVIL WAR

In terms of the definition of the fundamental part of the Constitution, the transfer of power from the President to Parliament generated a tension that was not solved until the government of José Manuel Balmaceda (1886–1891). Balmaceda governed with parliamentary political groups and later dispensed with them at the end of his government, which started off the 1891 revolution. The result of the civil war, which took place during the time of José Manuel Balmaceda, was to settle the debate, which had started soon after the enactment of the 1833 Constitution, regarding the supremacy of the President (Heise 1996: 91; Correa et al. 2001: 18). Several causes for the 1891 civil war have been highlighted: the weakening of the conservative spirit, also called "portaliano" [Portalian], from the influence of Minister Diego Portales; the development of new political parties and practices; the struggles for constitutional and electoral reforms; and also the special characteristics of President Balmaceda's government (Carrasco 2002: 135). Ricardo Donoso combines political, economic, social, and even psychological explanations:

> Among the first, Chilean historians include the fervent eagerness to attain a regime of a balance of powers and to break the presidential absolutism, which found its most prominent manifestation in the intervention by the Executive in the elections of congressmen and of the President of the Republic; among the second, the first attempts by international capitalism, linked to the nitrate industry, to bring their weight to bear on government policy; among the social reasons, the desire of the agricultural and banking plutocracy for absolute domination, which did not have the counterbalance of the middle class, who were disconnected from all political power; and finally among the psychological reasons, the disproportionate egomania of President Balmaceda, the most fickle and false of Chilean statesmen.
>
> (Donoso 1967: 273)

The electoral intervention of the Executive meant the control of the structure and operation of Congress. Members of Parliament sought to audit government in the exercise of their democratic representation, and at the same time, governments wanted to ensure their authority – in some cases, such as that of Balmaceda, to adopt dynamic policies of economic and social transformation. One of the methods of parliamentary control was applied through processing the so-called *Leyes Periódicas* [Periodical Statutes] that were sent to the Legislative every year for approval. These laws included the national budget statute, the collection of taxes and rates, and the staffing of the armed forces. In 1890, the Legislative rejected it and this impacted significantly on the power of the Executive, as the country could not function without it being approved. Its processing was subject to Article 42 of the 1833 Constitution, which established that the subject of a proposal rejected in Congress could not be discussed again until a year later, which left the budget unlegislated for a year.

At the beginning of the 1891 revolution, the supporters of Balmaceda organized a considerable military and bureaucratic force, centralized the power of the State in the executive function, censored newspapers, imposed conscription, confiscated assets, prohibited their sale or transfer, established a secret police, suspended ordinary tribunals and imposed military tribunals, controlled correspondence, tortured political prisoners, and, in practical terms, abolished civil liberties and personal rights. Additionally, during the civil war, three generals were made Senators and five colonels were made Deputies. Despite all these changes and the loyalty that the Army showed to Balmaceda, he suspected that the military could rebel against him and try to return to constitutional government (Zeitlin 1984: 212–213).

While playing down and justifying these measures, Julio Bañados, a constitutionalist supporter of Balmaceda, maintains that excessive self-interest and political ambition, the faults of the constitutional regime and the unconstitutional behavior of the parliamentary majority, generated the 1891 rebellion or civil war (Bañados 2005: 54–55). According to Bañados, the rebels had, as main false reasons, electoral freedom, parliamentarianism, abuse of individual guarantees, budget control, and maintenance of armed forces without the authority of Congress (ibid.: 35). Bañados' accusation also includes the *Acta de Deposición del Presidente Balmaceda* [Act Removing President Balmaceda], which, despite being signed by the majority in Parliament, had formal defects because it was not drafted during a formal session and was not communicated to the accused. Moreover, Bañados argues that Balmaceda did not have the opportunity to refute it, and that the right to insurrection exercised by Parliament could not be delegated and could only be exercised directly by the people (ibid.: 55).

The Battles of Concón and Placilla, which cost ten thousand lives, resolved these differences, and from 1891 onwards there was a consolidated practice in Chile, of a parliamentary government that some authors have categorized as one of assembly (Amunátegui 1951: 199; Barros 2000: 89–98). It has been mentioned above that Heise maintains that Chilean parliamentarianism emerged before 1891, which seems correct. The way in which Heise explains its development also seems accurate:

> The triumphant bourgeoisie in 1891 limited itself to continuing the parliamentary practices from before the revolution. Nobody thought to establish the closure of debates, nor the presidential faculty of dissolving the lower Chamber, nor the regulation of interpolations which are essential elements of government by Cabinet. Therefore, it is described as an incomplete parliamentary regime ... The powerful attributions which Congress could wield without counterbalance were prudently argued, with equanimity and profound democratic feeling, managing not to damage the harmony and collaboration between the public powers. The same happened with the serious and frequent conflicts created by the autocratic presidentialism enshrined in the 1925 Constitution.
>
> (Heise 1996: 91–92)

In December 1891 the Conservative Commission was given the faculty of summoning Congress to extraordinary sessions, and in 1893 a constitutional reform was approved, in which the Chambers, in the face of a presidential veto, could persist with a two-thirds vote (Campos Harriet 1956: 378). The parliamentary audit of government was also increased. The compatibility of functions between parliamentary and executive positions, which was authorized by constitutional regulations, was used to control the Executive. The compatibility of functions allowed Ministers of State themselves to be Members of Parliament. The audit could be carried out with questionings and votes of no confidence, without having the Members of Parliament in Cabinet. In the final analysis, the political regime emerging in 1891 lacked many elements that are central to parliamentarianism – for example, government was not carried out with a prime minister, and the President of the Republic was elected by universal suffrage. For this reason, Amunátegui comes to believe that it was condemned to expire by dissolution (Amunátegui 1951: 200–201).

Despite the progress that can be highlighted in this period, Alberto Edwards and others have spread a smear campaign of conservative derivation that denounces the irresponsibility and obstruction of Parliament, excessive ministerial rotation, low morale, inefficiency, and lessening of the government's actions and their inability to face the "social question," which supposedly would have characterized the political institutionality of the time (Edwards 1993: 188–198; Andrade 1963: 16–20; and also other more contemporary commentators, such as Vial 1987: 495–617; and Carrasco 2002: 139).

This is a criticism more rooted in ideology than in reality. For example, the great traditionalist historian Mario Góngora has clearly explained that, among the political groups, the least interested in the "social question" was the conservative group, and according to him, the liberals and radicals dedicated themselves to the cause with more concern than other groups. According to Góngora, even the small conservative faction, which at the beginning of the twentieth century was interested in social themes, did not question significantly the liberal and parliamentary regime of the time (Góngora 1986: 98–105). It is mainly the period after 1891 which some have linked to an era of stagnation in relation to social needs, and which is perceived as wrapped in an atmosphere of fraud and apathy, in the face of growing urbanization and industrialization (Keen and Wasserman 1984: 323–324). This way of judging the Chilean reality is very often inspired by a comparison with the North American political reality, and therefore is not able to perceive the potential germ of authoritarianism that was later reflected in the presidentialist emphasis of the 1925 constitutional reform (ibid.: 327). Furthermore, it must be considered that in the West there is strong criticism of liberalism, which is accentuated after the First World War and which culminates in the emergence of Nazism and Fascism until the middle of the 1940s, and of communism during the whole of the twentieth century.

In Chile, the 1891 revolution finishes the consolidation of the parliamentary regime whose origins are found in the previous constitutional reforms of the 1870s. The ownership of power is transferred to Parliament, without modifying the letter of the Constitution, but altering its original presidentialist spirit. According to Manuel Rivas Vicuña, the 1891 revolution: "had the purpose not of reforming the Constitution, but of making it complied with. It is true that it served to sustain the presidential regime; now, without changing the letter it will embody in its spirit the parliamentary regime" (Andrade 1963: 15).

4.3 THE NEW EXPRESSIONS OF CHILEAN CONSTITUTIONAL LAW IN ROLDÁN AND LETELIER

It is regarding this doctrinal and organic constitutional context that the work of Alcibíades Roldán, *Elementos de Derecho Constitucional de Chile* [*Elements of Constitutional Law in Chile*], takes its stance. This work has the virtue of being a modern treatment in which Roldán unfolds a debate regarding the sources of the law, in a systematic way that no other Chilean author has previously used. In it, he distinguishes, for example, between interpretative and other laws (Roldán 1913: 21). This distinction is of particular relevance because the new category of interpretative laws is considered as a special kind of source for constitutional law. In the work of Roldán, the study of the organic or structural element is also important – that is to say, the debate regarding the forms of power of the State, to the detriment of the rights of the individual and their guarantees. This new way of perceiving constitutional law rooted in positivism is, in some versions, anti-liberal because it considers as exaggerated the idea that the main objective of the State is the protection of individual rights. According to Roldán:

> The assertion of these rights in general and philosophical form was developed in the eighteenth century and deduced from the origin that was attributed to the State. Every man was invested with these rights from birth; therefore, they preceded the formation and organization of society. Conceding that part of their independence that was necessary to the constitution of those rights with political character and aims, they were understood that they would preserve what was left of that independence, that is, the set of freedoms not required for the organization of the State. It was incumbent on the authorities to ensure the preservation of these freedoms; and therefore any legal obstacles that opposed the development of the individual's faculties should be eliminated. The excessive extension of such ideas will later make it said that the center of society is this latter and that the main, if not the only mission of the State, is to guarantee this right.
>
> (Roldán 1913: 52)

Another author who acquires great relevance in this same period is Valentín Letelier. In his work *Génesis del Estado y de sus instituciones fundamentales* [*Genesis of the State and its Principal Institutions*], he considers different perspectives to explain the government's functions. Among them stand out the historical, psychological, political, and legal perspectives. Letelier, in his explanations related to the law, teaches us regarding the most appropriate way of understanding it, and in the first place he refers us to exegesis and its historical and empirical methods. According to Letelier, the first is directed to determining the rationale giving origin to laws, what the legislator had in mind when enacting them, which has the advantage of avoiding arbitrariness, being thus more adequate for the administration of justice. For Letelier, the best way to understand what he calls constitutional freedoms is that they do not exist in the abstract, nor by their nature do they belong to citizens, but they are to do with the simple and prudential limitations of public powers. In his explanation, Letelier proposes to give the necessary flexibility to the laws, so that with the same legal regulations, radicals, liberals, and conservatives could govern (Letelier 1917: 11). But these two exegetical methods as a whole are not sufficient to understand the law because – and this is one of the main points in his work – a great part of the legal regulations have not been sanctioned by the State, nor reduced to written formulae. It is thus that Letelier ascribes central importance to custom as a source of the law, recognizing it as the legal expression par excellence which springs spontaneously from the needs of society, which is at the origin of the State and all institutions, which is indeed the respected and practiced law, and which counts on more coercive power than the public powers to comply with its regulations. If the laws do not adapt to social changes, if they do not respond continually to what is needed, according to Letelier they lose the most indispensable condition of their existence and remain on paper as empty and inapplicable formulae.

> Right, the positive method teaches us that the true law is nothing but the expression of those relationships, coercive in character, that are established spontaneously among men; that the laws established by the legislator's external impulse do not create a right unless they are sanctioned by tradition and social assent; and that the written law is never perfect because it is never rigorously developed to meet the needs and traditions of the people.
>
> (ibid.: 36)

And even if it seems rather paradoxical, it is in the ordering of public affairs where Letelier recognizes that tradition has greater domination, there being many cases in which the law is no more than an aspiration of the legislator. Thus, regarding the political regime in Chile in 1917, Letelier indicates that if we listen to the law, the conclusion will be that Chile is a democratic republic, but the reality does not allow us to arrive at that conclusion:

> Suppose that we want to study the Chilean political regime to know if it is democratic, aristocratic, oligarchic, or autocratic. The exegesis will take as a source of study the written legislation and will soon arrive at the conclusion that this Republic is a perfect democracy, constituted as it is on the legal basis of universal suffrage, because all the males over twenty-one years old who can read and write have the right to vote. But if the law is not law unless it is a fact, science does not only need the written rule; it must discover the reality, and what there is in reality is: first, that no more than a fifth of the population of the Republic knows how to read and write; second, that of this portion, not even a fifth is registered in the records; third, that of those registered, more than half do not go to vote; fourth, that of those who go to vote, three-quarters delegate their conscience to the priest, the landowner, or the chief of police. Conclusion: while the written law flatters us with the illusion that we live in a perfect democracy, the real law, the law ignored by the exegesis, has us subjected to an oligarchy as corrupt as it is tiny.
>
> (ibid.: 13–14)

The importance that custom has in public law is also manifest in another reference that Letelier makes regarding the Chilean regime. He highlights the development of parliamentary law in Chile, a law that is not written in any text, but that has been formed almost exclusively by established practice, as has happened in all nations ruled by this system:

> The complete life of ministries, their organization, relationships with each one of the Chambers, their abilities to fill public offices, and so on, are subject to certain rules that every Member of Parliament knows and that no minister would dare to contravene. But this legal body of rules has not been instituted by the Constitution, nor by any law. If the President of the Republic must govern according to the majority in both Chambers; if he has to choose his ministers from among those citizens who have the more or less conditional support of one or other Chamber; if a Minister of State cannot oppose legislation proposed by any of his colleagues; if at the least insinuation of one or other branch of

> Congress the minister must resign his duties; if the election of
> a chairman hostile to the Cabinet is cause for imposing resignation,
> and so on; all this takes place, not because some written law prescribes it,
> but because parliamentary practices have established it.
>
> (ibid.: 21)

Despite the importance that Letelier gives to parliamentary practices, Góngora has argued that he also criticized the parliamentary
system because it cancels out the action and responsibility of the
government. Góngora says that in 1891 Letelier was a supporter of
deposing Balmaceda because, in his opinion, in a free country it cannot
be accepted that the Head of State changes the existing political regime
by himself. This critical way of thinking regarding the Chilean political
reality that we find in Letelier is explained, according to Góngora,
because his way of thinking combines a conception of moderate
authoritarianism, an academic socialism of German origin in social
matters, and a Jacobinism in what is religious (Góngora 1986:
106–107).

4.4 THE RELATIONSHIP BETWEEN THE SOCIAL QUESTION AND LIBERAL CONSTITUTIONAL REPUBLICANISM

The social question is a set of problems that can be characterized as
follows:

> From the last third of the nineteenth century, the high levels of
> violence, the filthiness, the overcrowding, the promiscuity, the deteri-
> oration of housing, the spread of contagious diseases, came to intensify
> the poverty observed in the cities. The explosive growth of the urban
> centers, fed by the migratory movement of important sections of the
> population, made evident problems that until then were unprece-
> dented, giving birth to the "social question" recently mentioned.
> The expression is eloquent in itself because it refers to a variety of
> conflicts glued together as though one, which, given the convergences
> in terms of origin and spread of the problems, needed global
> treatment.
>
> (Correa et al. 2001: 50–51)

During this period, the discussion in Chile regarding the "social
question" became a serious challenge to the political and legal system,
and generated a wave of growing unrest, in particular in the big urban

centers and in the mining establishments. This process of changes generated a series of strikes, which between 1902 and 1908 numbered 84, according to the North American historian Peter DeShazo (Correa et al. 2001: 60).

In Chile, two positions were initially established in relation to this "question." The first, conservative in character, assumed that poverty was of an individual and moral character and therefore tried to give paternalistic and not institutional solutions. The second position that was adopted by some liberal, radical, and social democrat groups consisted of recognizing the structural character of poverty and attributing it to the existence of disadvantaged groups who required preferential legal regulation to emerge from exclusion and marginalization. In the second position, the subject of poverty was thought of as linked to the exercise of certain rights and as an effect of inequality. This strategy is the one that prospered and served to inaugurate an era of social laws and new policies in terms of trade unions, labor relations, wages, rest periods, and so on.

Some authors have argued that liberalism was left silent and defenseless, and finally was overwhelmed by the social question. They believe that the moment of emergence of the "social question" marks the decline and replacement of liberalism by more progressive currents, in particular the ultramontane version of social Christianity, which arises in Christian democracy under the shelter of a confused understanding of social encyclicals. A more unhurried analysis of the social issue in Chile shows that the liberal contribution to this topic was substantial. It was the liberal position, related to the social issue in terms of content, but not regarding its form, that came to be imposed by force in the 1924 military intervention.

This is how James Morris has explained it in his work related to the polemic about the social question, in which he sets out the complex process of political and intellectual fermentation that for at least two decades took place in Chile, concluding with the adoption of the first social legislation in Chile, adopted in 1924 and consolidated from 1938 (Morris 1966: xv; Cristi and Ruiz-Tagle 2006: 307–308). The so called "social question" has served to put forward all kinds of arguments regarding a supposed additional weakness of political liberalism in Chile. In fact, Morris maintains that from the beginning of the twentieth century in Chile, the social question had a very broad meaning, and that attempts were made to encompass within this concept the social, labor, and ideological consequences of the processes of industrialization and urbanization of the twentieth century. These consequences referred to matters of wages, workers' living conditions, health, trade union organizations, and the answers given by the system to the revolutionary ideas regarding poverty. Morris explains how in Chile there existed a conservative and a liberal plan, which came face to face in their basic precepts and viability (Morris 1966: xv–xvi).

The conservative project, of Catholic inspiration and whose author was Juan Enrique Concha, put the emphasis on psychological, religious, and moral factors to solve the social question, and proposed as a solution a greater benevolence and a better treatment of the workers. The conservative plan introduced in the Senate in 1919 had as components limited improvements in working conditions, the establishment of industrial trade unions in businesses, and compulsory systems of conciliation and arbitration to resolve collective labor disputes. There was reference to a personal change of a moral kind, limited wage improvements, and limited participation in the profits of the business. The effect of the social legislation proposed by the conservatives, inspired by the social encyclicals, was intended to reduce the negative consequences of what were perceived as the non-Christian attitudes of employers (Morris 1966: 263–273).

That is why, according to Morris' explanation, there were significant differences between the conservative proposal and that of the *Alianza Liberal* [Liberal Alliance]. The *Alianza Liberal* consisted in those days of liberals, radicals, and other progressive sectors, in which were involved Arturo Alessandri, Jorge Errazuriz Tagle, Eleodoro Yáñez, Ramón Vicuña Subercaseaux, Malaquías Concha, Pedro Luis González, Jorge Gustavo Silva, and many others. The liberal proposal was a collective project prepared in the Law Faculty of the Universidad de Chile, that was preceded by many theses, academic reports, and comparative law studies, and which finally took shape in several legislative proposals (Morris 1966: 164). The liberal project contained a more comprehensive plan of legislative reforms, which included more substantial salary improvements, freedom to form trade unions, and formulae to solve labor conflicts. This proposal was introduced to Congress in 1921, in the form of a code, and it was based on the idea of establishing free trade unions and replacing the employers' control, proposed by the conservatives, with State intervention that would ensure labor stability (Morris 1966: 144–171).

The liberal proposal met fierce opposition from the conservatives, the Catholic hierarchy, and the *Sociedad de Fomento Fabril* [Manufacturers' Association], which meant that both sectors agreed a deal that consisted of adopting the conservative proposal of Juan Enrique Concha as a minimum, an idea supported mainly by Eleodoro Yáñez (Morris 1966: 225). The 1924 pro-military coup was opposed to this deal. Inspired by Arturo Alessandri, they demanded by decree the same legislation that in its time the *Alianza Liberal* had proposed (Morris 1966: 232–240). It is not strange that the social question was a subject on which the liberals had much to say, because one of the liberal concerns has always been the fight against privilege and in favor of equality.

4.5 THE NEW POLITICAL ACTORS AND THE COUPS D'ÉTAT THAT DESTROYED THE THIRD REPUBLIC

In an assessment of the Third Republic, the liberal and parliamentary shift should be highlighted as something new that emerges and that did not exist in the Chilean Second Republican period. Submission to the rule of law by the President of the Republic and the titleholders of the executive function was achieved, together with limiting the power of the military and the Catholic Church. A liberal conception of rights was developed, which gave predominance to the legislative function in the organization of government, and the extraordinary faculties of the Executive came to an end. Parliamentary acts abolished Spanish legislation and created a Chilean republican legislation, the first in South America.

Various strong and organized political parties appeared as new political actors, such as the *Partido Radical* [Radical Party] (1857), the *Partido Conservador* [Conservative Party] (1856), and the *Partido Liberal* [Liberal Party] (1850). At the same time, at the end of the Third Republic, new political parties were created, such as the *Partido Democrático* [Democratic Party] (1887) and the *Partido Obrero Socialista* [Socialist Workers Party] (1912), which gave expression to the aspirations of the middle class. The historical backgrounds of these new parties went back to social groups already in existence at the beginning of the Republic, made up of craftsmen, traders, miners, and rural landowners, those who gradually became employees during the Third Republic thanks to the public education system (González 2011: 365–370).

However, just as in the First and Second Republics, during the Third Republic power was concentrated and centralized in Santiago. During this period, liberal principles were adopted, which characterized in part the evolution of the First Republic. These liberal principles were expressed in the fight against the kinds of domination which ecclesiastical privileges constituted, to do with cemeteries and the control of marriages and education, and even the social question, as has already been explained, among many other issues.

The participation and deliberation of the governed in public issues and the right to dissent were considerably expanded. Respect for the law, as an expression of republicanism, occurred increasingly, and political participation and the fight against excessive power concentration were gradually advanced. This expansive political process was interrupted by the 1924 coup d'état.

CHAPTER FIVE

FOURTH REPUBLIC: THE DEMOCRATIC REPUBLIC, 1932–1973

It is no accident that in 1924 there was a military intervention. From the beginning of his government, Arturo Alessandri visited barracks and had innumerable meetings with the military. His purpose was to get them involved in political life, to reinforce his own power, reform the Constitution, and enact the social legislation that the country needed. That is how the figure of Alessandri became a neo-presidentialist model – that is to say, an executive authority that governs with an iron fist, that imposes order and prevents subversion, and that promises to confront oligarchs and exploiters (Correa et al. 2001: 128). The coup d'état of September 11, 1924 closed the National Congress, expatriated the President, and suspended the constitutional regime. This period of interruption to republican life came about, according to Amunátegui, because there were: "Congresses that, in one way or another, agree to reward their members and that become closed down by public force; government instability and constant rotation; short-lived cabinets; restriction of individual rights" (Amunátegui 1951: 202).

During the period 1927 to 1931, a military dictatorship was installed, presided over by General Carlos Ibáñez, with a clear anti-republican profile (Keen and Wasserman 1984: 328). In 1931, the Ibáñez dictatorship fell and was succeeded by a series of military coups d'état, whose leaders declared respect for the Constitution; nevertheless, they openly and repeatedly violated it, moving away from the republican practices that had been established in Chile (Vicuña 1938: 183–202). At the end of 1932, a constitutional government was finally consolidated, even though some authors have maintained that the period of validity of the 1925

Constitution began in the same year, 1925, and that it was never interrupted (Bernaschina 1958: 47). The Constitution returned the titleholder to the executive function, a pre-eminent position, and subjected all constitutional bodies to the legal regulations that emerged disproportionately from the President's initiative. The division of the exercise of power gave way progressively, each time more in favor of the authoritarian presidential figure, a situation that generated increasing tensions with Parliament. This tension was not resolved, and it could be said that it is one of the precedents of the constitutional conflict that would occur later, in 1973.

5.1 PRESIDENTIALISM, THE USE OF EXTRAORDINARY POWERS, AND THE JUDGMENT OF HANS KELSEN

In relation to the organic part of the 1925 constitutional reform, there is no better judgment, nor a more complete assessment, than that of Hans Kelsen. Upon knowing in 1926 the regulations of the reformed Chilean Constitution, Kelsen stated:

> The new Chilean Constitution is the result of that anti-parliamentarian movement that today is also spreading everywhere in Europe ... Already, the way of nominating the President through direct elections (Art. 63) and the setting of his period of six years show a tendency to organize Chilean democracy under the form of a Presidential Republic. Altogether, the Constitution includes a series of regulations leading from there up to very close to the frontiers of that format that today is usually called dictatorship. This can be seen especially in the legislative field. It is true that the legislative body, the National Congress, made up of the Chamber of Deputies and the Senate, can in no way be distinguished, in terms of its nomination, from the usual models of representative systems. However, the legislative process is regulated in a way that ensures that the President has a decisive influence. Indeed, the role of the President is not limited merely to enacting statutory laws. The Constitution reserves to him the right to approve the bills proposed by Parliament (Art. 52). It is true that withholding this approval only has the effect of a suspensory veto. However, against the President's wishes, Parliament could only realize its legislative intention by persisting in its decision with a majority of two-thirds in both Chambers. If it is, on the other hand, about a constitutional reform, the President can go to the people in opposition to that qualified majority and call a referendum (Art. 109). This means, in practice, that a statute cannot be enacted against the President's wishes. Nevertheless, the decisive deviation in

respect of the parliamentary principle is apparent in the fact that the Constitution does not depart from a principle that even characterizes constitutional monarchies, which is: that – apart from exceptions expressly mentioned in the Constitution – the regulations, in general, can only originate in the form of statutes, or as decisions of the representatives of the people ... In summary, it could be said that the South American Republic has solved this problem in a relatively moderate way, so that it has avoided, in the well-understood interest of the nation, abandoning the parliamentarian regime and falling into the opposite extreme of a dictatorship *lacking a Parliament*.

(Kelsen 2003: 643)

Amunátegui assumes a similar critical position in relation to the 1925 Constitution because it does not correspond to the Chilean social system:

We are among those who believe or feel that the governmental system established in Chile by the 1925 Constitution not only has not been realized; worse than that, it has been refuted. More, much more serious still: it is a government regime in conflict with our social system, with our social reality ... Chile, in its social and public system, is a country of parliamentary soul ... In the critical analysis of the Chilean political regime ... we arrive at the conclusion that, from the doctrinal point of view, our governmental system responds to the concept of systems of collaboration of powers or flexible separation, with marked predominance of the executive power.

(Amunátegui 1951: 218–219)

The 1925 Constitution requires, regarding Members of Parliament, a greater dependence on their parties because, according to a new theory of delegation, the parliamentary function becomes the exercise of a mandate that the political parties have conferred on Members of Parliament; consequently, they are its trustees and not representatives of the people (Heise 1996: 123). Therefore, it is not to be wondered at that after describing the organic part of the 1925 Constitution, Amunátegui incorporates a justification of parliamentarianism, which, in the Chilean case, is based on the system of political parties:

The following factors distinguish the regime of political parties in Chile: (a) it is a system of multiple parties, where not one of them forms a majority; (b) it is a case of flexible parties, that is to say, the leadership does not have great authority over its followers; (c) its legal formation is rudimentary; and (d) they have an important, direct, and indirect influence on the Chilean political regime.

(Amunátegui 1951: 220–221)

Amunátegui's call to adopt parliamentarianism in Chile, which should be based on the structure of parties, is not satisfied just with the development of practices that promote a constitutional mutation towards this type of regime. It also requires the adoption of certain constitutional dispositions that enable the consolidation of this governmental regime, among which Amunátegui highlights:

> The post-war parliamentarian system is made unique by regulating, in the constitutional text itself, the mechanism of the system which in its origin was based on mere practices and precedents. This regulation must consider the following bases: (a) formation of the Cabinet; (b) audit and censorship by the political Chamber; (c) dissolution of the Chamber by the Executive. Within this problem, we consider it appropriate to maintain our double Chamber system, with the addition of technical advisors of a consultative character, similar to the system established by the present French Constitution.
>
> (ibid.: 230–231)

Despite the richness of Amunátegui's democratic and liberal conception, both doctrinal and organic, it has to be recognized that Chilean constitutionalism, for reasons difficult to determine, and perhaps due to the influence of an out-of-date version of legal positivism or of legal formalism, lost its continuity and attractiveness, even before the 1973 breakdown. Mario Bernaschina, in one of his main works, analyzes the fall of the parliamentary system and states that the system existing in Chile imitated French parliamentarianism, which had many defects in terms of homogeneity of cabinets and the ability of the President to dissolve the Chamber (Bernaschina 1958: 328). The works of Bernaschina, even though precise in their sources, manage to distance themselves from political practice, and therefore sometimes lack a critical perspective in relation to the defects of the Chilean system.

It was during the same period that Francisco Cumplido justified the first forms of constitutional justice, by observing the defects of positive legislation. From there he concluded the need to create an institution like the *Tribunal Constitucional* [Constitutional Tribunal] in our country. There is, from his point of view, a substantial incoherence between the regime introduced with the 1925 reform and the Constitution, which is reflected in the kind of legislation emerging under its protection, which appears fragmented and as having lost its general character (Cumplido 1970: 179). The analysis of this author is based on the observation of daily politics. Cumplido presents the duties of public

111

law, and in particular of constitutional law, as an attempt to categorize the debate of the parliamentary sessions and their relation to the outcomes of legislation, and with it distances the constitutional law from its role as a doctrinal academic and comparative discipline. Constitutional law is transformed in this way into a description of political practice (ibid.: 180).

However, as Weston Agor shows in the study of the Senate in Chile of this same period, in the context of the 1925 Constitution, categories of comparative constitutional law were used and some powers of the Senate were exercised, such as the legislative initiative and the capacity of delaying, modifying, or rejecting legislative proposals originating in the Executive. Also, Agor was able to explain the power that the Senators exercised over the bureaucracy, civil service, and administration, their ability at exercising their sponsorship, articulating their interests, and solving political and legal conflicts (Agor 1971: 7). Consequently, when comparing Agor's work and conclusions with the study of Chilean constitutionalists of the same period, it is possible to perceive the loss in great part of local constitutional law, which was bottled up in mere short-term political contingency.

In any case, the most important conflict during the period of validity of the 1925 Constitution is that based on the discussion about the prerogatives of traditional rights in the face of economic and social needs. In particular, conflict arose over property and the successive experiences of agricultural reform. In the final stages of the Fourth Republic, there was a debate regarding State intervention in the economy, and there ensued the nationalization of most banks, industry, and the large copper-mining sector, with measures that were adopted after an intense electoral and parliamentary dispute.

The foregoing is not by chance, because it was a momentum typical of the growth of the State which can already be observed from the beginning of the twentieth century. Authors as perceptive as Max Weber, even though they considered in their work the incipient demand for State intervention in areas not required before, could not imagine the complexity that would be implicated in the contemporary phenomenon of growing State activity and regulation (Weber 1994: 1047–1066). Something similar could be said of the regulation emerging in this same period in the USA (Sunstein 1993: 11–46). This new State intervention, in the form of administrative regulation, in areas that before were given to the market, naturally presented problems regarding the legality of such actions. The permanent nature of the problem of the legality of State intervention was a consequence of the relationship between constitutional law and administrative law. From Otto Mayer, administrative law can be understood as the definitive constitutional law, and the question of the legality of the administration's power was centered on its justification or constitutional rationale (Schmidt-Assmann 2003: 100). That is to say, at the beginning, administrative law only had to configure the areas of action of the State administration as constitutionally determined. But the incipient widening of State intervention cast serious doubts on the aforementioned traditional conception. This interpretation has been recognized by Nicola Matteucci, who says: "the jurisdiction of the administration assumes ever more importance with the arrival of the Social State, that is to say, with the generalization of the economic and social activities of governments that could easily harm the legitimate interests of the citizens" (Matteucci 2010: 286).

5.2 THE NEW SOCIAL CONSTITUTIONALISM AND THE SUBSEQUENT EXTENSION OF RIGHTS

During the Fourth Republic, the constitutional rights of individuals were extended through legislative interpretation, and the use of extraordinary faculties given to the government was increased. Additionally, the concept of citizenship and of representation or political inclusion was gradually extended, until it included eighteen-year-olds among the voters, accepted female suffrage, and did away with bribery by introducing a unique identity voting card. This meant the consolidation of a republican, social, and democratic form in terms of dogma and the exercise of rights, and a presidentialist (neo-presidentialist or hyper-presidentialist) and in some ways corporativist, form in terms of the definition of its constitutional fundamentals.

The changes brought together by the 1925 Constitution were a reflection of the growing democratization and greater State intervention arising mainly from the country's industrialization (Heise 1996: 116). The constitutional conception emerging in 1925 was, for some, the expression of the crisis of a parliamentarian system that did not prosper for lack of the necessary political education, and the absence of a solid and disciplined system of political parties (Estévez 1949: 37). A change in the electoral system also took place, which caused ministerial paralysis and intransigence; the workers organized themselves into trade unions and a new social mentality emerged; in addition, the military decided to intervene in a more active way in politics, overthrowing and installing governments (Mirow 2011: 1187).

The new democracy established only at the end of this period, which Heise calls "social democracy," received the support of the popular masses, presenting the State with very different problems from those faced by the preceding liberal democracy (or "political democracy"), valid until 1925, and which allowed the political and social supremacy of a high class with privileged access to property and education (Heise 1996: 127). The new democracy was supported by the constitutional recognition of a new concept of property law which included its social function, by the introduction of social security, the indemnification of those whose cases were dropped and acquitted, compulsory primary education, and the scaling of taxation (Heise 1996: 137; Bernaschina 1958: 143). In 1931, once General Carlos Ibáñez leaves government, President Arturo Alessandri returns to Chile from exile. In December 1932, general elections are again organized and Alessandri is elected President. The new Constitution, approved by plebiscite in 1925, as a reform of that of 1833, does not take full effect until the end of 1932. According to Amunátegui, the main characteristics of the new Constitution are:

1. The reformed Constitution of 1833. The great doctrines that enlightened it – national sovereignty, representative government, separation of public powers – and the structure of the government bodies, are identical in both texts;
2. The political experience of parliamentary government, developed in Chile from 1891 to 1924, and against which there was a precise reaction by replacing the system of government; and
3. The influence of neo-contemporary political doctrines [sic]. In this sense, we must observe that, even though our Supreme Charter was enacted in a time of newest constitutions, these had little influence on it.

(Amunátegui 1951: 204)

It is noteworthy that Amunátegui highlights the relative lack of influence on the new Chilean Fundamental Charter, of other contemporary constitutional experiences, which he calls *newest constitutions*. Heise, on the contrary, perceives the influence of the 1917 Mexican Constitution, the 1918 Soviet Constitution, and the Weimar Constitution enacted on August 11, 1919. The Mexican and Soviet models inspire the creation of new governmental structures of social services, which deviate from classical constitutionalism (Heise 1996:

121). More than the influence of the Soviet Constitution, it is possible that the ideological conception underlying the 1925 Chilean constitutional reform was influenced by the ideas of Italian fascism and some of the doctrines of French public law. The 1925 Constitution recognizes the doctrine of social and economic rights and emphasizes the protection of jobs, industry, and the interventions of social welfare. It guarantees the citizens a minimum welfare that includes the State's duty of caring for health. Furthermore, in due course, constitutional reforms that validate the processes of the expropriation of agricultural, banking, and industrial property are enacted, promoting the dividing up of property and the establishment of family ownership (ibid.: 122). Sergio Carrasco, quoting Bernaschina, summarizes the objectives of the 1925 constitutional reform, enumerating them as follows:

1) Change the pseudo-parliamentarian system of government, establishing a presidential regime.
2) Define the sphere of action of the powers of the State.
3) Eliminate the pseudo-parliamentarian excesses.
4) Establish religious freedom.
5) Put the Constitution in tune with social rights.

(Carrasco 2002: 158)

The 1925 Constitution enshrines a presidential regime, but deviates from the original model of the United States of America. Despite concentrating power in the President, it officially recognizes the role of the political parties, and, by alternating presidential elections with parliamentary ones, ensures that no President may control the legislative branch on taking up office, favoring multi-party representation (Loveman 1988: 219). Amunátegui explores the common features between the Constitution of Philadelphia and that of Chile in 1925:

In a brief investigation, we note: (a) the concept of an exclusively representative government; (b) the political non-accountability of ministers; (c) the incompatibility between parliamentary and ministerial posts; and (d) the faculty of the judiciary power to declare the unenforceability of the statutes. But the main principle that characterizes the political regime in North America – that is, that the legislative function is only fulfilled by Congress – has been violated in our system of government.

(Amunátegui 1951: 211–212)

As for the structure of rights contained in the 1925 Constitution, we can observe its complexity thanks to Gabriel

Amunátegui, one of the most outstanding exponents of the democratic republican liberal tradition during the twentieth century in our country. In his work, he continues the development begun by Roldán and Letelier, starting with the analysis and criticism of the dispositions of the 1925 reformed Constitution. He appears greatly influenced by the French schools and develops a complete conception of the sources of constitutional law, and a range of sophisticated ideas regarding constitutional law which originates in the debate about the 1925 Constitution, and which, in its doctrinaire conception, endures with full validity to the present time. His conception is revealed by the use granted, for example, to comparative doctrine and law, and also, to political science as important elements of his analysis (Amunátegui 1953: 76). At the same time, Amunátegui contrasts in its conception a range of definitions of constitutional law, contraposing his own, which he defines as "a branch of the public national law whose regulations have the prioritized objective of organizing the State, determining the attributes of government and guaranteeing the exercise of individual rights" (ibid.: 73). In his definition, he includes, with emphasis, the idea of constitutional guarantees, and he gives great importance to the procedures for protection of these rights. However, his work attributes excessive importance to political science as an inspiration for new constitutions. In any case, his analysis of constitutional law, in relation to other branches of the law, such as international, administrative, criminal, procedural, and private law, anticipates some of the forms adopted by constitutional law in our time. He also distinguishes between regulations that should be constitutional, as opposed to those that must have regulatory treatment. Similarly, he describes constitutional law as the permanent conflict between what is individual and what is collective, from which emerge three possible forms of government: tyranny, despotism, and constitutionalism; this last, according to Amunátegui, is typical of civilization, where government directs and the governed control (ibid.: 74–76).

The features of Chilean constitutional law, according to Amunátegui, can be summarized as follows:

(1) A sophisticated notion of the sources of constitutional law.
(2) An explanation regarding the relationship between constitutional law and other branches and disciplines. The connection that he

makes between constitutional law and private law is important; the latter is seen to be influenced by the former, mainly in private law regulations that concern public order.

(3) An explanation about the relationship that must exist between governments and the governed: the government directs and the governed control.

(4) The idea of constitutional supremacy.

(5) The importance of resources and actions in relation to people's rights.

(6) The importance that he attributes to the different kinds of guarantee in relation to people's rights.

Additionally, Amunátegui analyzes the way in which constitutional law is structured in the context of his explanation regarding the essence of the constitutional problem. He identifies the essence as the harmonization of State power and individuality, as the interrelation between authority and freedom: "The essence of the constitutional problem ... consists of harmonizing the State with its authority, and the individuals with their freedom" (ibid.: 303).

Constitutional rights are changing constantly, which does not mean that there can be no going back in relation to them. This process evolves through the inspiration of a series of intellectual struggles and through the ideological disagreements that characterize political rivalry, and the constitutional debate which takes place in an open society with alternative points of view. Amunátegui assigns the following characteristics to constitutional rights:

> (1) They are the patrimony of the human race, as such, without regard for nationality, domicile, and civil status, and so on. (2) The constitutional recognition of the rights of the individual is not necessary for their exercise; the law being silent, men are empowered to use them, comprehensively. (3) They do not allow an accurate enumeration to be made of them because civilization determines that man progressively develops their faculties and the political Constitution limits itself to recognizing their existence. (4) They are subject to limitations motivated by the existence of rights of other individuals and by the harmony that should exist between the rights of the authority and those of the individual. (ibid.: 306–307)

As a consequence of the above, the recognition and protection of constitutional rights, for Amunátegui, has a function that fulfills three important purposes:

(1) To guarantee: the Constitution establishes rights in broad terms, in several areas, such as appeals for legal protection, petition, and, of course, unenforceability.

(2) To regulate: the individuals in the development of their material and intellectual capabilities should respect the rights of other individuals, and the sphere that is typical of the State's authority. The regulation, according to Amunátegui, will be mainly a matter for the law, so as to avoid arbitrariness.

(3) To restrict and suspend: this will be necessary mainly in cases of "*constitutional emergency*," linked to the states of emergency, structured without too much detail in the 1833 and 1925 Constitutions, situations that we find with much more regulation in the present Constitution.

(ibid.: 307–313)

Finally, Amunátegui classifies constitutional rights in two large groups. The first group is composed of civil equalities, which in the 1925 Chilean Constitution would be understood as equality before the law, equality of due process, and equality before public responsibilities and positions of public office. The second group is composed of freedoms, which are divided into a first group, including material freedoms, sanctity of home, freedom of work, trade and industry, property rights, and personal freedom; and a second group of intellectual freedoms, among which are freedom of thought and opinion, of conscience and religion, freedom of the press, education, correspondence and other means of communication, of meeting and association, and the right to petition (ibid.: 313–314). In relation to the right of equality, Amunátegui recognizes the special importance of equality before the law, the other equality rights being specifications of this, noting that "equality before the law derives its conception from the typical human personality which, before the law, recognizes the same capacity in all individuals" (ibid.: 314). Therefore, there is, according to Amunátegui, a link between equality and personality, which is an idea very close to the concept of "dignity." This can be the first foundation in Chile of the law that the German constitutional doctrine has called "the right to free development of the personality" (Heise 1996: 85–107). Furthermore, equality before the law is the essence of the democratic conception and of the general soundness of the law, and therefore of the state of constitutional law.

Amunátegui's sophisticated conception of the law, which is founded on the dispositions of the 1925 Constitution and its reforms, contrasts with the Chilean political reality characterized by the continuous application of extraordinary faculties that governments use to restrict the constitutional rights of citizens and which persist during almost the whole of the Fourth Republic (Ruiz-Tagle 2002: 189–211). In relation to this, Sofía Correa states:

> Arturo Alessandri governed for several years with extraordinary faculties given by Congress, where he had a majority. This meant, in practice, giving the Executive the power to watch people, to move them around the country, to confine them in their homes or in places that were not jails, to suspend or restrict the right of meeting, to restrict the freedom of the press and broadcasting, by being able to exercise prior censorship and banning the distribution of printed documents, make investigations with forced entry, decree the vacancy of public office positions … As well as the above-mentioned, at the beginning of 1937, legislation was enacted that sanctioned offenses against the internal security of the State, which allowed restriction of public freedoms without the need each time to have Congress's approval … under the González Videla government it was replaced by the *Ley de Defensa Permanente de la Democracia* [Permanent Defense of Democracy Statute], which outlawed the Communist Party and removed its militants from the electoral registers … This legislation was in force without interruption for ten years, between 1948 and 1958, and even during its validity under Carlos Ibáñez the state of siege was also declared to restrict public freedoms even more.
>
> (Correa 2000: 118)

To this picture of restrictions on public freedoms, it is important to add the limitations existing to the right of suffrage, which were maintained in Chile until the 1970s. In this period, the constitutional argument in Chile intensifies, in an effort to stamp out electoral fraud through the progressive extension of civil and political rights. The feminine right to suffrage is recognized in Chile, to be exercised for the first time in 1935 in municipal elections, and later approved by statute in 1949, to be exercised from 1952 in presidential and parliamentary elections (Cruz-Coke 1984: 42–43). Professor Correa has summarized the evolution of suffrage in Chile as follows:

Universal male suffrage existed in Chile from 1874, and from then until 1973, the proportional system that allows the parliamentary representation of minorities. However, it was not until the middle of the twentieth century that women could exercise in full our citizens' rights, participating for the first time in 1952 in the presidential election and in 1953 in the parliamentary election ... The registration in electoral records was not compulsory until 1962, and the proportion of the population with the right to vote and registered initially was low, even though constantly increasing: 23 percent in the 1930s, 32 percent in the 1940s, 40 percent in the 1950s, 50 percent in the 1960s; and in the 1970s registration became compulsory ... Only the 1958 electoral reform, which established the unique identity voting card, finally ended bribery because it made it impossible to know how a person had voted and therefore to control the effectiveness of the operation of buying and selling votes. From then on, electoral expenses were entirely orientated towards propaganda.

(Correa 2000: 118–119)

The question of the effective validity of the rule of law and the widening of rights is a legal-political discussion that is not peaceful, and which admits legal formulations of wide application. In any case, as a central question linked to the structure of rights, we have to recognize that in Chile there arises a well-developed doctrinal argument around property law, which acquires a prominent place in the doctrinal and political debate of the Fourth Chilean Republic, which we have called the Democratic Republic, and which begins with the full coming into force of the 1925 Constitution in 1932 and lasts until 1973.

5.3 THE SOCIAL FUNCTION OF PROPERTY AND THE AGRICULTURAL REFORM PROCESS

The 1925 Constitution contained a system of property guarantees which reproduced some ideas from the 1833 Constitution, such as understanding the diverse forms of possession, in the context of the industrial development which characterized Chile in this period, but its regulations announced a new conception of property. Obviously, the Constitution recognized the limitations, obligations, or easements that could be attached to property, and in the case of industrial property, also arranged that indemnity should be forthcoming in the case of expropriation. At the same time, the regulations in the 1925 Constitution treated property, following the model of the 1833 Constitution (Faúndez 2011: 87), but were contained in the same chapter as that dedicated to constitutional guarantees. There, the following is set forth:

Chapter III. *Individual guarantees*

Art. 10: The Constitution ensures to all inhabitants of the Republic:

10. The sanctity of all property without distinction. No person can be deprived of property, its possession or any part of it, or of the right to it, unless by virtue of a legal sentence or expropriation for public interest, qualified by statute. In this case, an indemnity will previously be given to the owner as agreed with him or as determined by a corresponding judgment. The exercise of the property right is subject to limitations or regulations demanded by the maintenance and advancement of social order, and in this regard the law may impose obligations or public utility easements in favor of the general interests of the State, of citizens' health, and of public sanitation.

11. The exclusive ownership of any discovery or production, for the time allowed by statute. If this latter should demand its expropriation, a corresponding indemnity will be given to the author or inventor.

        . . .

14. The State will tend to the fair division of family property.
(Valencia Avaria 1951: 224–225)

M. C. Mirow has explained the way in which the writings of León Duguit were the most influential source for installing, at constitutional level in Chile, the idea of the social function of property, and how this influence was expanded from its introduction by Arturo Alessandri in the debates of the 1925 Constitution, to later be used in the most diverse political contexts, including being appropriated by political leaders as varied as Eduardo Frei Montalva, Salvador Allende Gossens, and even the supporters of Augusto Pinochet Ugarte (Mirow 2011: 1185). Even though the expression "social function of property" was not reflected in the original text in the 1925 Fundamental Charter, in the debates, Arturo Alessandri and José Guillermo Guerra mentioned the idea that property must reflect modern legal practice and tendencies, as expressed, for example, in Article 153 of the Weimar Constitution of 1919, which recognized the idea that property is guaranteed by the Constitution and that its limits are defined by law, as well as that property implies duties and its use must be in the service of all (ibid.: 1194).

These concepts came up against the idea of thinking of property as a natural inviolable right and/or of maintaining the regulations of the 1833 Constitution, a position in which Luis Barros Borgoño and Domingo Amunátegui were prominent. The idea about property that finally prevailed was a deal between the main conceptions of this right, which consisted of maintaining the idea of the inviolability of all forms of property, ensuring indemnity in case of deprivation of this right, and giving the statutory law the possibility of setting limits in order to maintain the progress that is needed for social order (ibid.: 1203–1205).

This new constitutional concept of property adopted in Chile following the 1925 debates allowed successive governments to sustain the law in the proposals for colonization and allocation of land in the south of Chile, such as Aysen and Magallanes; to establish statutes covering urbanization, construction, and development, and regulations regarding public works, such as roads and sewerage, to set taxes and prices; to intervene in the economy and develop industry with a protectionist slant, among other subjects (ibid.: 1207). From the middle of the 1960s, the idea of the social function of property was a controversial issue in Chile, although it was a completely accepted notion that crossed the whole spectrum of legal understanding (ibid.: 1210).

For example, the ideas on agricultural property reform, which arose in Chile before the Alliance for Progress, were based on this social conception of property and, as such, allow us to fault the theory that assumes that it is only through an external issue that this process started in Chile. As Pía Muñoz has explained in her thesis, at least two relevant references are considered in relation to this, such as the following:

> the ideas of Leoncio Chaparro Ruminot, who was the managing director of the Caja de Colonización Agrícola [Agricultural Colonization Fund] between 1939 and 1942, and already in a work published in 1932, the *Agricultural Engineer*, noted that "among the main causes of the anemia that overwhelms our young race, we have to point out (together with a disorientated and inefficient education) the bad allocation of land ... that took place in Chile from the start of the twentieth century without counterbalance, encouraging land grabbing, land that had been unjustly allocated even from the beginning of the Conquest of our country."
> (Muñoz 2015: 18)

The second direct reference to the subject of agricultural property before the Alliance for Progress, found by Pía Muñoz and which she analyzes in respect of its relevance, is as follows:

On June 27, 1945, the then *Ministro de Obras Públicas y Vías de Comunicación* [Minister of Public Works and Communications], don Eduardo Frei Montalva, went to Congress with the objective of presenting the "*Plan de riego y rescate de la plusvalía de las tierras mejoradas por el Estado*" [Irrigation and retrieval of the added value of the land improved by the State], which addressed the problem of distribution and low productivity of agricultural land. Of pertinence here, Title III of the draft bill called *De las expropiaciones* [On expropriations] gave the President of the Republic the faculty of declaring subject to public use certain lands considered strategic for the general irrigation plan, and which, because they were uncultivated land, rough pastures, or were not exploited appropriately, could be expropriated by the State in virtue of such declaration. Meanwhile, the message from the Executive to the National Congress, presented by Eduardo Frei Montalva, explained that the irrigation work carried out by the State had the effect of increasing the added value of the land benefitting from the new irrigation network, which translated into a considerable increase in the market value, to the exclusive benefit of the owners of such farms. Thus, the main objective of the draft bill consisted of introducing corrections to such undue enrichment, so terminating "the unjust situation that only benefitted some from the efforts of the whole society." In this way, the proposal sought to obtain for the State a sum equivalent to the increase in commercial value of the farm from the benefitting owners, otherwise, that the State should receive a certain portion of the land, in keeping with its greater value.

(Muñoz 2015: 23)

In this new conception of property, the social doctrine of the Catholic Church also has influence, and the land reform process began with the Chilean Church giving its land to the farm workers. The debate regarding the agricultural reform generated many controversies, and a great number of arguments were put forward in favor of or against this process. It started out as an argument founded on the economic viability of the Chilean agricultural sector. Later, to these arguments were added others of a political nature, such as the need to dignify, give recognition, and citizenship to all farm workers. It was supposed that the backwardness and paternalism existing in the Chilean farming sector, and the great stretches of badly exploited land, called *latifundios* [large farms], were contrary to modernity, and that the farm workers, as a way of being liberated from a backward and subordinate situation, should participate in this political change. Some of these theories were put in doubt by the empirical evidence. As is evident in the work of professor and sociologist Raúl Urzúa, in the Chilean countryside there were a great number of small owners and *minifundios* [small farms], which obliged one to revise the idea of the predominance of *latifundios* (Urzúa 1969: 91–100). Furthermore, after studying a sample of country people in the basin of the Maule River, in the *Valle Central* [Central Valley] in Chile, Raúl Urzúa concluded:

> the more subordinated the position occupied by an individual in the rural social structure, the less ready he will be to support changes to this structure ... due to the strong pressures to resign himself to the expectations that are created by a paternalistic type of authority, we have also maintained that individuals subjected to this type of authority would be significantly more unwilling than other sectors of country workers to accept structural changes (ibid.: 227).

However, the political decision to deepen the agricultural reform was already taken, and despite the evidence that showed the complexity of the process, this intensified. In the agricultural reform, the leadership of Bishop Manuel Larraín stands out initially, and later, the ideas of Jacques Chonchol acquire special influence, with Chonchol expressing his proposal in the *Revista Mensaje* [Magazine Message], founded in 1951 by the Jesuit Alberto Hurtado. Pía Muñoz explains how the initial argument in favor of agricultural reform, which was focused on justifying the changes in order to increase agricultural productivity, was transformed into a secondary topic under the growing influence being won by the ideas of Jacques Chonchol, Julio Silva Solar, and others, who championed the introduction of a form of collective or communal property in the Chilean farming sector. These ideas alienated the initial support for agricultural reform shown by some liberal and even some conservative politicians. The agricultural reform was necessary, and the many ideological justifications on which it was based and the different directions in which this process advanced, generated great social tension. With such profound reforms, the conditions were created for the right of property and its usage, and those damaged by these measures, to become perhaps some of the main protagonists in the political rupture in Chile that concluded with the 1973 coup d'état. Muñoz summarizes the evolution of the new idea of agricultural property:

> According to Bishop Manuel Larraín, there was a "unanimous agreement to declare family property as the stronghold of Christianity and democracy, and, at the same time, the most efficient kind of agricultural exploitation." Furthermore, Larraín answers three essential ideas about

property contained in *Mater et Magistra*, that is: the importance of family property, the social function, and the relationship between property and freedom. Additionally, in the same year, an article was written by Jacques Chonchol, who would carry forward the agricultural reform process in the Frei and Allende governments. In this article, Chonchol defends the need for agricultural reform that would lead not only to a redistribution of land, a process that must be massive and drastic, according to the author, but also to the integration of the community of farm workers into all aspects of national life.

(ibid.: 39)

On how these changes are embodied in legal regulations, the concise explanation of Professor Enrique Evans stands out. His interpretation includes the changes that characterized the agricultural reform process, but also takes in other reforms to the property right that took place during the life of the 1925 Constitution, which are just as meaningful. In his work *Los Derechos Constitucionales* [*Constitutional Law*], Evans distinguishes four main stages. These stages, following Professor Evans, are summarized and synthesized in the next four paragraphs.

The first stage corresponds to the original text of the 1925 Fundamental Charter, which introduces three changes distinguishing property law from the 1833 Constitution: (1) substitutes the expression "the sanctity of all properties without distinction between those that belong to private individuals and those belonging to communities," with "the sanctity of all properties without any distinction," which implies the recognition of property rights to anything that has patrimonial value; (2) changes the expression "use of the State" as cause for expropriation, to "public use," which includes not only the interest of the State, but also the "health of citizens" and "public sanitation"; and finally, (3) adds a new insert, at the end of Article 10, No. 10, which subjected to the exercise of property law "the limitations or rules that the maintenance and progress of social order demand," granting statutory powers to the law to impose obligations and easements of public use. According to Evans, these regulations allowed for the *Código de Aguas* [Water Code], the *Ordenanza General de Construcciones y Urbanización* [General Code on Construction and Urbanization], the *Ley General de Ferrocarriles* [General Statute on Railways], the *Ley de Servicios Eléctricos* [Electrical Services Statute], the *Ley General de Caminos* [General Highways Statute], and others, to impose limitations on private property without affecting the sanctity of the right ensured by the Constitution (Evans 1999: 214).

The second stage corresponds to the constitutional reform enacted in 1963 during the government of Jorge Alessandri Rodríguez, by Law No. 15.295, which governed with special regulations the expropriation of abandoned or badly exploited country properties, in respect of which the consignation of 10 percent of their value was demanded before the expropriator took possession, with the balance of payment due in no less than fifteen years. Furthermore, in the case of expropriation for urgently required public works, the expropriator could take material possession of the expropriated assets before the agreement or final legal resolution regarding the amount of indemnity had taken place (ibid.: 215).

The third stage, beginning in 1967 during Eduardo Frei Montalva's government, modified property law through Law No. 16.615, allowing by statute a new term in the Constitution, to establish limitations and obligations to possession, in order to ensure its social function and to make property accessible to all. The constitutional requirement of prior total compensation to the expropriated was eliminated, and it was established that in the matter of expropriating country estates, compensation will be equivalent to the current valuation, plus the value of the improvements not included in this valuation, and that it could be paid in annual installments for up to thirty years. Furthermore, the statute is empowered to incorporate into national possession for public use all waters existing in the national territory. According to the Frei government, this reform had two objectives: to deepen the agricultural reform process, for which Law No. 16.640 was enacted on July 28, 1967, and to facilitate the refurbishment and modernization of the main urban centers in the country and the execution of public works of regional importance (ibid.: 218).

Finally, the fourth stage corresponds to the government of Salvador Allende Gossens, which by Law No. 17.450 reformed the property law in the Constitution, to allow the nationalization of the *Gran Minería del Cobre* [Large-Scale Copper Mining] and the *Compañía Minera Andina* [Andina Mining Company]. The process of nationalization ended when the dictatorship negotiated compromises with the copper companies over the pending lawsuits between the former owners of the mines and the State of Chile.

It should be remembered that the process established by the transitory regulations referred to here resulted in the companies whose assets were nationalized having no right to any compensation, for which reason they initiated the above judicial cases. The nationalization was transformed into a constitutional regulation, and empowered the statutory law to expropriate or reserve for the State the exclusive possession of natural resources, production assets and others that were declared of pre-eminent importance for economic and social activity (ibid.: 218, 221).

Consequently, the political and legal system that emerged from the 1925 Constitution, which took its republican form only after 1932, a period that we have called the Democratic Republic or Fourth Chilean Republic, established more developed forms of a Chilean conception of property at the constitutional level. The civil conception of property changed because new forms of property were created, and also because the idea of its social function was gradually introduced (López 2014: 59–92). This last idea was influenced by the work of León Duguit (1975: 235–245), among others, which was introduced into Chile through Arturo Alessandri Palma and Arturo Alessandri Rodríguez (son of President Arturo Alessandri Palma), to finally become part of the constitutional text (Alessandri, Somarriva, and Vodanovic 1993: 91; Mirow 2011: 1185–1210).

As Professor Hernán Corral has very generously pointed out, one has to be careful about identifying the book De los bienes [Regarding Assets], containing the transcriptions of lectures compiled by Antonio Vodanovic, with the ideas and doctrine of Professors Arturo Alessandri Rodríguez and Manuel Somarriva. Neither Alessandri nor Somarriva wrote this work, nor did they approve or authorize its publication. The teachings of Professor Arturo Alessandri Rodríguez on the subject of property must be found in the typed notes of his lectures, which inspire more confidence because they reproduce his own ideas, and even though Antonio Vodanovic declares that the content is "based" on the lectures, it is not clear what this means, what corresponds to each one of the authors, nor what is attributable to the editor.

However, despite the objections presented by Professor Corral, the work De los bienes contains a substantial explanation regarding forms of property that finds its foundation in the constitutional regulations of 1925, and therefore, in the paragraphs that follow, we make direct reference to this work. In relation to the conception of property developed by Alessandri Rodríguez, this is expressed in a masterly way in the famous lectures of the course on Civil Law that were assembled by Vodanovic in De los bienes. There, a deep reflection on property is presented, with special reference to the Constitution, which includes the treatment of the following issues: the reasons that justify the existence of property; the criticisms of property law; the modern tendencies: historic evolution and origin of property law in Chile. Also included are references to the material and legal faculties inherent in possession, the different categories of properties, the obligations or liens over property, and restrictions on property of generic type, such as the theory of abuse of the law, or specifics referred to only as the faculty of exclusion or due to limitations on possession. There are extensive explanations of joint ownership and horizontal property, among other forms, and several related matters. Meanwhile, the doctrinal work *De los bienes*, by Alessandri, Somarriva, and Vodanovic (1993), describes a complete systematization of the forms of property that are integrated by constitutional law with civil law, together with a comparative doctrine and specialized legislation and jurisprudence. To this, the León Duguit exposition has to be added regarding the social function of property, together with the ideas about property emanating from the papal encyclicals and the social doctrine of the Catholic Church, all matters about which Alessandri and Somarriva say:

> All the present-day theories coincide in that possession of wealth should not be, at national level, a way of abusing the economically weak, and they assert, with more or less emphasis, the social function of private property, and defend its adaptation to the general interest. The Constitutions enacted after the last two wars, even ours, embrace, in a more or less intense way, these principles. Perhaps none more categorical, in this sense, than the German Constitution of May 23, 1949, which states: "Property obliges. Its exercise must serve at the same time the common good." (Art. 14, Sec. 2)
>
> (Alessandri, Somarriva, and Vodanovic 1993: 44)

That is why it is no surprise that in the text *De los bienes*, in relation to the regulation on property law in the 1925 Political Constitution, Alessandri and Somarriva maintain: "In relation to property, in general, the Constitution contains two fundamental ideas: the inviolability and the limitations in the exercise of this right" (ibid.: 49).

As a summary of their explanations, the text of Alessandri Rodríguez and Somarriva concludes with a list of issues that explain the change regarding property law in what is called "present day," which they detail as follows:

1. Moveable property, not appreciated before, today, due to industrial progress, is more important than real estate.

2. Alongside individual property, different forms of collective property have developed, like family or social property, this last comprising the property of the State.
3. The limitations that restrict private property rights are many today, if compared with previous centuries, in particular those of public law.
4. Private property in countries where free enterprise is dominant, according to the law, is permeated by a certain more or less strong social orientation, according to the country.

(Alessandri, Somarriva, and Vodanovic 1993: 46)

It is important to note also that in the 1974 edition of the work *De los bienes* written by Alessandri Rodríguez and Somarriva, which was published originally by Editorial Nacimiento, two special sections are included, with the numbers 186a: *Formas de propiedades, la de derecho privado y la de derecho público* [*Forms of Property, that of Private Right and that of Public Right*], and 186b: *La propiedad en los países socialistas* [*Property in Socialist Countries*]. These two sections have been conveniently and suspiciously suppressed in the 1993 re-edition of the same book by Editorial Jurídica. This suppression represents another example of the imposition of a narrow privatist legal idea in our doctrine, which does not hesitate at the mutilation of our best legal doctrine in terms of property. In the cut sections, Alessandri Rodríguez and Somarriva return to conclude the following: "Today, to a greater extent, it is recognized that together with property of clearly private right, there are other forms of property that are of public right" (Alessandri, Somarriva, and Vodanovic 1974: 144–145).

Despite this concealment and doctrinal distortion that seeks to deny a place for public property, it is clear how León Duguit and others that try to limit private property influence the systematization and doctrinal self-understanding of the 1925 Constitution in Chile (Duguit 1975: 171–178, 235–245). This concept is finally incorporated as explicit text in the 1970 constitutional reform, and has direct incidence in the subsequent debate regarding agricultural reform, nationalizations, expropriations, and the legal political issue that was presented at the beginning of the 1970s concerning the differentiated regulation of the three areas of the economy. In 1970, the Chilean Congress enacted the nationalization of the large-scale mining sector, which implied the acceptance of a very special manner of acquisition, which is nationalization, because it consisted of taking away an asset, generally a juridical universality, from the private sector and transferring its title to the State (Novoa 2006: 43–56).

Professor Corral has also brought to my attention that Professor Luis Claro Solar, who wrote the famous treatise, *Explicaciones de derecho civil chileno comparado* [*Explanation of Chilean Comparative Civil Law*] (with the exception of the first two volumes), in the twentieth century (from 1925 to 1945, when he died), in the volume, *De los bienes y los derechos reales*, presents one of the most extended treatments of property law (cf. Claro Solar 1939: vol. VI, part I, nos. 283ff., 325ff.), where he expressly comments on the 1925 Constitution, with mention of the other transactions by the editing commission (ibid., nos. 308, 361ff.). Also, Luis Claro Solar critically refers to Duguit's ideas because, according to the Chilean jurist, Duguit denies that individual property is a right and admits it only as a social function. Regarding this point, Claro Solar describes how some proposed to establish this theory in the 1925 Constitution, but it did not prosper because the majority were in favor of keeping it as a right, albeit with restrictions to avoid abuse and to protect collective interests (ibid., no. 328: 408–412). In any case, Claro Solar interprets Article 582 of the Chilean Civil Code. He says it is not individualistic in essence, making clear the sense of "arbitrarily," and pointing out the restrictions of the property right (ibid., no. 289). In the work of Luis Claro Solar there also appears a consideration of several special forms of property, including that of family property, where he mentions the institution of the homestead (ibid., no. 324ff.: 391–405). At the same time, in the work *De los bienes y los derechos reales* he gives separate consideration to mining property and to intellectual and industrial property.

In addition, Professor Hernán Corral has also remarked, in relation to the civil dogma of twentieth-century property in Chile, the need to refer to the work of Professor Alfredo Barros Errázuriz (1921), *Curso de Derecho Civil* [*Civil Law Course*], and also the work of Victorio Pescio (1978), *Manual de derecho civil, de las personas de los bienes y de la propiedad* [*Civil Law Manual, Regarding Persons, Assets, and Property*], and remarks that the latter makes many references to the Constitution, not only that of Chile, but also Latin American and European constitutions.

Likewise, on the subject of property, Professor Corral points to the need to include the analysis of the evolution of property rights in the work of Pedro Lira Urquieta (1944), who discusses the issues in his book *El Código Civil y el nuevo derecho* [*The Civil Code and the New Law*].

All these references are very valuable and I am happy to mention them, but at the same time I warn the reader that in this book there is no intention to be exhaustive in the treatment of property rights, but rather to highlight some ideas that refer to the domain and its limitations under Chilean law.

Therefore, we do not say anything new when we recognize that during practically the whole of the twentieth century, property was the subject on which the main controversy of Chilean constitutional law was centered. Agricultural property was discussed in depth during the agricultural reform process in Chile, which started at the beginning of the 1960s and continued until the middle of the 1970s. The controversy also extended to the debate about the nationalization of mining property and State intervention in the banking sector, telecommunications, and other strategic sectors of the country (Cristi and Ruiz-Tagle 2008: 257–258).

All these very significant legal-political processes implied a transformation of the concept of property, linking this right to its social function, distancing it from its conception of the absolute and arbitrary ownership of the individual private proprietor. These processes suppose an understanding of the right of property as an economic and social right, whose regulation belongs preferably to the legislator. During this period, efforts were made to establish a relationship between the continuous limitation of property and the scarce activity of the tribunals to defend the rights of private persons, which, added to the absence of a court of administrative disputes, gave greater importance to the execution of the functions of the *Contraloría General de la República* [Comptroller General of the Republic] (which had just achieved constitutional rank) and, in particular, its function of recording, which monitors the legality of public administration in its actions, such as the decrees for resuming work and other measures of State intervention (Faúndez 2011: 87).

5.4 CORPORATISM, THE GROWING FOREIGN INFLUENCE, AND MILITARISM

Meanwhile, another important factor to highlight is the political corporatism that existed in the 1925 constitutional regime. Regarding this issue, Sofía Correa points out:

> we cannot conclude our characterization of Chilean democracy in the middle of the twentieth century without referring to the corporative representation that existed in parallel to electoral representation in the

political system. Indeed, the four entrepreneurial associations of the nineteenth century: SNA (*Sociedad Nacional de Agricultura* [National Agriculture Association]), SFF/SOFOFA (*Sociedad de Fomento Fabril*, [Manufacturers' Association]), SNM (*Sociedad Nacional de Minería* [National Mining Society]) and *Cámara Central de Comercio* [National Chamber of Commerce], were, from the 1920s, represented in the State bodies in charge of economic and social administration and regulation. This was such an extended practice that in 1964, for example, the SFF named directors for twenty government agencies and eight government advisory boards.

(Correa 2000: 120)

The corporatism that developed in Chile with such strength during the twentieth century is a precursor of the *gremialismo* [corporatist trade unionism] that would be a distinctive feature of the anti-republican and anti-democratic plan of the dictatorship that began in 1973, and was later picked up in the constitutional text adopted in 1980. *Gremialismo* defends the idea of the separation of politics and trade union activity, in particular at union level and within student organizations. Corporatism is contrary to the tendency of the Fourth Democratic Republic because it is a force opposed to people's political participation and to any more egalitarian idea of democracy. In corporatism, the entrepreneurial sectors, trade unions, and other entities with parallel power to the political parties have privileged access to the State and maintain a social and economic power that is independent and impervious to citizens' power.

At the same time, during the Fourth Republic one has to note an increase in foreign influence in Chilean political activity. During the nineteenth century, foreign influence in Chile was mainly in the area of business and of the UK Government, which shared power with other European countries and the USA. From the beginning of the twentieth century, the influence of the USA and the Soviet Union was accentuated, along with that of Cuba, which adopted a more direct form of military collaboration. This influence is framed by the tensions of the cold war, and after the presidential elections of 1964 and 1970, the USA became involved in active foreign intervention in Chile. The project to prevent the rise to power of Salvador Allende in 1970 brought some civil servants, citizens, and others with close links with the USA to provide assistance and financing to groups that acted in Chile in criminal and military operations (Carrasco 2002: 212–214). Armando Uribe, in his work *El libro negro de la intervención norteamericana en Chile* [*The Black Book on North American Intervention in Chile*], describes some of the kinds of intervention: "To conclude, the US Government wanted to maintain links of any kind with the Chilean armed forces, as a basic instrument of its hegemonic possession and whatever might become of North American private interests in Chile, because such a relationship enshrined Chilean dependence in relation to the center of the imperialistic system" (Uribe and Opazo 2001: 32).

It must be taken into account that between 1970 and 1975, Chile sent more soldiers to receive training in the *Escuela de las Américas* [US Army School for the Americas] than all other countries in the whole of the decade. In total, during the period, more than 1,500 Chilean officers received education on how to face the internal enemy, which in the cold war era, in the middle of the twentieth century, was identified with left-wing political groups (Gill 2005: 111–112).

5.5 THE STATUTE OF CONSTITUTIONAL GUARANTEES AND SALVADOR ALLENDE'S SOCIALIST REVOLUTION

In this context, Salvador Allende's triumph, with a relative majority of 36 percent of the vote, forced Congress to elect between the first two majorities and lay down the basis for a complex and tense political negotiation. As had happened in 1946 with Gabriel González Videla, in 1952 with Carlos Ibáñez, and in 1958 with Jorge Alessandri, Congress had chosen the first relative majority to serve as the President of the Republic. However, a climate of political turmoil and mistrust required that there should be put into place, as a precondition of that election, what was called the *Estatuto de Garantías Constitucionales* [Statute of Constitutional Guarantees]. The Statute, according to Evans, consisted of a constitutional reform whose justification was as follows:

> The whole reform . . . emerges from the heart of the *Democracia Cristiana* [Christian Democratic Party], which made its position quite clear to Mr. Allende: "We recognize in you a democrat, but there are sectors who support you that do not deserve our democratic trust; therefore to have our support in Full Congress we believe it indispensable that a broad constitutional reform may seal and guarantee during your government the full validity of some freedoms and rights that we consider essential".
>
> (Evans 1973: 104)

The dispositions of the Statute of Constitutional Guarantees, proposed to support the election as President of Salvador Allende, were as follows:

> I. Constitutional recognition of a statute of political parties; II. Constitutional guarantee of a statute for social communication media: press, radio, and television (freedom of opinion); III. Explicit constitutional provision of an independent educational system, mixed and pluralist (freedom of education); IV. Protection in an adequate form of the freedom to meet, personal freedom and the sanctity of correspondence; and V. Constitutional provision of a new statute on the public forces of law and order.
>
> (Evans 1973: 105–116)

The Statute of Constitutional Guarantees sought to ensure the concept of citizenship by giving broad recognition to the freedom of expression and recognizing the right to organize political parties and militate in them. It guaranteed the freedom of internal organization of the parties, including ideological and programmatic freedom, the right to present candidates, the right to participate in plebiscites, and the right to publicize in State media. Freedom of opinion was guaranteed without previous censorship and with the right of reply, and the following rights were all assured: the egalitarian access of individuals to communications media, the right of universities and political parties to organize and establish communications media, the legal reserve of the communications media regime, together with the freedom to import and commercialize books, written documents, and magazines, and the freedom to circulate these documents; it was also prohibited to discriminate against the owners of these media.

In relation to education, the right to open and maintain educational establishments was guaranteed, along with the right of parents to select teachers for their children. A private and public system of education was established, with autonomy in terms of its organization and freedom to contract personnel, the right to receive State assistance, and with a *Superintendencia Educacional* [Educational Supervisory Board], overseen by a pluralist *Consejo Directivo* [Advisory Board]. Additionally, a statute for universities granted them the character of entities of public law, with autonomy in their administration and in their academic and financial aspects. Freedom of teaching at universities was enshrined, and access to universities would depend on the capabilities of applicants.

In relation to the rights of association, personal freedom, and sanctity of correspondence, a legal reserve was established in order that a parliamentary bill or congressional statute would be required in order to impose limitations on these constitutional rights, which could not be affected by executive order, regulation, or decree alone. It also considered the new social rights, such as freedom of work, the right to receive a just salary, the right to belong to a trade union, and the right to strike, together with the right to social security and the right to social and community organizations participation, such as neighborhood committees, women's institutes, and trade unions. In relation to the law enforcement establishment, it was defined as professional, hierarchical, disciplined, obedient, and non-deliberant (Evans 1973: 107–121). This constitutional reform, of republican inspiration, was approved by the whole Congress, with 117 votes and 24 abstentions, and enacted by Law 17.398 on January 9, 1970.

Despite these safeguards, it was difficult for the Allende government to reconcile its socialist revolutionary process, inspired by ideas of a more radical constitutionalism, with the republican constitutional forms, more conservative and liberal, which, until then, had characterized Chilean politics. For example, during the Unidad Popular Government, presided over by Salvador Allende, constitutional rights were affected, in particular property rights, when trying to impose a socialist revolutionary program. In the words of Gabriel Salazar and Julio Pinto:

> the main objectives of his program were to radically modify the ownership of the means of production and to increase popular participation in the distribution of political power and economic income. This was to be achieved by combining a strong redistribution policy with what was called the socialization of basic means of production, among which were the big agricultural estates, basic mineral wealth (copper, nitrates, iron, and coal), the banking system, the industrial, distributive, and foreign trade monopolies. All these resources would be concentrated in an *Area de Propiedad Social* [Social Property Area] administered by the State, which, together with the *Areas de Propiedad Mixta y Privada* [Mixed and Private Property Areas], would become the new economic model, which, in the opinion of its agents, would overcome the chronic problems of inequality, underdevelopment and dependence that afflicted the country.
>
> (Salazar and Pinto 2010: 45)

To achieve this transformation, the attributions of the President of the Republic were used to pass regulations and take measures that allowed the government to take control of businesses and the economy. As the historian Enrique Brahm has explained, the use of regulations for requisitions by the government to control and administer directly different enterprises became an ever more intense process: "during 1970 we only found one decree of requisition, by 1971 there were 70, rising to 113 in 1972, and to 219 between January and September 11, 1973. Industries affected were of different sizes, outstanding in importance being: Yarur, Nescafé, Calaf, CCU, Loza Penco, Cimet, Fantuzzi, Fensa, Lucchetti, and Pizarreño" (Brahm 1999–2000: 338).

It is true that during the governments of Carlos Ibáñez and Eduardo Frei, on countless occasions use was made of delegation from Parliament to the Executive, in order that compulsory decrees, with the signature of the President and all the ministers, would oblige the Comptroller General of the Republic to approve them, despite being illegal or unconstitutional (Carrasco 2002: 205–206). That explains why the use of the kinds of legislation emerging from the Executive in President Allende's government was not initially contested. But that did not stop the most conservative institutions and those charged with control of the government from criticizing energetically the actions of President Allende, and accusing him of exceeding his authority and violating the rule of law. For example, this is how the *Corte Suprema de Justicia* [Supreme Court of Justice] pronounced on the obstruction of legal action and of police forces carried out by government officials in positions directly responding to the President of the Republic:

> This Court must present to Your Excellency for the umpteenth time the illegal attitude of the administrative authority by their illicit interference in legal matters, as well as the obstruction of *Carabineros* [Police] in fulfilling the orders given by a Criminal Court that according to the law must be executed by such body without any obstacle; all of which amounts to an open persistence in rebelling against judicial resolutions, disregarding the disturbance that such attitudes or omissions cause to the legal system, which also means, not only a crisis of the Rule of Law as it was presented to Your Excellency in the previous document, but an absolute or imminent collapse of the legal system in the country.
>
> (Bravo 1978: 226)

The answer from President Allende to this and other written communications was extensive and reflects the notable differences that

existed in relation to ways of understanding the constitutional regulations and their linkage with the process of change through which the
country was passing. Allende responded:

> By express constitutional mandate, the President of the Republic has the
> duty of conservation of public order. This presidential duty is fulfilled in
> the area of Interior Government of the State by *Intendentes* [Intendants],
> *Gobernadores* [Governors], and subdelegates, in whom is rooted – accord-
> ing to Article 45 and others of the internal regime – the duty of
> maintaining peace and public order . . . an evident lack of understanding
> by some sectors of the judiciary power, in particular by the Superior
> Tribunals, of the process of transformation taking place in the country
> and that expresses the yearning for social justice of the great held-back
> masses, results in practice in both the law and legal procedures being put
> to the service of the interests affected by the transformations, with
> impairment and damage to the institutional regime and to the pacific
> and normal coexistence of the various hierarchies and authorities.
>
> (ibid.: 227, 235)

In monitoring of the legality of the actions of President Allende's
government, the Courts of Justice, Comptroller General of the
Republic, and the *Consejo de Defensa del Estado* [State Defense
Council] participated jointly, along with the *Tribunal Constitucional*
[Constitutional Tribunal] that functioned in Chile from 1971 and
which had a highly relevant role, summarized as follows:

> The Constitutional Tribunal was fully functioning from 1971 until the
> end of President Salvador Allende's government; during that period this
> body of magistrates managed to pronounce on sixteen issues that were
> brought to its attention. Among the grounds mentioned, one of the
> issues aired before this judicial body corresponded to the conflict origin-
> ating from the proposed constitutional reform, presented by Senators
> Juan Hamilton and Renán Fuentealba, which had the objective of giving
> effective regulation to the proposal of the *Tres Areas de la Economía*
> [Three Areas of the Economy], presented in the executive program,
> because after several months in government Salvador Allende and his
> advisors still had not sent the relevant proposal to Congress, and fur-
> thermore, in practice, this aspect of the political program did not have
> a legal purpose, meaning that one was faced with no more than
> a declaration for propaganda that had led to controversies in relation
> to property, because the said part of the program opened doors to
> interpretations that translated into legal uncertainty.
>
> (Durán 2015: 130)

The controversy had its origin in a proposal for constitutional reform presented by Senators Juan Hamilton and Renán Fuentealba, which imposed the principle of legality in relation to any encumbrance of property, constraining the requisition with a transitory provision of the Fundamental Charter that lessened all its possibilities of encumbrance of private property. Once the reform was presented by Senators Hamilton and Fuentealba, the government of President Salvador Allende presented its own proposal that validated the administrative measures to affect property, and gave more leeway to the authorities to apply the means of requisition in relation to property. In Congress, the reform proposed by Hamilton and Fuentealba was approved and President Allende exercised his right to veto at the moment of its promulgation, substituting and eliminating parts of the approved proposal. In this instance, a constitutional question was raised because the government defended the idea that the vetoed proposal would require two-thirds of the Members of Parliament to be rejected, and the opposition majority in Congress argued that only a simple majority was required because it was a constitutional reform proposal. The government took this issue to the Constitutional Tribunal. It was even proposed that the issue between the executive and the legislative powers should be solved by a referendum. The Constitutional Tribunal, by sentence of June 2, 1973, role number 15, declared itself incompetent to deal with the government requirement because it was not within its powers to pronounce itself on constitutional reform proposals, and with that it validated the proposal regarding the three areas of the economy that were presented by Senators Hamilton and Fuentealba and approved by Congress.

Despite the importance of the opinion of the Constitutional Tribunal, it should be recognized that among all the documents that criticized President Allende for his political and administrative actions, most prominent is the *Acuerdo de la Cámara de Diputados* [Agreement of the Chamber of Deputies] about the serious breach of constitutional and legal order in the Republic, adopted on August 23, 1973. This Agreement recalled in its drafting the document that Parliament had approved in 1891 as a justification for the removal of President Balmaceda. The Agreement criticized the call from President Allende to the armed forces to incorporate themselves in the government, and accused him of interfering with the authority of Congress, the Tribunals, and the Comptroller General of the Republic, and of violating the constitutional guarantees of equality before the law, freedom of expression, university autonomy, right of meeting, freedom of education, right to property, personal freedom, right to work, freedom of movement, and freedom to leave the country (Bravo 1978: 257–261). The Agreement gave grounds to the opposition to the Unidad Popular regime to justify a coup d'état in 1973. President Allende, on reading the contents of the document, responded: "The approved Agreement, more than violating, denies the substance of the entire Constitution . . . The opposition is abjuring the bases of the political and legal regime established solemnly in the 1925 Constitution and developed in the past forty-seven years" (ibid.: 262).

5.6 THE NEW POLITICAL ACTORS AND THE 1973 COUP D'ÉTAT THAT DESTROYED THE FOURTH REPUBLIC

In summary, while considering the main characteristics of the Fourth Republic, it is important to keep in mind that from 1932 there was a swing in the liberal parliamentary spirit of the Third Republic towards a presidential constitutionalism. The submission to the rule of law of the President of the Republic, of the titleholders of the executive function, of the para-state bodies, and especially of the armed forces, was weakened during the course of the Fourth Republic. A conception of rights was developed that accentuated the democratic-social aspects of its application and that gave predominance to the legislative function.

The parliamentary proceedings established, in agreement with the Executive, a robust economic social legislation. In line with the policies inspired by the New Deal, schemes of redistribution and State intervention in the economy were emphasized. In this sense, the Fourth Republic was founded on principles of civic republicanism, but the Unidad Popular Government did not have the support of the necessary majorities for its program, and did not stick to the generally accepted forms of law to validate their processes of change, which affected the possibility of success in their ambitious project of great social, political, and economic transformations.

The reform of the new property regime that approved the nationalization of copper mining with the 1925 Constitution, in the National Congress, was not able to be established in full because the mining companies sued the Chilean State and blocked the shipments of copper overseas (Ruiz-Tagle 2001c: 159–162). Neither was it possible to institutionalize the proposal to organize the economy based on dividing it into three areas: (1) social or State area; (2) mixed area; and (3) private area.

The progressive broadening of suffrage, together with the adoption of a proportional representation electoral system, led to the proliferation and fragmentation of political parties, which during the Fourth Republic came to number more than twenty (Etchepare 2006: 191–288). In the public sphere, there also emerged and acquired importance innumerable entities of corporative or trade union representation, such as student federations, professional trade unions, farm workers' associations, and so on, which competed to impose themselves as political actors, sometimes even over the political parties, in organized political representation and participation.

The participation and deliberation of the governed in public issues and the possibility of dissent were considerably broadened, and there was a resistance against certain kinds of domination, in particular, forms of economic and social inequality. Foreign intervention was substantially increased in the context of the cold war during the Fourth Republic. For example, the presidential elections of 1964 and 1970, and also the military coup d'état of 1973, show several forms of direct international intervention in Chilean affairs.

Together with the violent removal of President Allende through the 1973 coup d'état, a right-wing military dictatorship was installed in Chile, where the de facto control of power was assumed by the armed forces and the police, with their respective commanders-in-chief. Thus, the Fourth Republic was destroyed, and with it collapsed the republican ideals, both democratic and liberal, that supported it. The dictatorship presided over by Army General Augusto Pinochet lasted seventeen years, and only in 1990 did a transition to democracy begin, allowing Chile to recover its ability to govern itself.

CHAPTER SIX

THE DICTATORIAL IMPOSITION OF
AUTHORITARIAN CONSTITUTIONALISM,
1973–1990

The deep conflict that arose between the supporters of the Unidad Popular and its opponents was not solved peacefully. On September 11, 1973, a coup d'état interrupted Chilean Republican life and suspended until March 11, 1990 the republican, liberal, and democratic constitutional project that had retained its validity from the dawn of independent Chile. The statement of Keen and Wasserman is controversial, according to which the Chilean coup d'état ushered in the most brutal and largest-scale repression known in the history of Latin America (Keen and Wasserman 1984: 339). The Chilean dictatorship did not cause as many victims with its repression as the Argentinian dictatorships. Neither did it last as long as the Paraguayan military dictatorship of Stroessner. Nor did it have as much power and continental influence as the military dictatorships in Brazil.

One of the major paradoxes in our political history is that some of the main grounds that were presented to justify the 1973 coup d'état were similar arguments to those used to justify the political and legal basis of the de facto government known as the Socialist Republic in 1932. In Table 6.1 it can be seen that to justify the dictatorships in 1932 and 1973, the same factual political identity was invoked by the *Junta de Gobierno*. Furthermore, the same grounds were used to state that "the Constitution and the laws of the Republic will be respected as far as it is compatible with the new state of affairs," in the case of 1932, and "the Constitution and the laws of the Republic will be respected insofar as the present situation in the country allows it," in 1973. Ultimately, in both cases, the Constitution and the law remained subject to merely

TABLE 6.1 Comparison of de facto decrees of 1932 and 1973

1932 Junta de Gobierno	1973 Junta de Gobierno
Republic of Chile, *Diario Oficial* [*Official Gazette*] No. 16,292. Tuesday June 7, 1932 Ministry of the Interior Constitution of the *Junta de Gobierno* No. 1728. Santiago, June 4, 1932. The Most Excellent *Junta de Gobierno* has decreed on this date as follows: We, the subscribed, constitute a *Junta de Gobierno* that will be in charge of public business. **This Junta, in the exercise of its mandate, will maintain the judiciary power and will respect the Constitution and the laws of the Republic insofar as they are compatible with the new state of affairs.**[*]	Decree-Law No. 1. Santiago de Chile, September 11, 1973 The Commander-in-Chief of the Army, Army General don Augusto Pinochet Ugarte; the Commander-in-Chief of the Navy, Admiral don José Toribio Merino Castro; the Commander-in-Chief of the Airforce, Air General don Gustavo Leigh Guzmán; and the Director General of the Police, General César Mendoza Durán, meeting on this date and Considering: 1. That the Public Force, constitutionally composed of the Army, Navy, Air Force and the Police Force, represents the organization that the State has provided for the safeguard and defense of its physical and moral integrity and of its historic-cultural identity; 2. That, therefore, its supreme mission is to ensure, above all other considerations, the survival of such realities and values, as are superior and permanent of the Chilean nationality; and 3. That Chile finds itself in a process of systematic and integral destruction of these constitutive elements in its being, by the effect of the intrusion of a doctrinal and discriminatory ideology, inspired by foreign Marxist-Leninist principles; Have agreed, in compliance with the urgent duty that such a mission imposes on the organs of defense of the State, to dictate the following: Decree-Law: 1. On this date the *Junta de Gobierno* is constituted and assumes the *Mando Supremo de la Nación* [Supreme Leadership of the Nation], with the patriotic obligation of restoring *Chilenidad* [Chilean way of life], justice and the destroyed institutions, conscious that this is the

Take note, communicate it, publish it, and insert it in the *Boletín de Leyes y Decretos del Gobierno* [*Bulletin of Government Laws and Decrees*]. ARTURO PUGA. Carlos Dávila. Eugenio Matte H.

only way to be true to the national traditions, to the legacy of the nation's fathers and the history of Chile, and to enable evolution and progress in the country to be vigorously channeled through the routes that the dynamic of the present days demands from Chile in accordance with the international community of which it is part.

2. Appoint Army General don Augusto Pinochet Ugarte as the President of the Junta, who assumes, with today's date, such position.

3. **Declare that the Junta, in the exercise of its mission, will guarantee the full effectiveness of the attributes of the judiciary power and will respect the Constitution and the Law in the Republic, insofar as the present situation in the country permits for the best fulfillment of the actions that it decides.**

Record it in the *Contraloría General de la República* [Comptroller General of the Republic], publish it in the *Diario Oficial*, and insert it in the official bulletins of the Army, the Navy, the Air Force and the Police Force, and in the *Official Gazette* of the said Comptroller. *JUNTA DE GOBIERNO* OF THE REPUBLIC OF CHILE. AUGUSTO PINOCHET UGARTE, Army General, Commander-in-Chief of the Army. JOSE T. MERINO CASTRO, Admiral, Commander-in-Chief of the Navy. GUSTAVO LEIGH GUZMAN, Air General, Commander-in-Chief of the Air Force. CESAR MENDOZA DURAN, General, Director General of the Police Force. Transcribed by: René C. Vidal Basauri, Lieutenant Colonel, Head of Department. Special Issues, Acting War Deputy Secretary.

---

* The text in bold comes from the author. The transcription was done by Alexis Ramírez from the primary source.

optional conditions, which the real power of the *Junta de Gobierno* bent to their will.

The great difference arises in that in 1932 no constituent power was attributed to the *Junta de Gobierno*, and by no means was it taken away from the citizen population; whereas, as explained above, the 1973 coup d'état set out to transfer the constituent power from the people's political entity to the *Junta de Gobierno*, which is a demonstration of its anti-republican character. To the foregoing should be added the constitutional simulation that characterized the dictatorship, beginning in 1973, which invokes in its justification the defense of and respect for the 1925 Constitution and its laws, on the one hand, but, on the other, and in contradiction to this declaration, orders in secret, from September 13, 1973, the preparation of a new constitutional text, to replace the other, as is borne out by the *Actas Secretas de la Junta de Gobierno* [Secret Acts of the Government Council] (Cristi and Ruiz-Tagle 2008: 174–175).

During the Chilean dictatorship, starting in 1973, a new constitutional ideal of anti-republican orientation is installed by force. This process was consolidated in 1980, when Pinochet "granted" a Constitution that, together with assigning the military a political function not subordinated to the civil power, sets out to institutionalize a neoliberal conception in respect of the laws and authoritarian in respect of government, inspired in Friedrich A. Hayek and Carl Schmitt and, in the Statute of Constitutional Guarantees, adopted as law in 1970.

According to Cristi, the notion of original constituent power is used to legitimize Pinochet's military dictatorship. This notion was extracted from Chilean disciples of the Spanish jurists Luis Sánchez Agesta, Alvaro D'Ors, and Luis Legaz Lecambra, who elaborated this idea in the shadow of Carl Schmitt and Juan Donoso Cortés (Cristi 2000: 77). Bringing this notion of original constituent power to the fore allowed the destruction of the 1925 Constitution to be decreed, arguing that constituent power no longer lies with the people, but with the military junta. Thus, the Schmittian idea of sovereign or revolutionary dictatorship is made implicit, as opposed to a merely commissarial dictatorship. The Decree-Laws 1, 9, 27, 50, 128, 527, and 788, passed by the military government, show how the anti-republican action of the Junta was being channeled in the direction of a sovereign dictatorship.

The same September 11, Decree-Law No. 1 declared that the Junta "will guarantee the full effectiveness of the attributes of the judiciary power and will respect the Constitution and the Law in the Republic, insofar as the present situation in the country permits for the best fulfillment of the actions that it decides" (Transcription of Decree-Law 1, No. 3, in Table No. 1). From September 11, 1973, the *Junta de Gobierno*, composed of the Commanders-in-Chief of the Army, Navy, Air Force, and Police, assumed the executive, legislative, and constituent powers, leaving in operation the judiciary power, whose representatives, by ideological affinity, are obedient to the real power of the dictatorship. In fact, the judiciary power's authorities gathered together at the *Escuela Militar* [Military Academy] to validate the coup d'état and made themselves available to the military authorities. The aforementioned supposes that from September 11, 1973, the 1925 Constitution would maintain its validity, in all that which does not get modified by Decree-Laws of the dictatorship. Also, in September of that year, Decree-Law No. 9 was promulgated, which provided that the President of the Junta would be the person who promulgates the regulations and supreme decrees, and who assumes the regulatory authority. Decree-Law No. 27 dissolves the National Congress, and Decree-Law No. 50 appoints *Rectores Militares* [Military Rectors] or *Delegados de la Dictadura* [Representatives of the Dictatorship] in the universities.

On November 16, 1973 the promulgation of Decree-Law No. 128 attributed the ownership of the constituent power to the *Junta de Gobierno* (usurping it from the people), together with the attribution of the powers of the Legislative and Executive. This decree stated that these powers will be exercised through the decree-laws, and that the President of the Junta will pass supreme decrees and resolutions. At the same time, it provided that the 1925 Constitution, and the laws linked to it, will maintain their validity until they are modified, and those modifications, once promulgated, will be part of their texts and will be treated as incorporated into them.

On June 26, 1974, Decree-Law No. 527 was promulgated, which contained an *Estatuto de la Junta de Gobierno* [Statute of the Government Junta], recognizing the legislative commissions as bodies that advise the dictatorial government in its tasks, and appointed a President, together with a system of replacements and precedence of its members. On December 4, 1974, Decree-Law No. 788 was enacted, limiting the possibility of bringing an action of unenforceability for unconstitutionality before the Supreme Court, through a limitation of the actions that recognize the rights of the workers. Additionally, it declared that all the decree-laws promulgated at that date are of a modifying character to the Constitution, even though this modification may be understood only tacitly. It also refers to the regulations that expressly amend the Constitution, to which constitutional rank is attributed, and therefore, in relation to which, it is not possible to bring an action of unenforceability. Finally, it was declared that the sentences of tribunals that have been processed and that have been declared at that date, will be respected, and that in the future it will be expressly declared when the *Junta de Gobierno* makes use of the constituent power.

The Constituent Commission, also called the Ortúzar Commission, being the surname of its President, was created secretly from September 13, 1973 (Cristi 2000: 93). In March 1974, the Junta emitted a *Declaración de Principios* [Declaration of Principles], which made apparent the idea of destroying the 1925 Constitution, and which appeared in *El Mercurio* newspaper in 1975 (ibid.: 82). This constitutional destruction is what gives Pinochet and the Junta a sovereign character, similar to that of the European absolute monarchies of the seventeenth and eighteenth centuries (ibid.: 83).

From January 9, 1976, the Constitutional Acts emerge, which in reality are decree-laws enacted by the *Junta de Gobierno* in the exercise of the self-attributed constituent power. These acts are so-called by virtue of the matters they deal with, and their name was probably inspired by similar documents used in the Nazi collaborationist regime of Vichy in France. Regarding this issue, it is important to note that Maurice Duverger explains that in 1940, the National Assembly of the IV Republic met to give full constituent powers to Marshal Pétain, so that in one act, or in a series of acts (origin of the Constitutional Acts of Vichy), a new Constitution is enacted, and with that, total power was given to the authorities, collaborators of Nazism, in France, which gave rise to the Vichy Nazi regime (Duverger 1970: 587–588).

In Chile, Act No. 1 created the Council of State, an advisory body appointed by the *Junta de Gobierno*, formed from collaborators with the dictatorship. Act No. 2 contained a first version of what would be the first chapter of the 1980 Constitution, and it referred back to the bases of the institutional framework, for which reason it contained dispositions regarding the nature of the State and of government, and the relationship between the State, the family, and the individual, among other important matters. Constitutional Act No. 3 (which corresponds to Decree-Law No. 1552) contained a legal recognition of the rights and duties of the individual and their guarantees, and revoked previous regulations that were contrary to the new dispositions, such as the old articles Nos. 10–20 of the 1925 Constitution. It also introduced the lawsuit (or appeal for protection) and regulated the lawsuit (or writ) of protection that were forms of judicial guarantees destined to protect constitutional rights. Act No. 4, promulgated successively after Act No. 3, provided that in states of emergency – that is, during practically the whole period of the dictatorship – limitations and restrictions were imposed on the constitutional rights recognized in Act No. 3. Decree-Law No. 1684, with constitutional status, decreed that the lawsuit or writ of protection does not proceed when there are states of emergency such as those that occurred throughout the time of the dictatorship, from 1973 to 1990.

The Ortúzar Commission, for its part, concluded its work on August 16, 1978, handing over to Pinochet the *Anteproyecto constitucional y sus fundamentos* [Constitutional Draft Project and its Foundations], from now on called the Draft Project, in which was reiterated the reason that it was necessary to enact a new Constitution, which must be more than a mere reform of the 1925 Fundamental Charter. The Draft Project pointed out that the political regime instituted by the 1925 Constitution:

> finally fell into crisis with the coming of a totalitarian regime of hate, violence, and terrorism, contrary to the character of our people. A system, therefore, that led the country to the greatest moral, political, social, and economic chaos in its history; that could not preserve the dignity, freedom, and the fundamental rights of individuals and which not only brought the nation to the breaking-up of the institutional framework and collapse of its democracy, but also exposed it to the imminent risk of losing its sovereignty, obviously was a regime that by 1973 was definitely finished.
>
> (Comisión de Estudio de la Nueva Constitución Política de la República 1978: 7–8)

During this period occurred the collapse, not only of the Fourth Republic, but also of the republican institutionality that was forged in Chile from its independence. The catalyst of this collapse was the decision to transfer constituent power from the people to the military junta, headed by Pinochet. This transfer had no previous precedent in the republican history of Chile, and therefore broke with our political and constitutional tradition, begun at independence. What was not taken into account, was that, in this way, it was depriving the main work of the dictatorship – that is, the 1980 constitutional text – of any democratic legality, as was shamefully recognized in the *Declaración de Profesores de la Facultad de Derecho de la Pontificia Universidad Católica de Chile respecto de la Convocatoria a Plebiscito para Ratificar la Constitución* [Declaration by the Professors of the Law Faculty at the Pontificia Universidad Católica de Chile in relation to the Call for a Referendum to Ratify the Constitution] of August 24, 1980. This Declaration asserted the non-democratic nature of the referendum called to approve the Constitution because the Junta in no way tried to activate the constituent power of the people. According to the Declaration, the military junta "as the titleholder of the original constituent power" was legitimately qualified to present the Constitution without the need for a referendum, which only "out of prudence and not for legal necessity" decided to have it ratified. This confirmed the annulment of the constituent power of the people and its usurpation by the military junta.

Pinochet's Draft Project of the constitutional text was submitted for the consideration of the Council of State, which was an advisory body whose members were appointed by the same Junta in 1976. For its part, in the middle of 1980, the Council of State provided an alternative draft to that of the Ortúzar Commission, so that both drafts were presented for the consideration of the military junta, which, having assumed constituent power for itself, would make the final decision. Meanwhile, from 1976, the Junta was promulgating acts and statutes of constitutional status, as has been noted already. On September 11, 1980, the referendum for a new constitutional text took place. Without electoral registers or public freedom, this referendum not only lacked the minimum necessary conditions to become an act of free expression of the people's will, but also it was considered by the military and their civil advisors as a mere mechanism for ratification of the Junta's decision. In fact, as has just been explained, some people postulated that even if there were to be a referendum, constituent power would remain with the military junta, possessor of the final word in relation to constitutional order.

The new constitutional text was enacted six months after the referendum. It consisted of two different parts: transitional provisions, which must be valid for eight years, and the permanent provisions, which would operate in the following period. With the transitional provisions, the military dictatorship's State of Exception was simply ratified: the power would continue to be concentrated in the military junta, and in Pinochet as President, and the fundamental rights would not be in force. In its permanent articles, the main forces and ideological tendencies of the military regime were gathered. On one hand, the tutelage of the military over political institutionalism was established. On the other, the neoliberal conception of rights was embodied, insofar as pre-eminence was given to property rights and to the freedoms understood as non-interference, and economic-social rights were recognized only in the form of a weakened guarantee. Also, the Catholic corporatist aspect of the fundamental bases of institutionalism was included, according to which, intermediate entities, such as the family, must be protected against the individual and the State, which puts the objective of the common good as a limit to popular sovereignty. There would converge in all these doctrinal aspects expressed in these manifestations of authoritarian constitutionalism, a marked devaluation of the importance of citizenship, the civil and political rights that characterized the present Constitution.

Thus, due to the validity of the permanent articles, the approval of the constitutional text did not lead to liberalization nor any political transition – on the contrary, it had the effect of petrifying the dictatorship until the referendum of October 5, 1988, in which the people could decide if they wanted to continue with Pinochet as President or not: the majority of citizens said: "No."

Even though the transitory provisions gave the exercise of constituent power to the *Junta de Gobierno*, this remained subject to referendum approval. That is why, in July 1989, after the triumph of "No," a referendum was called in relation to the first reforms to the constitutional text; in this act, constituent power returned to the people, at least in part, and from then onwards, it can be said that there was an actual Constitution, and the overcoming of the pre-constitutional period marked by the military dictatorship.

The reforms approved by referendum were the result of a hard negotiation between the political opposition that had triumphed on October 5, and the civil advisors to the military regime. In December that year, presidential elections were carried out in which the opposition, the *Concertación de Partidos por la Democracia* [Coalition of Parties for Democracy], triumphed; thus, in March 1990, the Coalition assumed control of the Executive. From then onwards, a push was given to the process of transition to democracy, which was marked, from the legal perspective, by innumerable reforms to the Constitution, none of which has left Chilean citizens satisfied; new modifications are forever being proposed, and even, in recent years, the adoption of a new Constitution.

The 1989 reforms repealed Article No. 8 that prohibited the existence of Marxist political parties, but in part, these proscriptions were maintained in the legal form of the right to association, and in the effect of exclusion produced in the binomial electoral system (Ruiz-Tagle 1989: 189–211). At the same time, it was not possible to dismantle the provisions that gave the military tutelage over the institutional framework. In fact, those articles that gave the armed forces the character of guarantors of the institutional framework were left valid, and at the same time, they continued to be members of the *Consejo de Seguridad Nacional* [National Security Council], a constitutional body created by the 1980 constitutional text and unheard of in Chilean history. The appointed Senators were also maintained, among whom were the four ex-commanders-in-chief of the armed forces and police. The Constitutional Tribunal continued to be integrated by members appointed by the armed forces. The commanders-in-chief remained unmovable. Very high quora were maintained to reform the Constitution and Constitutional Organic Statutes, always forcing a negotiation, generating through legal and political means a kind of draw of the majority with the minority, who were identified with the supporters of the military regime.

The 1980 constitutional text, with which the transition to democracy began, concentrated an enormous number of powers in the President of the Republic, among those some belonging to the legislative function. The legislative power remained very debilitated, the Senate had non-elected members – that is, appointed and lifelong Senators – and parliamentary majorities had difficulty in reflecting the majority of citizens, establishing a binomial electoral system that obliged the political parties to concentrate in blocks and favored the representation of the second minority. However, it would be the interpretation and application of, and the partial reforms to, the Constitution in the new political context, inaugurated in 1990, which would add democratic legitimacy to a constitutional design that, in its origins, comes from an authoritarian mold.

CHAPTER SEVEN

FIFTH REPUBLIC: THE NEOLIBERAL REPUBLIC, 1990 TO DATE

The constitutional government which arose in 1990 adopted in part the text of the 1980 Constitution, of authoritarian and neoliberal stamp. On the defeat of Pinochet in the referendum of October 5, 1988, the negotiation continued between the representatives of the dictatorship and those of the democratic opposition, who agreed on fifty-four reforms to the 1980 constitutional text, which later was subject to a referendum in the middle of 1989. That is why, even though, materially, there are coincidences between the 1980 constitutional text and that of 1990, it is formally another Constitution because it was the people who gave life to it, who, after the referendum with valid electoral registers in 1989, recovered their place as an entity of the constituent power. At the end of the day, this is what the return to democracy means. However, with the passing of time, it has become evident that constituent power has been left in the people's hands, but the neoliberal and authoritarian character, which the military government gave it, persists.

The sovereign will of the people is distorted by the partial survival, within its text, of the anti-republican provisions of the 1980 Constitution. A paradoxical situation has arisen, through which the constituent power of the military junta persists and continues to uphold a Constitution that has been claimed by the people in Chile since 1990. A formal recognition to the effect that the entity with the constituent power continues to be the military junta, appears in decisions of the Constitutional Tribunal (hereafter, "TC," for its acronym in Spanish) from 1990. Renato Cristi rightly criticizes the TC judgment of

March 18, 1998, which displays the state of confusion into which Chilean constitutional law has fallen, because in this decision the constituent power is still recognized as rooted in the *Junta de Gobierno* (Cristi 2000: 145–146). This paradox is observed early on by Juan Andrés Fontaine:

> Paradoxically, even though led by their political adversaries, the emerging Chilean democracy seems not to differ much from that foreseen by the architects of the military government's plan of transition. In present-day Chile, the range of individual liberties has increased enormously, thanks to the free market reforms applied in previous years. Intervention by the State has decreased significantly and the probability of returning to the redistribution policies of pre-1973 seems more distant each day.
> (Fontaine 1993: 275)

Without drawing on legal references, Fontaine makes it clear that in Chile it is through force that the neo-conservative revolution manages to succeed, which rises against the New Deal and the redistributive State which fails in the USA during the Ronald Reagan and George H. W. Bush presidencies. In 2005, the Chilean model of social security, supported by President Bush and promoted from the *Cato Institute* by José Piñera, did not manage to achieve the approval of a Congress dominated by Bush's own party. This would indicate that there can be no neoliberalism in democracy, and that a neoliberal policy has to be imposed by authoritarian fiat.

7.1   THE NEW CHILEAN CONSTITUTION THAT EMERGED IN 1990 AND ITS SUCCESSIVE REFORMS

Of all the Chilean constitutions, the present Charter is the one that has had the greatest number of reforms to its text. Despite this, it has not changed significantly in its fundamental aspects. After the reforms of the 1989 referendum, the amendments have been realized according to the Constitution – that is, as a presidential initiative and with Congress's agreement fulfilling the high quorum of approval in both Chambers. The Constitution has been modified by more than twenty statutes of constitutional reform – among which should be highlighted that of 1989 (already mentioned) – and the modifications add up to more than 300, if the changes to each article reformed are counted.

Among these modifications, the President's powers to dissolve once the Chamber of Deputies before its last year in place were removed, and also a series of regulations were repealed that limited the exercise of the legislative power located in the National Congress; the number of Senators elected by universal suffrage was increased from twenty-six to thirty-eight; and in relation to the right to freedom of expression, the *Consejo Nacional de Televisión* [National Television Council] was created. The duty of all State entities was to respect and promote the fundamental rights enshrined in the Constitution, as well as those international treaties ratified by Chile and still in force, which left the door open for a broadening of the catalog of rights, incorporating those contemplated in the international treaties on human rights; also repealed was the regulation that prohibited the existence of Marxist political parties.

Furthermore, within the constitutional reforms that followed, it is important to mention that of 1991. This reform modified the regulations regarding regional, provincial, and communal administration, advancing towards a major administrative decentralization, without losing the unitary character of the State. At a regional level, the *Consejo Nacional de Desarrollo* [National Development Council] was closed down, composed of the intendant, governors, representatives of the armed forces, other public and private bodies, and other functional representatives from each region. It was replaced by the *Consejo Regional* [Regional Council], integrated by councilors representing the municipalities in the region. At a municipal level, mayors became directly elected, instead of being appointed by their respective regional development councils from among the elected councilors. Another amendment that is important to highlight is that originating on the occasion of the reform of the administration of criminal justice, also called criminal procedures reform. In addition, the Supreme Court and the tribunals were restructured to make them more compatible with the needs of a democratic government. In this respect, it was established, for example, that Ministers to the Supreme Court would not be elected by themselves and the government, but should be designated by the President of the Republic, in agreement with the Senate, and that their maximum age in the position is seventy-five.

In 1999, Article 1 of the Constitution was modified, establishing that all persons (not just men) are born free and equal in dignity and rights; and that "men and women are equal before the law." In 2001, film censorship was repealed and the freedom of creation and broadcast of the arts was assured. In 2003, it was established that secondary school education was compulsory and that the State must fund a free system to ensure access for all the population, up to the age of twenty-one. Finally, it is important to highlight the most extensive constitutional reform, that of 2005, which achieved the elimination of several authoritarian provisions and of military control over the institutional system. When President Ricardo Lagos enacted it, he thought that these reforms had managed to create a new Constitution that would put an end to the period of transition and inaugurate a properly democratic era, which is why he put his signature to the constitutional text, replacing that of Pinochet. However, from that date onwards, almost all the political parties and social groups have insisted on a deeper reform and even on the drafting of a new Constitution, and on the repealing of several organic constitutional statutes, as was the case of the partial modification of the *Ley Orgánica Constitucional de Enseñanza* (LOCE) [Organizing Constitutional Statute of Education], now called the *Ley General de Educación* (LGE) [General Statute of Education].

Among the most important modifications enacted in 2005, it is worth mentioning the elimination of appointed and lifelong Senators, leaving the National Congress constituted exclusively by members elected by civic suffrage, and the elimination of the armed forces' role as guarantors of the institutional system, which now belongs to all State bodies. That is to say, significant progress was made on the recognition of the principle of democratic representation and the principle of the subordination of the armed forces to civil authority, which is one of the basic assumptions of a democratic constitutional system. Furthermore, in the same way, the power of the President to order the retirement of the commanders-in-chief of the armed forces was restored, after informing the National Congress. The Chamber of Deputies was given the power to call Ministers of State to render account of the progress of their portfolio, establishing the practice of interpellation of ministers, even though the political responsibility of ministers is not affected by it (that is only possible to realize through an impeachment, requiring a high quorum of the Chamber for its approval). The Constitutional Tribunal was modified, with its ministers appointed by the Senate, the Supreme Court, and the President of the Republic, and the National Security Council no longer participating in these appointments.

The National Security Council was maintained, which is still questionable for being contrary to democratic constitutional principles because it has attributes such as the making of pronouncements regarding the bases of the Chilean institutional system, even though it can only be summoned if required by the President of the Republic. The obligation of holding presidential elections jointly with those of Senators and Deputies was established, for which coordination with presidential terms was sought, reducing their duration to four years, which has been the subject of criticism for the brevity of the time allocated, but in truth it has served to reduce the excessive power of the President of the Republic.

As for rights, the principles of disclosure, transparency, and probity were established at constitutional level, which implies a new conception of the exercise of public authority, which obliges it to inform the people about what is happening. Additionally, the constitutional states of emergency were modified, restricting the scope of their application. This supposes that the limitations and suspension of constitutional rights should be subject to more control by Parliament, the tribunals, and the constitutional authorities.

All in all, the constitutional amendments enacted in 2005, despite being relevant, do not amount to a new Constitution. In the present text there remains, for example, excessive predominance of the Executive over the National Congress, which undermines the division of power. In terms of rights, the right to property is still too privileged in relation to equality and political rights, and in general, the idea of reinforcing aspects of liberty and not the equality of all rights is emphasized, in particular those defined as economic and social. For example, freedom of education is assured, but not equal access to education; freedom of work is assured, but not equality of treatment and non-discrimination at work.

One of the more urgent pending reforms in order to progress towards greater democratization was the changing of the present binomial electoral system for another that would allow representation in Congress of the ensemble of more diverse opinions that the people might express. Finally, in 2014, the electoral system was modified to establish one of proportional character, which recognizes quotas for feminine representation and was in place for the 2017 congressional election.

Still awaited and required in order to achieve a better balance between the public powers (National Congress – President of the Republic), and to promote more leadership from the Constitutional Tribunal, is a commitment to give effect to the Fundamental Charter and to move forward in the consolidation of representative democracy in Chile, leaving behind the military government's ideas that are incompatible with constitutional government. Finally, and no less important, it is necessary to eliminate the doctrine of national security from the constitutional text, as well as the restrictive vision of the guarantees by which economic, social, and cultural rights are protected.

These outstanding tasks are seen, in turn, as challenges within the democratic life in our Republic, and make us realize that Constitutions are not abstract and petrified things, but that they evolve through time, updating their ways of organizing power and the rights enshrined in them, according to the historical moments in which they are applied.

Only with the 2005 reforms does this paradox, of the authoritarian link that our Constitution has in its origin, begin to become clearer, even though it is right to recognize that the task is still unfinished. The neoliberal and authoritarian guidelines are maintained, which creates difficulties for the re-emergence of the republican spirit inspiring much of our historical evolution since independence. The present constitutional regime preserves the attributes of the titleholder of the executive function, thus subordinating the legislative function. With that, it debilitates the division of powers in favor of a neo-presidential authoritarian figure and maintains a tension with Parliament which continues today.

7.2   THE CONSOLIDATION OF EXECUTIVE CONSTITUTIONALISM IN CHILE

It is interesting to consider the apprehensions of Bruce Ackerman in his work, *The Decline and Fall of the American Republic*, published in 2010, which recounts one of the most conspicuous signs of the decadence of the principles of republican constitutionalism in the USA. The foregoing is relevant because Ackerman's concerns refer in particular to what he calls the executivization process of constitutional law. That is to say, the process whereby the government executive function, under the provisions of *administrative regulation,* has upset the equilibrium of checks and counterbalances that the republican constitutional model implies. And on this point, it is worth pausing for a moment, because it is surprising the degree of similarities it has with the development of Chilean constitutionalism. On this, Ackerman describes a series of institutions within the presidency of the USA that allow it to become a power, challenging the traditional role of the Supreme Court (as an institutional counterbalance) (Ackerman 2010: 87). Ackerman highlights the fact that constitutional law seems to be more amenable to ideological assumptions than the constitutionalists traditionally thought. The consequence of this idea is that the presidency has generated what the author calls *executive constitutionalism*, which is the most powerful threat to the republican and democratic ideals of the modern world.

Meanwhile, the problem generated by this executivization of constitutional law is one of legitimacy of the jurisdiction of the State. For the actions of the administration must be conceived in broader terms than the sole satisfaction of legality. It is already a reality that we have to presuppose the existence of a broad interpretation of the jurisdiction of State administration, based not only on constitutional regulatory considerations, such as that of constitutional law in practice, but also derived from the multiplicity of kinds of intervention that, from the middle of the twentieth century, the actions of the administration of the State have been adopting (Sunstein 1993: 11–46). In this new context, which Chile also shares, it is necessary to understand the possible problems of legitimacy that this broadening of executive and administrative power could entail, because from a *limited* conception of the administration's jurisdiction, we have passed to the acceptance of a *broadened* conception.

The evident question is how a republican conception of constitutionalism should treat these problems of legitimization. As Schmidt-Assmann indicates, "to talk about the legitimacy of the power of the administration is to ask oneself about its justification and rationale" (Schmidt-Assmann 2003: 100). In this sense, Ackerman has verified that the presidency, in the case of the USA, has not only been transformed into the *great accelerator* imposing radical changes, but is also capable of convincing the other powers and the citizens that its actions are always legitimate (Ackerman 2010: 84). Ackerman, after analyzing the problems facing his country, proposes some possible ways out of these problems. Thus he draws up a strategy based on overcoming two generic problems, which he calls the politics of unreason and the culture of illegality. This is the main issue that drives his proposals.

In relation to the politics of unreason and illegality, Ackerman's purpose is to rethink the role that falls to the citizens (ibid.: 119–179). He considers the cases of professional politicians who act outside the system, the so-called "second-floor politics," in which a group of advisors dedicated to increasing the popularity and influence of the person of the President, and acting exclusively on the basis of polls, have dulled the relationship between the government and the citizens, and have reduced their politics to merely taking part in elections. To overcome these problems, Ackerman proposes mechanisms to captivate the citizens anew, such as the Day of Deliberation and "vouchers," which are forms of subsidized funding of the citizens' petition, so that the media gives encouragement to deliberative politics and finally forces the President to present serious ideas, subject to the scrutiny of the people, downplaying the immediacy of re-election in exchange for constructive politics based on ideas. Ackerman's objective is to generate and propose measures which are in tune with the politics of the twenty-first century in order to rein in the excessive power that the President of the Republic holds at present.

In Chile, this phenomenon also finds expression, as will be shown, in the direction taken by some aspects of the development of administrative law in the 1980s. Then there was demonstrated a public law conception that made a show of the rhetoric of a State at the service of mankind and of the need to set limits to abuses of authority, but the truth is that some of these pro-administrationists were among the most enthusiastic supporters of the broadening of the powers of de facto governments, even to validating violations of human rights and keeping silent when the reason of State was cited (Caldera 1979: 71–98).

During the Fifth Republic, this executivization finds its place in the governments of the Coalition of Parties for Democracy, which developed a normative-regulatory structure destined to oppose the privileged conception of the right of property that was erected as a limit to State intervention. This is another of the many barriers developed by the military dictatorship to protect the model of authoritarian constitutionalism. Paradoxically, the legal devices that have served to combat the supremacy that authoritarian constitutionalism assigned to the right of property have also served for the unjustified broadening of the administration's powers and to embed new forms of executive constitutionalism in Chile (Cristi and Ruiz-Tagle 2014: 159–161). In this undertaking, the *Contraloría General de la República* [Comptroller General of the Republic] and other controlling entities have also contributed; by self-limiting their functions, they have stopped supervising the responsible exercise of the power of the President of the Republic and resigned from their responsibility of public service in benefit of all Chileans (Ruiz-Tagle 2008: 241–251).

7.3   THE CHILEAN SYSTEM OF GOVERNMENT AND ITS MAIN CHARACTERISTICS

From the end of the 1970s until the beginning of the 1990s, there has been consideration through a high-powered discussion in academic and political circles regarding the type of government that Chile needs. Thereafter, and for almost twenty years, this debate was paralyzed and it has been reactivated in the last few years due to the problems building up from the effects of centralization and the strong concentration of political power in the President of the Republic. At the beginning of the 1990s, as in the present day, the Chamber of Deputies has taken a leading role in promoting this discussion and participating actively in it. A good summary of the discussion has been collected in the so-called Informe Ortega 1990 [Ortega Report] (preliminary report of the *Comisión de Estudio del Régimen Político Chileno* [Commission for the Study of the Chilean Political Regime]).

More recently, in a session of the *Comisión Especial del Régimen Político Chileno* [Special Commission of the Chilean Political Regime] in the National Congress of the Republic of Chile, on October 27, 2008, the following ideas of constitutional reforms were proposed: (1) to explore the idea of appointing coordinating ministers according to Article 33 No. 3, and to revise the parliamentary incompatibilities of Article 59 in order to give government more flexibility to organize its tasks; (2) to keep the bicameral system that some in Chile have proposed to eliminate and allow the President of the Republic to dissolve Congress once during his mandate in order to call early parliamentary elections; (3) to extend the presidential mandate to five or six years or allow re-election for one more term for four years; (4) to seek in Congress a greater balance between the representative system and participation in parliamentary representation, and finish with the project of political exclusion that has been consolidated by way of elections, repealing the binomial system; (5) to limit the indefinite re-election of congressmen to ensure the renewal of Congress, so that Senators can be re-elected once, and Deputies for a maximum of three successive periods; (6) to repeal Article 23 of the Constitution, which raises a corporatist barrier between Members of Parliament and social organizations; (7) to include forms of popular initiatives in the legislative and tax-setting parliamentary process; and (8) to revise the organic constitutional statutes.

The Constitution rests on a tangle of thorny bushes, which are those organic statutes whose revision has to be undertaken with the same force as applies to the Constitution. Some of the organic statutes are *leyes de amarre* [immobilizing statutes], which are not compatible with the principles of democratic constitutionalism.

In the academic world, one of the fundamental questions debated was whether the political crises that provoked the military intervention in the 1970s were intensified by the hegemonic presidentialism that was the rule in Latin America. It was argued that presidentialism did not have release-valves to overcome the crises, and therefore, the government regime played a dominant role. In this discussion it is possible to find two clearly differentiated trends.

The first is that maintained by Juan Linz (1990), according to which there is a direct relationship between the democratic breakdowns in Latin American countries and their systems of government. As a result, the political instability of these countries is due, to a great extent, to the presidentialist system. Accordingly, Linz recommended the introduction of a parliamentarian system as the best option for these countries, paying attention especially to the stability it generates (Zovatto and Orozco 2008: 11). Juan Linz's position has been characterized by Bruce Ackerman as follows:

> Linz argues that the division of powers has been one of the most dangerous exports from the USA, especially to the south of its frontier. According to Linz, generations of Latin American liberals have taken Montesquieu's theories together with the North American example, as an inspiration to create constitutional governments that divide the legislative power between elected presidents and elected congresses, only to see their constitutions succumb in the hands of frustrated presidents who disband intransigent congresses and install themselves as *caudillos* [leaders] with the help of the military or extra-constitutional plebiscites. From the comparative point of view, the results are surprising. Almost thirty countries, mainly in Latin America, have adopted similar systems to that in the USA. *All of them*, without exception, have succumbed to the so-called "Linzian" nightmare.
>
> (Ackerman 2007: 28–29)

Ackerman calls a scenario of constitutional rupture, a "Linzian" nightmare, where one or another power, in the effort to destroy a political rival, intimidates the constitutional system and installs itself as the only legislator, with or without the support of a referendum that endorses it. Dieter Nohlen has criticized Linz's arguments for proposing an ideal model towards which Latin American political systems should steer. The methodological approach proposed by Nohlen is a historical-empirical one, which consists of investigating, comparatively and qualitatively, the existing political institutional system, describing this institutional system in relation to the social, political, and cultural context of a given country (Zovatto and Orozco 2008: xvii–xviii). Nohlen's proposal is to carry out a controlled reform of presidentialism that contributes through its renovation towards a parliamentarian operation of the presidential system. For that, he proposes the strengthening of Parliament's authorities, and the improvement and relaxation of the relationships between the presidential entity and the parliamentary entity, with the triple objective of strengthening governability, increasing the effectiveness of public policies, and enhancing the degree of legitimacy of the political system (Zovatto and Orozco 2008: 7).

The proposals of Nohlen and Zovatto and Orozco seem to be better adjusted to the constitutional practices of Latin American countries. However, these proposals need to adapt to a new political scenario that does not dodge the debate regarding the kind of government regime necessary to avoid political crises. In Chile, and in the majority of Latin American countries, a political institutional system has been firming up and more value is given to the importance of maintaining this institutional system. Despite that, it is difficult to sustain the position that our regimes are completely legitimized by the people. On the contrary, surveys still show a lack of satisfaction with respect to the political actors and their capacity to provide answers to their citizens' demands. Thus, to think of reforms to the system of government is of the highest importance.

Consequently, beyond the archetype models of presidentialism and parliamentarianism, it is necessary to assess the functioning of the Chilean government system in its political context, and, based on that situation, to promote greater flexibility in the relationships between the executive and legislative functions so that they can increase the levels of governability and efficiency in public tasks, promote the legitimacy of the political system, and guarantee the principles of constitutional democracy. To an important degree, this flexibilization is achieved through practices, regulations, and principles that are adapted and promoted to confirm constitutional order. The concept of increasing flexibilization consists of a greater distribution of power among the political bodies mentioned, with the object of strengthening governability, increasing the effectiveness of public policies, and enhancing the legitimacy of the political system, beyond the labels with which final definitions have been given to each government regime in academic circles and professorial chairs (Zovatto and Orozco 2008: 14).

From this concept, it is not understood that President and Congress are separate entities that do not pretend to intervene in the tasks of the other. On the contrary, increasing flexibilization assumes adequate instruments of control of one body over the other. But a necessary requirement for an effective process of flexibilization to take place is that there is a certain balance in the powers of both bodies that needs to be schooled in flexibility and this is the central axis of our proposal.

If the Chilean system of government is analyzed only in terms of constitutional regulation, it could be concluded that it is essentially presidentialist, that is, a pure case of presidentialism, even when the 2005 constitutional reform reinforced the controls that Parliament, in particular the Chamber of Deputies, has over the governmental management of the President. Meanwhile, an analysis of this type would be incomplete without a revision of the main instruments that determine the Executive–Legislative relationship and how they function in constitutional practice. Only then is it possible to identify the critical problems that affect the Chilean system of government. Thus, an example of the relevance of the approach that puts emphasis on constitutional practice is that from the point of view of constitutional regulation, the most problematic rule, in terms of its effect on the balance of powers between the President and the Congress, is the power of veto that the Political Constitution grants the first, which could be qualified as a type of potent veto, because in the case of the Chilean Constitution, in addition to admitting partial, total, suppressive, additive, and suspensive types of veto, a super majority, or quorum of two-thirds in the Chamber, is required to overcome it. However, it is a reality that in constitutional practice, the veto has not been used very often, and the imbalance of powers between the political bodies does not arise from the use of this constitutional instrument of power.

In our opinion, there are in Chile four aspects that have unbalanced the executive and legislative powers in favor of the former, from the point of view of constitutional practice. These are: the exclusive initiative of the President of the Republic, the control of urgencies, the management of budgetary and financial issues, and the imbalance in technical capabilities between Parliament and the Civil Service.

One of the key purposes of the 2005 constitutional reform was to strengthen the control mechanisms of Congress, in particular the Chamber of Deputies, over the actions of the President. That is why the Constitution provided for the interpellation of ministers, the investigative Commissions, the faculty of drawing up agreements or putting forward observations, and the obligation of ministers to attend in person any special sessions that the Chamber of Deputies or the Senate might summon. Despite these new powers, no strengthening of the role of Parliament as the accepted place for democratic deliberation has been witnessed. Even more, there is general agreement that the use of these new instruments has not been the most appropriate.

With the purpose of seeking mechanisms that facilitate increased flexibility in the relationships between executive and legislative powers, it is useful to look at some comparative experiences where lessons can be learnt for the Chilean case. To that end, it has been relevant to take into account the methods set up by parliamentarian or semi-presidential systems for the creation and approval of bills and statutory law and control of power. Together with studying the differences and similarities that our system has with other legal systems in order to find flexible formulae to solve the problems of collaboration between President and Congress, and to consider institutional reforms, it is very important to focus attention on the need to have new sources of technical and political legislative advice established in Congress. There is also an urgent need to reinforce a culture of internal democracy in political parties, that they may become schools of civic behavior, giving political and technical support to this formula of flexibilization and equilibrium which must be ensured between the Executive and Congress of the Republic of Chile.

A presidential system, according to Sartori, is defined by three main features. First, the Head of State is elected (directly or semi-directly) for a fixed period of time. Second, the government (the presidential body in our system) is not appointed and cannot be unseated by the vote of the parliamentary body. Third, the Head of State leads or directs the government of the country. These three characteristics are established in the Chilean constitutional system and explain, in general, why Chile has a presidential form of government (Sartori 1996: 97–111).

In Chile, the attributions and powers of the President of the Republic have gone on being progressively reinforced, in particular from 1925 to date. This reinforcement can be seen in political, legislative, and, especially, in administrative matters, which does not prevent many of these reinforced attributes from not being exercised in the way which was envisaged at the time they were drawn up. Equally, since the 2005 constitutional reform, it has been possible to observe that the parliamentary body, in particular the Chamber of Deputies, has significantly increased its powers in political affairs. However, despite the introduction of more powerful supervisory tools in Chile, such as interpellations and the facility of creating Commissions, neither has produced the balance required between Congress and the Executive. To all the above must be added the phenomenon of the increasing inflation of powers of control in the organs of specialized justice and the autonomous constitutional bodies that in the present Chilean Constitution seem excessive.

It is not adventurous to say that in terms of structure, the other powers of the Chilean State, such as the Judiciary (without considering the power to resolve constitutional cases and appeals), have maintained their powers and functions relatively unchanged since 1833. The great reinforcement of organic powers that has appeared in the present Constitution refers, on the one hand, to the powers of the Constitutional Tribunal, the *Justicia Electoral* [Electoral Justice], the *Ministerio Público* [Public Ministry], and the Comptroller General of the Republic, which we call specialized justice, and, on the other hand, to the Central Bank and the *Consejo de Seguridad Nacional* [National Security Council], which we call autonomous bodies. These powers given to the bodies of specialized justice and to the autonomous bodies are particularly concentrated in the roles of political, legislative, administrative, judicial, economic, and also military control, and have become equated to and in some cases greater than the powers and functions that the President of the Republic, Congress and the judiciary powers have as a whole regarding these same matters.

In order to define our proposal of flexibilization, this analysis will be divided into two sections. I will review the relationship between the President of the Republic and the National Congress, from two perspectives: on the one hand, we will focus on the constitutional regulations, and on the other, we will center our analysis on the working of this relationship based on constitutional practice, to identify the critical problems that our current system of government presents. First, I will explain a brief version of Chilean political history that is based upon the ideas that I have shared with Professor Sofía Correa. Then I will work on a brief comparative analysis of the Chilean political system with the two most distinctive government systems: parliamentarian and semi-presidential. From this comparative analysis we will extract some institutions and practices that will serve to argue in a better way for the promotion of increased flexibility in the relationships between the President and Congress, with the objective of enhancing the levels of governability and legitimacy in our political system.

An initial diagnosis of the relationship between the Executive and Legislative cannot be complete if it only deals with the constitutional regulatory framework. It becomes necessary to revise how these regulations are taken up in the constitutional practice of the political institutions, in this case, by the National Congress and the President of the Republic. Thus, inspired by Zovatto and Orozco's model, let us analyze in this section the relationship between these two constitutional bodies (Zovatto and Orozco 2008: 18).

7.4 HISTORICAL EVOLUTION OF THE CHILEAN GOVERNMENTAL SYSTEM

Before immersing ourselves in the comparative analysis, it is necessary to reflect upon the institutional political history of Chile in the nineteenth and twentieth centuries. The perspective from which this history is viewed will condition decisions about the political regime desirable for the present and future of the country. Therefore, in this proposal of flexibilization, there is concern about the historiographical condemnation that the Chilean parliamentarian experience has suffered at the hands of several authors. This critical view of the parliamentary period is a feature of Chilean historiography of the twentieth century, in particular starting from *La fronda aristocrática en Chile* [The Aristocratic Frond in Chile] by Alberto Edwards, published as a book in its first edition in 1928. Its publication came hand in hand with the exaltation of the authoritarian presidentialism that preceded it, which has been called the "Portalian" regime (Edwards 1993: 15, 61–71). Edwards' interpretations coincided with those of Francisco Antonio Encina, who gave them wide dissemination in his work, *Historia de Chile* [History of Chile], in twenty volumes, which was profusely read.

Later, in the middle of the 1980s, the influential work of Mario Góngora, *Ensayo histórico sobre la noción de Estado en Chile en los siglos XIX y XX* [Historical Essay on the Notion of the State in Chile in the Nineteenth and Twentieth Centuries], gave new force and diffusion to the historiographical interpretation of Alberto Edwards (Góngora 1981). This vision, finally, has been reinforced from the middle of the twentieth century by Catholic historiography (Jaime Eyzaguirre and Gonzalo Vial) and by Marxist historiography (Julio César Jobet, Hernán Ramírez Necochea, and Luis Vitale). Paradoxically, both sides combined in condemning this historical era for its oligarchic, plutocratic character and for the frivolity of the political class, unable to solve the economic and social problems that accumulated without solution, in the midst of plenty that only they enjoyed. We have doubts about this interpretation because, in fact, the most recent studies on economic history of the period have demonstrated that a third of the wealth from nitrates was left in the State of Chile through the high taxes imposed on the export of nitrates and iodine, which reached more than 40 percent of the value of exports in the 1890s, after the civil war, at a time of full parliamentarianism (Cariola and Sunkel 1983: fig. 18 and p. 137).

This last interpretation, firmly anchored in the economic-social dimension, was added to the idea of political inefficiency that Alberto Edwards had raised. Just as Edwards maintained that nothing happened in Chile between 1891 and 1918, in the same way, this anti-oligarchic historiography installed the idea that nothing was left in the country from the wealth of nitrates, because all of it was spent in the frivolities of the oligarchy. Incidentally, all these lines of interpretation come together to the extent that they settle down into an anti-liberal and anti-parliamentarian ideological interpretation, which has to be overcome to be able to re-examine, without prejudices, this historical era. Accordingly, it is interesting to see how at the end of the 1970s, a critical vision begins to take shape about the presidential regime established by the 1925 Constitution. In this respect, a pioneering work was the 1974 study by Julio Heise regarding the parliamentary regime in Chile, which, in his opinion, extends from 1861, given its parliamentary practices and predominant ideas, until 1925. Heise proposed a reappraisal of parliamentarianism to demonstrate its virtues in opposition to the presidential regime. One of his main arguments aims to highlight the stability of the political regime under the Chilean parliamentary system, given its flexibility and ability to accommodate dissent, while at the same time pondering on its strengthening of public liberties, and rediscovering the broadening of political participation, as well as the subordination of the military to the civil power. According to Heise, parliamentarianism was a civic school for the Chilean people because through it they learned to be government and opposition, to exercise and respect public liberties, to compete politically within the Constitutional State. Published in 1974, almost immediately after the 1973 coup d'état, unfortunately, Heise's work did not then have the impact hoped for within academic or political circles.

Stemming from this historical revision that re-evaluates the virtues of parliamentarianism for Chile, the following section is dedicated to an analysis of comparative law in the Chilean system of government, with a brief approach to the general background of the two alternative systems of government to the presidential – that is, parliamentarianism and semi-presidentialism – and thereafter we will refer to features that could be applied to Chile.

7.5 THE RELATIONSHIP BETWEEN THE EXECUTIVE AND LEGISLATIVE FUNCTIONS

The attributes of the presidential entity are established fundamentally in the Political Constitution, apart from some legislative faculties that appear in the *Ley Orgánica Constitucional* [Organizing Constitutional Statute] of the National Congress. Its regulation occupies the whole of Chapter IV of the constitutional text, called "Government," and describes the functions of the President of the Republic, Ministers of State (immediate collaborators of the President), and the *Bases Generales de la Administración del Estado* [General Bases of State Administration] by constitutional regulation after the 2005 reform (Carmona 2006: 85–129). The mission of the President of the Republic is dealt with in Article 24 of the present Chilean Constitution:

> The government and the State administration belong to the President of the Republic, who is the Head of State. His authority extends to everything that has the object of conserving public order in the interior and the external security of the Republic, according to the Constitution and the law.

The special attributes of the President are numbered in Article 32 and basically refer to the functions that correspond to him as Head of State, with ultimate responsibility for the functioning of public administration. In this context, regulatory power is included (autonomous and implementing), as well as the power to declare states of emergency, to appoint the principal officials of the Administration (ministers, undersecretaries, intendants, and governors), to conduct international relationships, and so on.

The 2005 constitutional reform introduced important modifications to the powers of the presidential body (Carmona 2006: 85–129). One of the reforms refers to the recognition of the presidential power to order

167

the retirement of the commanders-in-chief of the armed forces and the director general of the police force, before the completion of their respective terms. In order to take this step, the President must enact a decree explaining the motivations and inform Parliament of the decision prior to implementing it. The second modification refers to the power to appoint members of other State bodies. The number of members that could be appointed to the Constitutional Tribunal was increased: formerly, the President could appoint one out of seven; with the reform modifications, he can appoint three out of ten. A third modification consisted of the formalization of the public account that the President has to present to the nation every May 21st, which before was a practice not regulated constitutionally. Finally, the requirements concerning states of emergency were increased, with the objective of guaranteeing the protection of fundamental rights during those periods.

7.6   LEGISLATIVE FACULTIES OF THE PRESIDENT

Jorge Huneeus distinguishes between legislative and non-legislative attributes of the presidential body (Huneeus 1891: 44–45). The legislative attributes refer to the powers to generate draft bills and promote their approval, and these consist fundamentally of competences to control the legislative agenda.

A principal presidential legislative power refers to the legislative measure which gives recognition to the President. In this, the Latin American presidential system is different from the North American model, which does not grant the President the power to send draft bills to Congress (it is notable that in the opening of sessions in Congress, the President of the USA declares his interest in some projects). All Latin American constitutions grant their respective presidents the right to initiate legislation. Some countries, among which Chile is not included, extend this attribute to other officials of the Administration, such as ministers (Zovatto and Orozco 2008: 34). The recognition of this legislative initiative of the President is found in Article 65 of our Political Constitution, which provides that the statutes on economic and administrative matters (listed in the same article) can have their origin in a dispatch from the President of the Republic to the Chamber of Deputies or the Senate.

Meanwhile, in line with Latin American constitutionalism, but probably with more extensive regulation, the current constitutional text in Chile adds to the foregoing attribute the exclusive initiative of the President of the Republic, regulated by subsection 3 and onwards of Article 65 of the Political Constitution. The exclusive initiative means that legislative bill proposals on determined subjects can only be originated by a dispatch from the President of the Republic, independent of the subsequent parliamentary discussion. Among the subjects affected are those such as the alteration of the political or administrative division of the country, the financial or budgetary administration of the State, including the modifications to the *Ley de Presupuesto* [Budgetary Statute], the regulations related to the disposal, leasing, or concession of assets of the State or of the municipalities, the regulations that organize the air, sea, and ground forces in times of peace and war, tax statutes, and so on. There are some very broad subjects reserved to the initiative of the President of the Republic, such as that mentioned in Article 65 No. 6, which refers to regulations on social security or which affect it, both in the private and public sectors.

A second legislative attribute of the President is the veto, where there is greater concordance between the Chilean case and the North American model. As Zovatto and Orozco indicate, "The veto is the mechanism by which the President repeals or makes observations in relation to a draft bill or decree approved by the Legislative. It is considered as the main counterbalance of the Executive against the Legislative, and all the Latin American countries take it into account, with some variants" (Zovatto and Orozco 2008: 35).

The veto can be partial or total. When it is a partial veto, the President returns to Congress that part of the project that is rejected, but enacts and publishes the remaining part of the initiative. This type of veto is accepted in legislations such as Argentina, Brazil, Colombia, Panama, Paraguay, and Venezuela; however, it is not established in the same way in Chilean law. In the Chilean Constitution, the veto is regulated in Article 73:

> If the President of the Republic disapproves a draft bill, he will return it to the Chamber of origin with the appropriate observations, within thirty days. In no case will observations that have no direct relation to the original or fundamental ideas of the project be admitted, unless they were considered in the respective draft communication. If both Chambers approve the observations, the draft bill will have the force of law and it will be returned to the President for its enactment. If both Chambers reject all or some of the observations and insist, by two-thirds of their members present, on the totality or part of the draft bill as approved by them, it will be returned to the President for its enactment.

As can be seen, from the point of view of the regulation, the norm recognizes the presidential veto and grants broad powers to the President, because to defeat him, two-thirds of the members present are required for the total or part of the approved draft bill in each Chamber – that is, with the control of one-third plus one Member of Parliament in each Chamber, the President can block the Legislative's initiatives. This is what Shugart and Mainwaring call "strong veto," to differentiate from "weak veto," which only requires an overall majority to be defeated (Zovatto and Orozco 2008: 37).

The third legislative attributes are the declarations of urgencies, probably the most useful mechanism for controlling the legislative agenda. Through them, the President sets deadlines for the discussion of certain draft bills, with the consequent effect of defining the priorities of the legislative program. This faculty is only recognized in some Latin American countries apart from ours, such as Colombia, Ecuador, Paraguay, Dominican Republic, and Uruguay (ibid.: 46). The urgencies are regulated by Article 74 of the Political Constitution and in Articles 26 and 27 of the *Ley Orgánica del Congreso* [Organizing Statute of Congress] in the National Congress. Article 74 of the Constitution states:

> The President of the Republic can declare the urgency in dispatching a draft bill, in one or in all of its formal stages, and in such case, the respective Chamber will pronounce itself within the time limit of thirty days. The qualification as an urgency will belong to the President of the Republic, according to the organic constitutional law governing Congress, which will also set out everything related to the internal processing of the law.

Article 27 of the Organizing Statute of Congress declares:

> When a draft bill is qualified as of simple urgency, its discussion and voting in the required Chamber must be completed within thirty days; if the qualification was of extreme urgency, that time limit will be ten days, and if the request was for immediate discussion, the time limit will be three days, in which case the draft bill will be discussed in general and in particular at the same time. The communication or official letter from the President of the Republic which requires urgency will be taken account of in the earliest session celebrated by the respective Chamber, and from that date the time limit for its urgency will begin.

A fourth legislative faculty is the requesting of special sessions. This regulation (Article 32 No. 2 of the present constitutional text) was established in the 2005 constitutional reform, due to the suppression, in the same reform, of the distinction between *Legislatura Extraordinaria* [Extraordinary Legislature] and *Legislatura Ordinaria* [Ordinary Legislature]. Given the elimination of the extraordinary term, it was considered appropriate for the President to have the authority to summon Parliament to session when it was considered that there were issues requiring urgent attention. According to Professor Carlos Carmona, some of the features of this faculty are the following: (1) it does not exclude legislative issues – that is, the presidential body can summon the session to deal with a draft bill – however, legislative practice indicates that this is achieved through other instruments (agreements with the presidents of the Chambers or Committees), so its use makes more sense for non-legislative issues; (2) it concerns a faculty embodied in the Head of State, not in his ministers; (3) it is to do with a legally binding attribute that does not require the approval of Parliament; (4) the power means not only to convoke, but also to define the issues to be discussed; (5) there are no limits on the number of times that the instrument of convocation can be used; and (6) the session requires the general quorum required for the functioning of the Chambers (Carmona 2006: 85–129).

A final legislative attribute also incorporated in the 2005 constitutional reform is the faculty to enact rewritten texts. Such an attribute is established in Article 64, subsection 5, which states:

> Without prejudice to the provisions of the previous subsections, the President of the Republic is authorized to determine the rewritten, coordinated, and systematized text of the statutory law when it is appropriate for its better implementation. In the exercise of this faculty, changes in its form that are indispensable can be introduced, without altering, in any case, its true sense and scope.

This presidential power already existed; however, the novelty is in the manner of its regulation. Before the 2005 reform, by resolution of the Comptroller General of the Republic, legal authorization was required for the passing of rewritten texts because it was considered that they were *Decretos con Fuerza de Ley* [Decrees with Force of Law] (hereafter, "DFL," for its acronym in Spanish). Now such authorization is no longer necessary because it amounts to the faculty to enact special DFLs authorized by the Constitution (Carmona 2006: 85–129).

7.7 NON-LEGISLATIVE FACULTIES OF THE PRESIDENT

Concerning the non-legislative attributes of the President, following the proposals of Huneeus and Zovatto and Orozco, it is worth highlighting some elements. Firstly, and unlike the original presidential system which is the North American, where the Senate intervenes, in the majority of the Latin American Constitutions the appointment of ministers is the exclusive competence of the President of the Republic. That is how it is explicitly established in Article 33 of the Chilean Constitution. The same regulation establishes the possibility that the President entrusts to one or more ministers the task of coordinating their duties and the relationships between the government and the National Congress. Furthermore, the present constitutional text empowers the President to appoint some public officials of special importance, as, for example, three members of the Constitutional Tribunal (of a total of ten).

The Chilean Constitution, unlike other Latin American Fundamental Charters, does not give many political attributes to the ministers. In other countries, they participate in the declaration of the states of siege or emergency, in appointing important officials, in the granting of reprieves or pardons, and in summoning Congress, among other functions (Zovatto and Orozco 2008: 50). Among the attributes that the constitutional text grants to ministers are the endorsement of the regulations and decrees emanating from the President (Article 35), the possibility of attending sessions in Congress with preferential right to speak (Article 37), and the possibility that all their signatures, together with that of the President, may authorize payments not authorized by statutory law in cases of extraordinary emergencies, up to 2 percent of the *Ley de Presupuesto* [Budgetary Statute] of that year.

7.8 CONTROLS OF THE LEGISLATIVE OVER THE EXECUTIVE

The Chilean Parliament is bicameral, that is, it comprises two branches: the Chamber of Deputies and the Senate. Both chambers take part in making the laws and have all the attributes that the Constitution and the statutes grant them. The main difference between the Chamber of Deputies and the Senate is that the first has more powers in the field of political audit, while the second has more relevance in matters of approval and nomination of public positions and legal issues.

When referring to the controls that the Legislative has over the Executive, one is thinking mainly about the mechanisms that make it possible to control the activities of the Administration, independent of the legislative procedure by which statutory law is enacted. The faculties of Parliament in this matter are set out fundamentally in the Political Constitution and in Statute No. 18.918, the Constitutional Organic Statute of the National Congress. One of the major modifications of the 2005 constitutional reforms was the strengthening of the powers of political audit, in particular of the Chamber of Deputies (Carmona 2006: 121–129).

A first modification referred to the faculty of making agreements or putting forward observations (Article 52 No. 1(a)). The present constitutional regulation demands that such agreements or observations should have a well-founded response from the respective minister within a time limit of thirty days. These two requirements (substantiation and time limit) did not exist before the reform. A second reform that has had more public resonance refers to the interpellation of ministers (Article 52 No. 1(b)). The summoning of ministers is one of the exclusive faculties of the Chamber of Deputies and consists of the possibility of holding a special session to ask questions regarding the performance of the ministers. The assistance of the ministers is compulsory, as is the obligation to answer the questions put to them in such sessions. To summon a minister, a quorum of one-third of the Deputies sitting is required. Another limit imposed by the Constitution is that a minister cannot be summoned more than three times in the same calendar year. The third supervisory attribute added by the reform is the ability to set up investigating commissions (Article 52 No. 1(c)). Previously, this faculty was regulated by the Chamber of Deputies' regulations. The requirement to form these commissions is a quorum of two-fifths of the Deputies sitting. The objective of the commissions is to collect information in relation to determined acts of the government. For this purpose, they can summon officials involved or request background information. As with the previous attribute, it is established that ministers can only be summoned up to three times by one investigating commission. Finally, a new faculty granted by the 2005 constitutional reform, to both the Chamber of Deputies and the Senate, is the obligation that ministers have to attend in person at the special sessions that the Chamber of Deputies or the Senate calls to inform themselves about issues related to their office. These do not involve investigating commissions or public interpellations, but special sessions to discuss a topic. Here, the Constitution did not establish a limit in terms of the number of summonses.

All the other faculties of the National Congress are maintained more or less the same as before the 2005 reform. One can conclude that this process of reform held a special place in the balance of powers between the President and Parliament, in particular, increasing the institutional possibilities of political audit in the Chamber of Deputies.

Meanwhile, it should be said that with respect to the controls of the Legislative over the Executive, there are several Latin American constitutional texts that contemplate more intense and elaborate audit instruments than those adopted by the Chilean Constitution. There are two Latin American countries that take into account confidence motions, as steps before the composition of a *Consejo de Ministros* [Council of Ministers] – Peru and Uruguay. Additionally, twelve constitutional texts establish the motion of censure in relation to ministers, which in some cases requires the ratification of the President (Bolivia, Costa Rica, El Salvador, Nicaragua, Panama, and Paraguay), while in others it is binding – that is to say, the Parliament can end up dismissing one or more ministers (Argentina, Colombia, Guatemala, Peru, Uruguay, and Venezuela) (Zovatto and Orozco 2008: 56).

According to Chilean law, the only way that Parliament can dismiss a minister, or even a President, is through constitutional impeachment or a political trial, which is a way of control over the Executive's performance, but this kind of political-legal control is based on the inspection of illegal acts or non-compliance with duties associated with the position or constitutional offenses.

7.9   THE EXECUTIVE–LEGISLATIVE RELATIONSHIP IN CONSTITUTIONAL PRACTICE

If the Chilean government system is analyzed only in terms of constitutional *regulation*, it could be concluded that it is essentially and excessively presidential – that is, a pure case of presidentialism – even when the 2005 constitutional reform reinforced the controls that Parliament, in particular the Chamber of Deputies, has over the governmental administration of the President. Meanwhile, an analysis of this type would be incomplete without a revision of the main instruments that determine the Executive–Legislative relationship and how they function in constitutional *practice*. Only then is it possible to identify the critical problems that affect the Chilean governmental system.

An example of the relevance of this approach that puts emphasis on the constitution in practice is that from the point of view of constitutional regulation, the more problematic norm in terms of the effect on the balance of powers between the President and the Congress is the power of veto that the Constitution grants the former, which was described above as a powerful type of veto, because in the case of the Chilean Constitution, a super majority, or quorum of two-thirds, is required to defeat it. However, it is a reality that in constitutional practice the veto has not been used very often, and the imbalance of powers between the political bodies does not arise from the application of this instrument or constitutional authority.

7.10 THE IMBALANCE OF POWERS BETWEEN THE EXECUTIVE AND THE LEGISLATIVE

From the point of view of constitutional practice, there are in Chile four attributes that have unbalanced the powers of Legislative and Executive, in favor of the latter. As was mentioned before, these are: the exclusive initiative of the President of the Republic, the urgencies, the management of budgetary and financial issues, and the imbalance of technical capabilities between Parliament and the Civil Service, in particular the *Ministerio de Hacienda* [Ministry of the Treasury].

As seen in the previous section, as well as having the legislative initiative, the President of the Republic has the exclusive initiative over a great number of issues. This regulation, in practice, has resulted in the great majority of issues discussed in Parliament being projects sent by the Executive. It is feasible to envisage an active legislative power, even with the existence of the exclusive initiative, insofar as there are many issues that are outside the scope of its application. However, in reality, this regulation has meant a strong control of the legislative agenda by the Executive and the inhibition of the work of Parliament in the processing of draft bills. One Chilean Congressman indicated that 80 percent of the projects discussed in Parliament come from the President. The broad terms used in the constitutional text have contributed to this situation.

Nevertheless, even if it is recognized that the parliamentary activity in the preparation of draft bills has increased, the President continues to have a predominant role in generating legal initiatives. In the initiation of the process of forming statutory laws in the Chilean system, the President of the Republic is the main legislator.

The other instruments that have greatly helped the President to control the legislative agenda are the urgencies. Through this instrument, the priorities of parliamentary discussion are determined. As there are no sanctions for non-compliance with the time limits established for the urgencies, their use has been more relevant in the determination of the order of priority of parliamentary deliberation. In this sense, the control of the agenda by the President has been notorious.

Therefore, political deliberation takes place under the control of the Executive, which generates a strong incentive to discuss those projects sent by this power. Another possible explanation and justification for the use of this instrument is that the total days in the year for parliamentary discussion are not many, taking into account the district visit weeks, the number of weekdays in which there is no session, and a month's holiday every year. In order to complete the government program, the President has to arrange and adjust the debates in Parliament.

The previous point is evidence, in any case, that the urgencies amount to an anomalous instrument, if one is thinking about the balance of powers between the President and Congress. However, the strange thing is that, as the secretary of the Chamber of Deputies, Miguel Landeros, said in an interview of May 11, 2009 (a document also archived by the researchers who worked with the author of this study, which serves as the basis for this chapter), in the discussions of the 2005 constitutional reform, consideration was given to establishing a possible way of categorizing the urgencies, but the Members of Parliament themselves finally rejected this option. The categorization of the urgencies could have served to prepare Members of Parliament to participate in the final definition of priority in the processing of draft bills pushed by the Executive, but it was not approved.

A third critical aspect in the Executive–Legislative relationship are the powers in budgetary and financial matters. In the Chilean regime, the President has very wide powers over the elaboration of draft bills related to expenditure and financial administration, including, paradigmatically, the making of the budget. Furthermore, he has wide powers over the implementation and assessment of the expenditure. The role of Congress is limited to the discussion and negotiation of the budgetary headings and notes already presented for Parliament's approval by the Executive.

This is a particularly sensitive issue in Chilean constitutional history. In addition, as will be seen in the comparative analysis, in general, all political systems give control over budgetary and financial issues to the government because it is an instrument essential to the fulfillment of the programs needed to satisfy the citizens' requirements. Despite that, in the present Chilean regime there is an imbalance in these matters, where the role of Parliament is reduced. It is possible to think of several aspects in which the legislative power could have more prominence than at present, without taking away the preponderant role that the President should have, in particular in everything related to the budget. One of these aspects is control of expenditure, where Congress could play a more active role.

It is noted in the treatment of this issue so typical of the Chilean regime – that is, the imbalance of powers between the executive and legislative functions – that, as so rightly stated by Professor Sebastián Soto, there exist several informal institutions or "practices." These form part of our political culture and are able to generate new conditions of equilibrium between the executive and legislative functions. Sebastián Soto defines these informal institutions as "rules socially shared, usually not written, which are created, communicated and requested outside the officially established channels." In this definition, he draws upon the contributions of political science and applies the concept of informal institutions expressed by Helmke and Levitsky (Soto 2015: 31–32). In the Chilean case, Professor Soto explains that these practices are expressed in various very different examples, among which he highlights:

> the meetings between the government representatives and various Members of Parliament to discuss which projects are necessary and should be incorporated in the Executive's program. Equally, at the beginning of each period of sessions, the government authorities meet with Members of Parliament to decide the legislative priorities for the year. Later, representatives of ministers and of Members of Parliament who belong to different commissions meet periodically to discuss aspects of different draft bills that are being processed. In addition, the different Presidents of the Republic, records Siavelis, sometimes take part in these meetings so that they can determine the week's legislative agenda.
>
> (ibid.: 33)

From the compilation and analysis of these practices so thoroughly carried out, combining his parliamentary experience with that as legislative advisor in the Ministry of the General Secretariat to the Presidency, Sebastián Soto concludes that the legislative power is a lot more balanced and has more influence than is shown in the formal rules of the Chilean constitutional system (ibid.: 34). These informal attributes are expressed in a preferential way in the case of the determination of legislative urgencies, the veto, the exclusive initiative in legislative matters of the President of the Republic, and the proceedings of the statutory law approving the budget, to which annotations or "notes" are made and "protocols" are signed that mean commitments over specific political matters that are accepted between the representatives of the Executive and Members of Parliament. In the light of this informal reality, Sebastián Soto has proposed the introduction of new rules that could rationalize and improve legislative proceedings in Chile, and among them he highlights the idea of introducing a new kind of rule of constitutional closure that provides that all matters that are not the exclusive initiative of the President of the Republic are the exclusive initiative of Members of Parliament (ibid.: 270). This proposal, which I support, insofar as it aims to revise and eventually reduce the matters that are, at present, the exclusive initiative of the Executive, is based on the verification by Professor Sebastián Soto that not all matters of exclusive initiative have the same theoretical foundation. Additionally, Soto argues that all the draft proposals contain regulations of mixed presidential and parliamentarian initiatives, and therefore it would be advantageous if all proposals initiated by a presidential communication were also to be subscribed by a number of Members of Parliament at the time of their presentation (ibid.: 271).

Sebastián Soto has also highlighted some practices for dealing with the legislative urgency that the Executive imposes on the legislative proceedings that can generate conditions of equilibrium. If one is guided by what is contained in the regulations of the Chilean Constitution, the Congress Organic Statute, and the Chambers Regulations, the Executive's power and control over the degree of urgency of draft bills seems to be almost total. However, Professor Soto has indicated several factors that influence the way the Executive applies the legislative degrees of urgency:

> it is a permanent interchange of information by which the President, through the ministers, tries to set the agenda by using the degrees of urgency, but negotiates the rhythm of the draft bills proceedings and the real signals that it is desired to send to the Members of Parliament. The

> Members of Parliament receive the prioritization knowing that there is a range of factors that will put into context the purpose of the urgency, such as who is occupying the presidency of the commission, the interest of public opinion in the draft bill, the pressure of stakeholder groups, or the other projects in the legislative agenda.
>
> (ibid.: 299)

Faced with this reality, Professor Soto has proposed a reform of the Constitution and of the Congress Organic Statute that links urgencies with voting, and this means that if the time limit fixed for a project has expired and it has not been approved, it must be brought to a vote. Sebastián Soto says:

> the correct thing to do is not direct the rules towards dealing with the projects, but towards voting on them. In other words, it is not reasonable that non-compliance with the degree of urgency should lead, for example, to the approval of the project. It is reasonable, however, that its non-compliance provides a fast road towards taking the vote. This last puts the incentives in the right place.
>
> (ibid.: 302)

To these proposals, which in principle I support, and which show great knowledge of Chilean legislative practice, a capacity for analysis in the light of comparative law, and references to concrete cases, is also added the idea of eventually limiting the presidential veto. The proposal could be to eliminate all forms of partial veto, except in the case of the budget. Furthermore, Sebastián Soto explains that the presidential veto is only insisted on in relation to dispatches, and not parliamentary motions, and he covers with comprehensive knowledge other questions of major importance related to the institution of the presidential veto and the legislative process (ibid.: 171–183).

It is also to be noted that on the subject of the relationship between the Executive and the Legislative, the influence of a novel factor must be considered – that is, citizen participation. At least from Michelle Bachelet's first government, the Executive has incorporated in its public policies the concept of citizen participation, enacting a statute that promotes it and that incorporates it – for example, in the consultative councils of consumers, reinforcing transparency, rights of the patients, and so on. These forms of participation sometimes cause controversy within the Administration because, justly, it is on that entity that the implementation and provision of services falls, which, depending on the extent of the participation, has two effects: (1) either it is very little, and therefore, rather irrelevant or symbolic, and/or (2) it is an expenditure of institutional and strategic resources because it involves the citizens, and the Administration is forced to carry out and maintain its services at least with a minimum and dignified degree of participation.

In this context, the constitutional role of Congress in the promotion of citizen participation is limited to what its organic statute provides, which is that the Members of Parliament may have an office in the place that they represent, which suggests acceptance of the logic at its minimum level of a representative system. However, part of the lack of contact between Congress and the citizens and the uneasiness or dissatisfaction that public opinion today is expressing, could be due to the fundamental constitutional structure of Congress and the lack of attributes that might bring the citizen closer to the work of the Legislative. For example, what Congress does for the benefit of the population is not known. Therefore, together with the introduction of the popular initiative and other innovative measures for participation, there has to be a redoubling of efforts to make transparent or publicize the activities of Members of Parliament.

The above is directly connected to the last of the critical aspects of the Executive–Legislative relationship, which involves the imbalance in technical capabilities. The difference in technical capabilities is overwhelmingly in favor of the Civil Service that is lined up behind the executive power. This factor is of major importance in other identified critical aspects. Given a strong system of technical advice, Members of Parliament could generate a greater number of draft bills, improve the quality of political deliberation, and better supervise the performance of the Executive.

The Imbalance in Technical Capabilities between the Executive and the Legislative

The *Biblioteca del Congreso Nacional* [National Library of Congress] is not the only technical source for legislative work carried out by Members of Parliament, but it is the one that concentrates the greatest number of advisors and the one that contains the most sophisticated system of parliamentarian consultancy. In recent years, the National Library of Congress has become the central coordinating reference of technical support to Members of Parliament (Valdés and Soto 2009: 53–88). The Ministry of the Treasury is not the only source of technical consultancy to government, but it has become a central coordinating reference in the design of all the public policies carried out by the Executive. One of the most important reasons for the existence of this centralizing activity being established in the Ministry of the Treasury is that it concentrates all the necessary budgetary coordination for the design and implementation of public programs through one of its main services, the *Dirección de Presupuestos del Ministerio de Hacienda* [Directorate of Budgets of the Ministry of the Treasury] (hereafter, "DIPRES," for its acronym in Spanish).

Meanwhile, it has to be recognized that in government, technical capability is better distributed than in Parliament, because each ministry and public service intervenes in its own regulatory sector. However, if the important asymmetry of technical capabilities has to be demonstrated using only one of the ministries, then one would be verifying the general trend identified concerning the unequal situation in which Parliament finds itself in the production of its own high-quality regulations and legislation. There are other institutional entities of legislative support, such as the *Oficinas de Informaciones del Senado y de la Cámara de Diputados* [Offices of Information for the Senate and the Chamber of Deputies], the *Secretarios de Comisión* [Commissions Secretaries], the personnel contracted by each Member of Parliament, and the think tanks or non-governmental external organizations affiliated to political parties or stakeholder groups. However, these entities either have a low number of advisors or demanding administrative functions, or lack any political neutrality in terms of legislative consultancy. Therefore, the National Library of Congress is the best benchmark for making the proposed comparison. The distribution of technical capabilities among ministries is also not homogeneous. These differences are a matter deserving profound analysis to the extent that they also reflect the imbalance of powers, this time within the civil service. Also to be considered is the frequency with which expert or reputable private associations or organizations are invited to the discussions in Chamber and not in commissions – for example, on environmental issues.

The collected information demonstrates that a single ministry of the executive power practically quadruples in personnel the technical capability of the principal entity providing technical expertise to Parliament. These proportions may have changed, but I dare to hypothesize that since 2009, there has probably been an accentuation of the differences existing between the resources and costs of the advisors linked to the Ministry of the Treasury, in particular, DIPRES, in comparison with other advisors in the public sector. Naturally, as with any hypothesis, it needs to be verified.

More recently, in an undergraduate thesis in which the history of the budget in Chile is analyzed, referring, in particular, to the introduction of the system of assessment of budgetary control and management which anticipates an assessment of the instruments of budgetary control by results, there appears the fundamentally dictatorial origin of the centralization of the Chilean budget in the DIPRES. According to the records examined by Benjamín Alemparte, the following summarized judgment is advanced:

> the decree with force of law No. 106 of 1960 will reorganize the former Oficina de Presupuestos [Budgetary Office] under the new name Dirección de Presupuestos ["DIPRES," for its acronym in Spanish], establishing its dependence on the Ministry of the Treasury and establishing as its main functions the preparation of the budget and the implementation of budgetary policy. With that, the hierarchical status of this entity was enhanced within the administration and its attributes were also broadened, maintaining the role that it had in the examination and revision of the requests of the other public services, but also in the setting of limits on the amounts of expenditure for each service. The same decree established that the DIPRES should coordinate, as far as technologically advisable, the annual programs for legislation of executive initiative and advise on their economic and financial aspects, and in this way, the DIPRES became a key institutional actor in the design and planning of public policies by the government. The later years of the DIPRES, with the rise to the presidency of Salvador Allende, and the eventual political and social pressures of the time, will end in one of the worst institutional crises that our country has had since independence. The elements that will finally unbalance the system of financial administration are four: growing inflation, the low price of copper, the strong expansion of public investment, and the increase in remunerations that have exceeded all government targets. In this way, after the 1973 military coup d'état, the main reforms of the *Junta de Gobierno* will be focused on reducing public expenditure and continuing on the path of centralization of the financial administration of the State. The military dictatorship, in parallel with its plans to establish a new Constitution in its strategy of economic and political transformation, will establish unification as one of the most urgent measures. This coordination will be carried out in the future by the Ministry of the General Secretariat to the Presidency ["SEGPRES," for its acronym in Spanish], establishing two centers of power (DIPRES–

SEGPRES) essential for the legal initiatives of the Executive, controlling in this way the legislative agenda of the National Congress through Decree-Law No. 1263 of 1975, which repealed DFL No. 47. Decree 56 meant the reinforcement of the control of public finances by the Ministry of the Treasury, consolidating a center of political power that is recognized by everyone even today. The above was supported because for the military government, financial discipline was one of the best tools to integrate and develop the new economic model for the country. The *Decreto Ley Orgánico de Administración Financiera del Estado* [Organizing Decree-Law for the Financial Administration of the State], in its intention of modernizing the public financial apparatus, established among other novel things a new form of preparing the budget, setting up a system consisting firstly of a medium-term financial program. Together with the tax reform of the same year through Decree-Law 824, *Ley sobre Impuesto a la Renta* [Income Tax Law] and Decree-Law 825, *Impuesto a las Ventas y Servicios* [Tax on Sales and Services], it had a strong impact on public administration. According to Art. 10 of Decree-Law No. 1263, the financial program is an instrument for medium-term planning and financial management of the public sector, which comprises forecast income and expenditure, internal and external credit, public investment, acquisitions, and personnel requirements. The harmonization of these budgets enables a public-sector budget that is a financial estimate of income and expenditure for a given year, harmonizing available resources with the achievement of goals and objectives previously established. Furthermore, it was arranged that the budgetary exercise will coincide with the calendar year, fixing that the accounts of each year's exercise will close on December 31st, and from January 1st, the new year's budget will come into force, as laid down in the constitutional regulation. In this way, the DIPRES, understood as the "technical entity in charge of proposing the assignment of the financial resources of the State," will have as its exclusive competence the task of guiding and regulating the process of formulating budgets, as well as regulating and supervising the execution of public expenditure without prejudice to the attributes – in relation to the correct administration of State resources – of financial control and accountability, which will be concentrated in the Comptroller General of the Republic. With the return to democracy, the scheme of financial public administration inherited from the military government will not have major changes, and a fundamental role in the planning of public policies at national level will continue to be centered on the DIPRES.

(Alemparte 2016: 46–48)

Alemparte has explained the relationships between the budget and the possibilities of demanding social rights, as well as raising an idea regarding the intervention of the tribunals in guaranteeing these rights. It is a well-prepared and focused conclusion on one of the most important questions of contemporary constitutional law. Alemparte has concluded:

> From a theoretical perspective and following Rawls' approach, we checked that the budget can be seen as part of the basic structure of a country, as a power of transference, responsible for guaranteeing a social minimum necessary to satisfy the principle of difference. The budget is at the center of the debate for the insistence on social rights, where there is a permanent tension between the courts of justice and political powers. We have argued against the idea of placing such enforceability exclusively in the courts because it is not their work to supervise the government's social programs. The courts are unable to distribute the enormous budgetary appropriations that demand their guarantee, and their interference could lead to real political deliberation. Additionally, we point out that the power of discretion of the government and of the National Congress is different to that of the courts. Judiciary discretion is more restricted than the political because it intervenes in the scope of application of the statute; therefore, even though the statute can predetermine the substance of a social right, its limit and scale will be determined by the political powers. In Chile, when a President wants to be populist or wants to carry out major reforms that mean enormous budgetary efforts for the government, this is limited by the Ministry of the Treasury and the DIPRES, which have centralized budgetary discussion. We have checked that this centralization of the budgetary discussion is expressly contemplated in our Constitution. The President dominates the discussion through such attributes as the exclusive initiative, the presidential veto, and its regulatory power in the execution of the Budget. Through this last, the President draws up amounts and priorities for each sector, being able to modify the budget according to the possibilities that the statute contemplates. This vertical structure of the decision-making system also has an impact in terms of the decentralization of public administration. The regional governments, despite being recognized at constitutional level, are impaired by criteria of fiscal responsibility and of technical incompetence, which leads to their budgets being established as part of the Ministry of Interior, which consolidates the fact that they are subordinated to the intendant, a figure dependent on central government. The Ministry of the Treasury controls, to a great extent, the government's legislative agenda and the preparation of the budget, through the financial reports on draft bills and through the so-called "visaciones de hacienda" [treasury endorsements]. The "presupuesto por resultados" [budget by results] means a new

conception of the power relationships between the Executive and Congress. From the point of view of decision-making, the establishment of tools for follow-up, assessment, and incentive have unbalanced the institutional equilibrium even more in favor of the Treasury and the DIPRES. We studied how the DIPRES improves the strategic definitions of each service or public institution, and in coordination with the SEGPRES sets up a hierarchy of the government's political priorities and its legislative program. At the same time, through the *Balances de Gestión Integral* [Integral Management Balance Sheet], the DIPRES carries out a follow-up on the performance indicators of each institution or program, checking that the results achieved are not below previous years.

(Alemparte 2016: 113–115)

In their turn, Salvador Valdés and Sebastián Soto have set out another valuable description, and also some reform proposals regarding parliamentarian legislative consultancy, in an already cited work by the *Centro de Estudios Públicos* [Public Studies Center] (Valdés and Soto 2009: 53–88). In their study, they raise several criticisms about the advisory system, and therefore they propose a model that combines internal personnel with contracting external legislative advice, generated by think tanks and other institutions previously accredited. They propose that the internal advice should be made out basically by a body of civil servants who report to each Committee (political parties' bench) in one branch of Congress. This will reduce the risk that each Member of Parliament diverts the work of his legislative advisors towards his district responsibilities, allowing, at the same time, a greater closeness and loyalty between advisors and Members of Parliament that, in the authors' view, is not possible with neutral advice like that provided by the National Library of Congress. Therefore, they propose to restructure this last type of consultation so that it can fulfill a supporting role to the legislative work, generating neutral inputs that will be processed later by the advisors to the party benches. They also propose that part of the personnel should be used to work in the *Comisión Especial Mixta de Presupuestos* [Special Mixed Budgetary Commission], with the objective of strengthening the function of supervision of the commitment of public expenditure.

Valdés and Soto's proposal is clear and detailed. However, the emphasis on the consultation dominated by the benches and external think tanks could erode the feeling of togetherness and the republican spirit of the work that should be carried out inside the National

Congress. Dedicating large sums of money to finance studies coming from external institutions, many of which respond to private interests or factions and are sometimes politically, economically, or corporately not transparent, does not seem a reasonable solution. With adequate independence, more personnel, and a better infrastructure, the National Library of Congress could perfectly well carry out that work, from Parliament. Eventually, in qualified cases that require external inputs, the same Library could be in charge of tendering for studies and proposals, as it does at present. The proposal to transfer the legislative consultancy to one controlled by the political party benches must be analyzed, but again, the National Library of Congress seems to be in a privileged position to take the leading role in the selection, coordination, and assessment of those personnel, with the objective of reducing the risk of capture identified by the authors. A substantial improvement of the legislative advisory model includes the strengthening of public institutions that work in this area, and therefore, they should not forget the republican spirit of their work, which is to discuss public issues in an open and transparent space, with resource allocation that responds to a democratic representative logic and with broad social participation, expressing the ideals of all citizens, not only of the usual organized groups.

Assessment of Control Mechanisms by the Legislative
One of the key purposes of the 2005 constitutional reform was to strengthen Congress's control mechanisms, in particular those of the Chamber of Deputies, regarding the actions of the President. Thus, the Constitution provided for the interpellations of ministers, the investigative Commissions, the faculty of drawing up agreements or putting forward observations, and the obligation of ministers to attend in person the special sessions that the Chamber of Deputies or the Senate might summon.

It has already been explained that despite these powers, a strengthening of the role of the Chilean Congress has not been noticed as an exemplary place for democratic deliberation. The control mechanisms that the legislative power has, have not managed to turn back the established practice of the broad autonomy of the Executive in the process of government. In the management and inspection of public policies, the role of Congress is limited. If to the above are added the significant instruments that the President uses to control the exercise of legislative power, we have to recognize that in Chile, in theory and in political reality, a kind of presidentialism has established itself, which in the classification of Zovatto and Orozco, is of the predominant type.

Accordingly, in the diagnosis of the constitutional practice of the rule of the Chilean Government, we find four attributes that unbalance the Executive–Legislative relationship: exclusive initiative, urgencies, financial administration, and technical capability. These are not the only elements that need to be reformed, based on the concept of improving flexibility, but at the very least, they are perhaps the most critical points that degrade the quality of the present constitutional practice in Chile. In order to move forward in this reform, we present below some ideas of Comparative Constitutional Law, which we hope will help us to face our real situation and give further thought to some formulae of change and improvement.

7.11   THE CHILEAN GOVERNMENT REGIME COMPARED WITH THE PARLIAMENTARIAN SYSTEM

Parliamentarian systems envisage a set of provisions that regulate the attributes of Parliament and the government and, more importantly still, assume that in practice subtle and complex relationships are incorporated between the different actors in the political system. In these systems, government and Parliament are closely linked, both in forming the government and in the exercise of the functions of both bodies and in the maintenance of their power. The relationship of mutual trust is also manifest in the possibility that Parliament has to provoke the resignation of the Cabinet, and in the faculty of the prime minister to call for the dissolution of Parliament. Government and Parliament together lead the government and politics of the country, one of their means of operation being the drawing up of law.

Without prejudice to the foregoing, the work of Parliament is sharply differentiated from that of the government by its supervisory audit faculties. Of these faculties, those particularly pertinent to take into account in the case of Chile are the investigative and ministerial commissions, the questioning and interpellations, the debates, and the budgetary control.

The most important ordinary control mechanism in parliamentarian systems is, without doubt, the system of interpellations and questioning. These mechanisms are exercised regularly, every week, which allows Parliament to keep up-to-date with the activities of the government and with the most important topics of national significance, and its regularity avoids causing a destabilizing effect on the government being questioned. Another fundamental characteristic of these mechanisms is their publication, so that civil society can also take part in the task of supervision. The regularity of these interrogations is helped in the countries studied by the existence of time limits for carrying out each question and answer (five minutes, in general), as well as for carrying out the interpellations (ten to fifteen minutes).

At the same time, among the essential elements in parliamentary systems that can prompt interpellations and motions are the debates, which on any subject and without excessive regulation may arise in the Chambers or in the Commissions. It is in these debates where the main directives are formulated that Parliament imposes on the acting of the government. Within the debates that are held in the countries studied, there are two of particular interest. One is the Opposition Days in the United Kingdom, where the opposition has a number of days to debate the topics they wish. Another type of debate of great interest arises after the Queen's Speech in the United Kingdom, or the Annual Debate regarding the state of the nation in the case of Spain, where the annual government programs are assessed. In these countries, it is also possible for the government to put forward particular topics for discussion.

As for the Commissions, rather than those of investigations that do not allow effective control by the parliamentary minority, the commissions specializing in the control and performance of competences belonging to the government ministries are more interesting. Thus, in Italy there are commissions dedicated to a particular ministry of government, not only in relation to the legislation in that sphere, but also supervising and developing the competences peculiar to each ministry (something similar to the work that the Opposition Cabinet realizes in the United Kingdom).

Finally, it is important for the purpose of considering the improvement of the Chilean political system to highlight the work that Parliament carries out in Italy and the United Kingdom in terms of expenditure control. The government, in addition to the annual budget, must present to Parliament multi-annual budgets, in order to carry out a long-term review of the financial stability of the country. Additionally, in the case of Italy, the government must give account for the expenditure in the previous year. All this without prejudice to the interpellations, debates, and investigations by parliamentary commissions that may arise on this subject, at any time.

As already pointed out above, in parliamentary systems, government and Parliament are closely linked, both in forming the government and in carrying out the functions of both bodies and in the maintenance of their power. The relationship of mutual trust is also manifest in the possibility that Parliament has to provoke the resignation of the Cabinet, and in the faculty of the prime minister to call for the dissolution of Parliament. Government and Parliament together lead the government and politics of the country, one of their means of operation being the drawing up of laws. Without prejudice to the foregoing, the work of Parliament is sharply differentiated from that of the government by its supervisory audit faculties.

7.12 THE CHILEAN GOVERNMENT REGIME COMPARED WITH THE SEMI-PRESIDENTIAL SYSTEM

One of the main reasons in Chile to argue in favor of the adoption of the present presidential system is the stability achieved in the political system which favors large political coalitions. The semi-presidential systems that have been reviewed have produced the same effect. The government regimes in France and Portugal are characterized by three elements which, even if they do not define a semi-presidential regime, are the natural consequence of such, and are similar to the Chilean political context: (1) presidential elections that require an absolute majority, establishing a second-round election, or *ballotage*, if none of the candidates secures 50 percent + 1 of the votes; and (2) the configuration of political parties or political associations around the candidature or government of a President (Duverger 1970: 277–290).

The coalitions governing, as well as those that would like to govern, define themselves by the figure of the President or candidate as such. It is important to note the great internal and external presence that the leadership of Sarkozy and Royal had in the French political system, and the reform of the French Socialist Party that took place after the defeat of their presidential figure; and (3) the configuration of the party system in a stable framework, with two large balanced forces constituted by a coalition of parties. Until now, these two forces have maintained power, but it is possible that the scenario could change in the future. It has to do with an effect that, unlike the reasons that explain the phenomenon in Chile, has occurred particularly in France because of the second-round configuration of elections and the *presidentialization* of the political parties, which means that in order to have better possibilities of taking the presidency, the parties tend to reassure themselves through agreements with smaller groups in order to consolidate the votes that could reach an absolute majority.

Beyond the relationship that the *Consejo de Ministros* [Council of Ministers] has with the President, the possibility of dissolving Congress and submitting the government to the political approval of Parliament could have positive consequences in the Chilean system. Some consequences that would derive from the introduction of this mechanism are: (1) accountability of political groups in Parliament that refuse to approve or discuss public policies, or that use a policy of blocking government proposals; (2) elimination of the generalized qualified quorum from our political system, in view of the constitutional alternatives available to the President of the Republic to call parliamentary elections or to offer their resignation to Parliament; and (3) to have available democratic solutions in case of legislative impasses, when there are political majorities that cannot be reconciled with the President of the Republic of the day.

The range of faculties available to Congress for the revision of presidential performance is a consequence of its own role in the system because it is monitoring the person who was elected indirectly by Congress. However, Members of Parliament taking part in the budgetary discussion is a concept that is worth analyzing when giving more power to parliamentarians in the context of a presidential system.

The reform of the Chilean political system must take into account the modification of the regulations and practices that have accentuated the so-called "executive constitutionalism," which has already been explained (Ackerman 2010: 68–87), and which has led to the excessive increase of presidential power over constitutional deliberation (Ruiz-Tagle 2012: 229–247). For this reason, in this complex scenario of redistribution of political and constitutional functions that I propose, the concept of increased flexibility consists, on the one hand, of greater distribution of power among the political bodies that have more direct democratic legitimacy with the purpose of strengthening governability, and, on the other hand, at the same time through that legitimizing action, could increase the performance of public policies and enhance the legitimacy of the political system. From this point of view, it is not to be understood that President and Congress are separate entities that do not pretend to intervene in the work of the other, or that their attributes are balancing out or are resolved usually by a third party, such as a constitutional autonomous body. On the contrary, the project of flexibilization provides for the installation of adequate instruments of control by one body over the other, in particular, to bring about a result coordinated between the President and Congress. From the coordination between those two bodies with democratic representation arises the governability, technical coherence, and public policies that may provide additional cloaks or layers of legitimacy. A necessary condition for an effective process of flexibilization to take place is that there should be a certain balance in the powers of the bodies one wants to discipline, and mutual checks and balances. A proposal in order to address this idea of balance between the President of the Republic and Congress is in Senator Eduardo Frei's presentation before the *Comisión Especial del Régimen Político de la Cámara de Diputados* [Special Commission on the Political Regime of the Chamber of Deputies] of October 2008. These seven proposals were listed to achieve this balance:

1. *Cooperation between the President and Congress:* In terms of the substantive proposals, I believe that regarding the government regime the battle of the labels should be ended over presidentialism and parliamentarianism. We should look for a system that works and that can balance better the relationship between the President of the Republic and Congress. To make progress in that direction, it seems reasonable that Members of Parliament could be appointed Ministers of State so as to use the talents that are available in Congress for political tasks, and end with the categorical separation between these two powers so that they can collaborate closely.

2. *To reform attributes of the bicameral system:* Even though some have proposed the creation of a unicameral system, the political chamber, together with the institution of the Senate, should be maintained. To maintain the bicameral system of course assumes a revision of the existing districts and circumscriptions, and reinforces the attributes of the upper chamber so that it is a place of political deliberation at the highest level, as it was for much of Chile's history. For example, to the faculties of the Senate can be added that of approving, by a majority of its members, the appointment of Ambassadors.

3. *To modify the presidential term:* Additionally, with respect to the length of the presidential term, this should be extended to five or six years, without the possibility of re-election and it is proposed alternatively to maintain the term of four years with the possibility of immediate re-election for one more time only.

4. *Dissolution of the Chambers:* It is proposed also that the President may dissolve the Chambers and call for elections once during their mandate, and that this faculty can be used to generate a new majority that allows them to govern without stalemate and the feeling of being in a political mud bath.

5. *Reinforce the capabilities of Congress:* Other substantial reforms must also be made to the legislative process to ensure the technical quality of our laws. To this end, it could be appropriate to incorporate more and better professionals to advise Parliament as civil servants in the preparation of draft laws. These professionals, in turn, must be able to help in the evaluation of public policies linked to legislative initiatives and auditing experiences.

6. *Modify the legislative attributes of the President:* At the same time, the excessive presidential power should be revised in terms of the legislative initiative and the urgencies, in particular in relation to economic and budgetary matters. It is that without falling into the trap that the periodic laws were in our history, we must be able to learn from the forms of parliamentary budgetary control existing in other countries. We have seen how in the USA, due to the crisis in Wall Street and the Iraq war, Congress exercised its functions with more responsibility. This experience is not far from what we need to address complex reforms in similar areas.

7. *To restructure Ministries:* It is proposed to restructure the *Ministerio de Planificación* [Planning Ministry] so that it becomes a Ministry for the Coordination of Social Policies that can act, collaborate, and coordinate more directly with the Treasury Department.

These are some of the factors that are not present in Chile and that could be studied to improve our Constitution, in particular in terms of the exorbitant legislative attributes that the Executive enjoys, in terms of the exclusive initiative, control of urgencies, attributes in administrative and financial matters, and technical and advisory capabilities. Those who criticize this predominance of the Executive maintain that there is very little parliamentary influence in the preparation of the law in the Chilean presidential regime. At the same time as studying the differences and similarities of our system to other political systems to find flexible formulae, it has to do with solving the problems of collaboration between the President and Congress and thinking about institutional reforms. For it is very important to focus attention on the need for a new capacity, based in Congress, for technical and political legislative advice that, as has been explained, in comparison only with the Treasury Department is unbalanced, it being necessary also to reinforce a culture of political parties that practice internal democracy and are schools in citizenship, and which give political and technical support to this formula for flexibility and equilibrium that should be ensured between the Executive and Congress of the Republic of Chile.

A summary of some proposals emerging from this chapter in relation to the Chilean government regime, together with the articles in the existing Constitution that require reform in order to put these proposals into practice, are shown in Table 7.1.

TABLE 7.1 Proposals of President–Congress flexibilization

Source	Proposal	Justification	Constitutional or statutory regulations that require revision
Diagnosis of Chilean constitutional practice	1. Revision of the areas subject to the exclusive initiative of the President	Allow Parliament greater involvement in preparing draft laws	Article 65 Political Constitution
	2. Revision of the system of emergencies/ urgencies	Allow more intervention of Parliament in the definition of priorities in the legislative agenda	Article 74 Political Constitution Article 26 LOC National Congress
	3. More faculties for the National Congress to supervise expenditure	Achieve more control by Parliament over the commitment of expenditure	Articles 65 & 67 Political Constitution Article 25 LOC National Congress
	4. Increased technical capability of National Congress	Allow more dialogue between Congress and the civil service in the preparation and processing of draft laws	(New regulation)

TABLE 7.1 (*cont.*)

Source	Proposal	Justification	Constitutional or statutory regulations that require revision
Parliamentary government regimes	1. Regular system of interpellations and questions	Generate a democratic culture of constant dialogue between government and Parliament	Article 52 Political Constitution
	2. Open and flexible debates regarding alignment of government policies	Allow more intervention of Congress in the discussion of the basic government guideline	(New regulation)
	3. Legislative periods assigned to opposition	Generate more participation of the opposition in the preparation and processing of draft laws	Article 55 Political Constitution Article 6 LOC National Congress
	4. Parliamentary commissions by ministry	To boost the role of Members of Parliament in the audit of the government's performance, allowing them to specialize in the different government sectors	Article 52 Political Constitution
	5. New parliamentary institutional framework for the control of expenditure	Achieve more control by Parliament of commitment of expenditure	(New regulation)

TABLE 7.1 (*cont.*)

Source	Proposal	Justification	Constitutional or statutory regulations that require revision
Semi-presidential government regimes	1. Revision of mechanisms for dissolution of Congress and for submitting the tenure of government to the approval of particular laws	Introduce institutional mechanisms to solve political crises	Article 32 Political Constitution
	2. Eliminate the qualified quorum system	Respect the principle of majority and boost the efficiency of legislative work	Article 66 Political Constitution

In these proposals we have not taken a position in relation to the appropriateness of having a change of government regime in Chile that means a redistribution of the executive function, by adopting one that is more shared or dual in nature. In Chile, this function can have varied forms. I believe that it is not politically viable in today's Chile to think in terms of establishing a parliamentary monarchy that could represent the functions of the Head of State, nor of eliminating or substituting the President of the Republic, who should at least fulfill the functions of Head of State. However, the President can be accompanied when functioning as Head of State by a Vice President, who may or may not fulfill roles that are symbolic or as a replacement, or who may have more specific duties.

In Article 60 of the 1828 Constitution a Vice President was contemplated. The Vice President can be elected together with the President or can be appointed at the sole discretion of the President and can have a role in Congress, as in the USA, where the Vice President presides over its sessions and has a casting vote in the case of a stalemate. Also, the President can be accompanied by a head of government who can have their own political functions, which can include being the Head of the Administration. The head of government can be appointed by the parliamentary majority and be accountable to the trust of this majority – such a situation, by coexisting with the President, forms the basis of the French semi-presidential system.

In relation to the Chilean case, it is indispensable to consider Article 33 of the existing Constitution, which allows the President of the Republic to appoint a minister to coordinate the Cabinet (*primus inter pares*), who takes charge of the relationships between the government and Congress. The only element missing in this regulation is to add the possibility that the person can be removed by a no-confidence motion or by parliamentary majority, in which case the President could appoint another person who may or may not be a Member of Parliament. Naturally, this proposal requires "detailed engineering," but in reality it is clear that in the present regulations of our Fundamental Charter, we are not far from the regulations required to install in Chile the policy of a Cabinet and an accountable prime minister.

The effect of the electoral system on the government regime has not been the object of detailed analysis, nor are detailed proposals for change made in this work. However, the Chilean electoral statute was changed for the 2017 parliamentary elections, and a proportional system was introduced with quotas for women candidates plus the irruption of new political parties. It is very probable that this situation could arise in Chile because Articles 179 and 180 of the new Chilean electoral statute determine the districts of the Deputies and the circumscriptions of the Senators in a way that favors the big parties and coalitions, which means that probably in a high percentage of votes, a parliamentary representation similar to that of the present day will be reproduced in our country, in virtue of the binomial system.

Additionally, the decision of the electorate could imply that the reality of coexistence could not take place. Coexistence arises when, in the semi-presidential regime, the President governs with a head of government from a political party or coalition that is not his own.

Not discussed in these proposals are the ways in which representative or constitutional democracy can be complemented by mechanisms of participation or referendum, such as the political spaces open to marginal groups and those that do not feel represented by the system. These groups could play a greater political role through the introduction of participatory mechanisms, such as a referendum of annulment, or a referendum coming from the people's initiative that in truth can be very influential regarding the form of government, even though, in countries where these new forms of politics have had more success, they are used in a limited way, as a complement to the representation that continues to be a distinctive element of constitutional democracy, such as happens, for example, in Italy, where a quorum of 50 percent of the total electorate is required before they can be activated (see Article 75 of the Italian Constitution). Furthermore, these issues of the relationship between the structure of the Executive, the Legislative, and also the constitutional control bodies demand careful consideration that is beyond the scope of this work.

7.13   THE GENERAL CONCEPTION OF THE LAW AND ITS COMPARATIVE ANALYSIS

Concerning the conception of rights in the Fifth Republic, at this stage the right to property maintains a privileged place in comparison with other rights, in particular those that are defined as economic and social, which also maintain the libertarian or neoliberal character of all the rights. In today's Chile, an economic policy is applied which in its founding principles is basically neoliberal and which has blended together and expresses a series of very diverse ideas, such as Carl Schmitt's conception of fundamental rights, the *Estatuto de Garantías Constitucionales* [Statute of Constitutional Guarantees], which was required to be signed by President Salvador Allende in order for him to be elected in 1970, and the contribution of a "pontifical" doctrine, expressed, for example, in some of the work of Professor José Luis Cea Egaña. These very different elements that are examined in this section are part of the so-called general conception of rights that has a marked neoliberal ideological tint. In this conception, the notion of citizenship and of representation or political inclusion is inserted under the logic of a protected democracy, which has manifested itself in an electoral system that excludes minority political groups, in particular the Marxist left, which came to be called *izquierda extra parlamentaria* [non-parliamentary left]. Only a recent series of reforms and electoral results has incorporated this sector in the institutional political system.

In the Fifth Republic, a political form has been consolidated that is neoliberal in terms of dogma and the exercise of rights, and neo-presidentialist in terms of the definition of its constitutional fundamentals.

This is our paradoxical political and legal structure, born in 1990 and still valid at the time of writing this work.

However, the republican, democratic, and liberal constitutional conception, despite the difficulties of its survival in a predominantly neoliberal climate, surrounded by real hidden powers, is evident, at least partially, as Hernán Molina maintains. In his commentary, Molina strives to connect the text of the Fundamental Charter with our democratic constitutional tradition before 1973. He explains that the sources of our present Constitutional Law are similar to those indicated by Amunátegui in the 1950s. His contribution consists of the inclusion, within the conception of the sources of the Constitutional Law, of the rulings of the Comptroller General of the Republic, and of proposing a definition of Constitutional Law quite close to that of Amunátegui, as "the branch of public law that studies the set of legal regulations referring to the organization of the State, its government and the fundamental rights of the individual" (Molina 1993: 1).

What Molina considers innovation, in the sources of law in the present Constitution that inaugurates the Chilean Fifth Republic, are the international treaties referring to the fundamental rights, which are placed above all other sources, except the text of the Constitution itself and its interpretative laws. Another innovation detected by Molina relates to the law as the source of rights, especially in terms of its minimum legal domain expressed in Article 60. This means an important change in relation to the principle of legal supremacy that characterized the 1925 Constitution, because in the present Constitution, the regulation is the definitive word on the system of constitutional sources. With it, legislative neo-presidentialism is consolidated and it distances the law from the will of the people as expressed in Congress. Furthermore, Molina highlights how the new Constitution establishes a complex system of legislative "super majorities" in relation to determined matters, which include constitutional organizing statutes, qualified quorum statutes, amnesties, and reprieves.

A properly researched constitutional history of Chile cannot overlook that its characteristic intellectual activity consisted of pondering on and controlling politics from the perspective of the law. From 1925, this way of thinking about constitutional law changed because the main doctrinal theme became the discussion of property law and economic, social, and cultural rights. There can be observed, however, despite all these differences, a line of continuity in Chilean constitutionalism that seeks to give greater representation and to broaden suffrage. This means maintaining a compromise with constitutional equality as a political and legal principle, and also as a fundamental constitutional right.

From the previous explanations, the wealth of our constitutionalism before 1973 can be noted, and how this had been developing through the efforts of different people. Also, it can be understood how, as in other republican political experiences, our constitutional history has not only consisted of building the elements of the State, but has also witnessed a continuous tension between different fundamental rights.

For example, in the nineteenth century we find a way of discussion focused on equality that supposedly debated how to build Chilean citizenship. It also postulated the development of the rights of freedom of religion and conscience in the face of the prerogatives of the Catholic Church. This tension was partially solved with the separation of the Church from the State in 1925, and later, it was further resolved, until the end of the twentieth century, with the new statute on religious freedom enacted in 1999.

As for the form of these rights in Chile, constitutionalism is identified during the second half of the twentieth century with one of the most influential constitutional doctrinal structures, which we may call generically by the name "pontifical," because together with responding to the influence of papal encyclicals, it is based in the university institution that takes that name. This group of doctrines serves to justify the abrogation of civil and political rights during the military government, from 1973 to 1990; emphasizes the right to life among all rights, at the same time that it reduces the value of equality, and the importance of civil and political rights; and recognizes, in a precarious and partial form, some social economic rights, among which it emphasizes, in particular, the guarantee of freedom, such as non-interference by the State in private entrepreneurial activity. It also develops a conception of prioritizing local authority and of economic public order, which are confusing ideas that do not have a clear foundation in the text of the present Chilean Constitution (Ruiz-Tagle 2000b).

Alejandro Silva Bascuñán, distinguished professor at the Pontificia Universidad Católica de Chile, is the most outstanding exponent of this pontifical doctrine. When referring to the 1925 Constitution, Silva Bascuñán explains how this followed the predominant trend of classic constitutionalism in terms of the rights and duties of the individual. But at the same time, he postulates that the reality of these rights "arises from the nature of man," thus adopting a natural law conception of them (Silva Bascuñán 1963: 205). Silva Bascuñán also adopts the doctrinal nomenclature of constitutional rights and guarantees, and maintains that the 1925 Constitution refers to these guarantees not only to ensure them, but also to declare the limits of their reach or exercise, because they cannot be left to the mercy of a whim (ibid.: 206).

Professor Silva Bascuñán also maintains that the 1925 Constitution did not restrict the full use of freedom, but that it punished its exercise contrary to the law, and he sets out several criteria by which the Constitution restricts this. Among these, he highlights, in the first place, the need to prevent that the exercise of rights for some destroys or reduces the rights for others; secondly, what he calls the routing of the individual towards their full temporal and transcendent development; and third, the restrictions emanating from public order and common good (ibid.: 207). At the same time, he recognizes differences between constitutional rights that have constitutional limitation, those rights whose limitation is legal in nature, and those that are limited according to the Constitution in the interests of public order or good practices (ibid.: 207–208). Finally, he maintains the importance of legal resources in relation to these rights and he classifies them into freedoms and equalities, admitting that there are rights, such as that of association, which are, by nature, social in character (ibid.: 209).

Alejandro Silva Bascuñán, in his most comprehensive work, uses a terminology that includes the notion of individual rights and political rights, and he also adopts the classification of freedoms and equalities to reaffirm his natural rights posture and make it stretch to include the notion of human rights. More recently, Silva Bascuñán recognized in human rights the natural, inherent, individual, subjective, universal, and abstract characteristics, and added that States not only commit themselves to ensure these rights, but also to promote them (Silva Bascuñán 1997: 139–140, 153–155). In any case, Silva Bascuñán's position is highly discursive. Its intuitive and all-embracing character refers, if anything, to the justification of its limitations or restrictions on rights and to the homogeneous application of the ideas proposed in relation to all sorts of constitutional procedures.

On the other hand, the constitutional doctrine of José Luis Cea Egaña, expressed in his work *Tratado de la Constitución de 1980* [Treatise on the 1980 Constitution], which was published in 1988, represents another comprehensive proposal of understanding for our Constitution, in what we could call the pre-constitutional period – that is, before the return to democracy. Some of its ideas retained a substantial part of its influence, many years after 1990, in several versions published by

Professor Cea Egaña, such as the hierarchy of rights explained in *El sistema constitucional de Chile. Síntesis crítica* [The Chilean Constitutional System: Critical Synthesis] that was published in 1999 (Cea Egaña 1999: 171–175). Professor Cea Egaña's effort has to be recognized – to give coherence to the regulations of a Constitution that was not applied during a very extensive period of its validity, and which subsisted as a dead letter during the dictatorship, coerced by transitory provisions. His interpretation of the 1980 constitutional text had a decisive influence during the last two decades of the twentieth century. In the original version of his work, published in 1988, Cea Egaña did not criticize directly the neo-liberal conception of rights, nor the excessive neo-presidentialism with regard to its organic part, nor, in its conception, its distancing from the democratic and liberal republican development that Chilean constitutional endeavors had attained before 1973. As a sample of what José Luis Cea Egaña says in his work *Tratado de la Constitución de 1980*:

> The values that I will outline and that model the new Constitution are not those of the liberal individualism of the nineteenth century; neither are they those of provident and benevolent neoliberalism; nor are they, finally, those of democratic socialism or of another sort. On the contrary, gathered together in the first nine articles a categoric position is taken regarding the person, society, and the State which is congruent with the civilization, Western and in particular Hispanic, that we have inherited.
>
> (Cea Egaña 1988: 40)

These ideas, contained in the principal treaty of Chilean Constitutional Law, represent the going astray of constitutionalism in Chile at the end of the twentieth and beginning of the twenty-first century. When conceiving the Constitution as a unique phenomenon, Cea Egaña rejects its liberal, democratic, and republican roots. How could we think of a Western Hispanic culture outside the liberal or republican contribution? How could the present Constitution in Chile be an isolated case of legal or political principles? The foregoing quotation encapsulates what José Luis Cea Egaña maintains, by considering as possible and coherent a democratic constitutional system that is characterized by the anti-constitutional idea of a protected democracy (Cea Egaña 1988: 6). More recently, Professor Cea Egaña has stated that the original constitutionalism of 1980 is maintained in its main features, despite the innumerable constitutional reforms that culminated in 2005 (Cea Egaña 2005: 92).

It is important to recognize that José Luis Cea Egaña knew how to oppose the extreme demands of the supporters of the pontifical doctrines, and he was the only law professor at the Pontificia Universidad Católica de Chile who refused to sign the shameful *Declaración* [Declaration] of the academics that in 1980 attributed the constituent power to the *Junta de Gobierno*. Also, he dared to publish articles against the doctrines of protected democracy in the pontifical institution's *Law Review*. In his more recent work, Professor Cea Egaña has keenly criticized the organic structure of the present Constitution – that is, its authoritarian, neo-presidentialist features – but until now he has maintained his support and uncritical stance with regard to the neoliberal position that the doctrinal part contains in its formulation and guarantee of fundamental rights.

In any case, concerning the content and form of the rights in the Constitution of the Fifth Republic, we must recognize a collective responsibility. This is reflected in the content of some chapters of the Constitution – for example, the chapter on constitutional rights, which is the third chapter of the Constitutional text approved by Pinochet. This part of the Constitution was inspired by some ideas of Carl Schmitt and Friedrich A. Hayek, but it also collected ideas from the *Estatuto de Garantías* [Statute of Constitutional Guarantees] imposed on Salvador Allende by the Christian Democratic Party in the 1970 presidential election. The Statute of Constitutional Guarantees has a stronger structural influence, in the section regarding rights in the 1980 constitutional text, than the influence of either Schmitt or Hayek. This is the reason it has been so difficult to achieve a reform to this part of our Fundamental Charter.

Furthermore, it is important to recognize that from the doctrinal point of view, from the 1990s in Chile, constitutional rights have been conceived in the style of Hans Kelsen because they have been thought of in the form of a partial reductionism that only perceives them as a national positive right or as the counterpart of an obligation imposed on the public authorities (Kelsen 1995: 138–200). The Chilean constitutional doctrine has followed Kelsen's idea of the reconversion of fundamental rights into duties, which, paradoxically, has coexisted with postures that revive classical natural law. Influenced by John Finnis, there are also in our country certain ways of thinking about rights that are similar to what Gregorio Peces Barba has called improper *jus* naturalism, and also in authors of the closest tradition to new forms of positivism, such as Ronald Dworkin and Carlos Nino (Peces Barba 1999: 46, 49).

All these ideas have coexisted with a partial negation of the neoliberal type that is close to the ideas of Friedrich A. Hayek (Hayek 1975: 284–304), and which assigns a greater value to the rights of freedom and autonomy, rejecting in this way State interference in other rights that have a social or political character, such as economic, social, and cultural rights and those linked to the idea of citizenship.

In terms of the Catholic way of thinking that was most influential in Chile during the twentieth century, the thought process that prevailed was closer to the liberal ideas of Locke than to a total rejection of the subjective rights that the traditionalist realism of Michel Villey postulates (Villey 1976: 151–153, 242–244). This predominant conservative thought did not consist of a total negation of rights, but has served instead to impose an intuitive method of constitutional argument that rests on encyclicals and other Catholic documents, and which sometimes avoids legal argumentation and the contributions of comparative law (Ruiz-Tagle 2001b).

The doctrine has debated the way in which the Chilean Constitution has been the source of direct application by the political and legal authorities to solve conflicts of all sorts, and how its content aims to establish the recognition of certain values in its regulations and to express them in our legal system with a character of supremacy. However, in this effort, the constitutional values of dignity, equality, freedom, and democracy compete in our Constitution with doctrines of dubious democratic legitimacy, such as the doctrine of national security, subsidiarity, or the economic and public good order, which are constitutional doctrines that are based on questionable precepts and that express a confusing, discretional, and argumentative laxity (Ruiz-Tagle 2001a).

Today, Chile requires a new way of thinking about fundamental rights that must also be framed in a special theory of the rights of equality and freedom, among others. We also need to integrate in Chile the conception of the *Estado Social y Democrático de Derecho* [Social and Democratic State within the rule of law], so popular in European legal doctrine (Spanish, Italian, French, and German), to make real the importance of the right of equality and State intervention in social matters, until a more preponderant role than that which the constitutional doctrine now fulfills is attained. From the above can be deduced the importance of legal drafting and interpretation.

A major disorientation has arisen in seeking these legal criteria, and therefore, the intensive use of comparative law and the need to know about the previous endeavors that characterized Chilean constitutionalism before 1973 seem appropriate. In many of these previous endeavors, even though they might have been sporadic, the right to constitutional equality occupied a principal place (Ruiz-Tagle 2001b).

The introduction of the doctrinal status of fundamental rights in Chilean law that developed gradually from 1990 became entirely consolidated around 1997, with the ruling by the Inter-American Court of Human Rights regarding the film *The Last Temptation of Christ* by the director Martin Scorsese. In this case, the State of Chile was condemned for applying constitutional regulations on cinematographic censorship (Article 19 No. 12 of the Constitution) that were contradictory to Article 13 of the American Convention on Human Rights, Pact of San José, to which Chile was signatory. The condemnation meant approving a constitutional reform that would remove the censorship until it was compatible with Article 13 of the Convention.

Also it finished with the idea of the superiority of the Constitution over treaties on human rights, imposing a new vision of Article 5 and installing the notion of "constitutional bloc," which means interpreting the rights in the Constitution in relation to or in interface with human rights, which is the central idea of fundamental rights. This notion means considering our constitutional history and comparative law in the context of Latin American law (Garzón Valdés 1993c: 201–234; and for the Chilean case, Ruiz-Tagle 2001b). It also means treating our constitutional law as a continuous competition between different conceptions, among which the following are emphasized: (1) a natural law conception that in its main versions is conservative; (2) a liberal-republican democratic tradition; and (3) a set of social democratic or socialist ideas. These three conceptions have competed amongst themselves throughout our history, in order to express, in its best version, the principles and regulations of the Fundamental Charter. This competition arises in a similar way to how it happens in comparative law, for example in Germany (Ruiz-Tagle 2001c: 255–275).

It is our opinion that the catalog of rights in the Chilean Constitution must be interpreted from a republican, democratic, and liberal perspective. This interpretation is possible because the constitutional text ensures the rights of every person, and despite not protecting in the same way the right to participation or the right to social benefits, it is based on the principal separation of equalities and freedoms. However, this classification is not fixed, but provisional, and is only illustrative in character, because the relationship between the rights is determined by each particular case. In fact, a fixed classification should not exist, nor a hierarchy or priority among the fundamental rights. Additionally, a given right can be expressed in the form of a freedom or an equality, as, for example, the right to free (and equal) economic initiative enshrined in Article 19 No. 21 of the Chilean Constitution (Ruiz-Tagle 2000b).

In the republican conception that we propose as best-suited for the present Chilean Constitution, any classification of rights must be broad and flexible, and must avoid being restrictive; it must include and be integrated with the right to suffrage, economic and social rights, and those recognized in international law. At the same time, any form of classification must be linked to the values of freedom, equality, dignity, and democracy. Otherwise the classification fails. For example, the classifications that intend to isolate the right to life, health, or the environment, or any other right, from the values of freedom, equality, dignity, or democracy, run the risk of losing the support of the values of constitutionalism. The fundamental rights exceed the provisions of Article 19 of the present Political Constitution, and none of its classifications can be restrictive or complete enumerations, because they are, by definition, provisional, since they do not make reference to the constitutional acts that protect the rights in each particular case and do not include references to international treaties (Correa and Ruiz-Tagle 2010: 176–178).

It is not surprising that, as we have mentioned, another feature of the Chilean constitutional doctrine is that property occupies a principal place and that the legal guarantee of socio-economic rights is limited. The privileged status of property in Chile is not only maintained by the force of the original draft, which was embodied in the constitutional text ratified by the dictatorship. It can also be explained because the doctrine of Chilean public law has still not been able to organize a systematic and coherent account of the abundant jurisprudence that already exists in our country in matters of dignity, equality, freedom, and democracy.

In relation to the limits set for economic and social rights, the Chilean Constitution is contradictory because it confirms the essential content of all the rights, yet at the same time it decrees that some of them do not have the same judicial protection or legal guarantee. The essential content of rights in Chile has been identified with a restricted conception of subjective rights, but the direct effectiveness of the

fundamental rights does not seem to be limited. The study of fundamental rights and duties in Chile from the democratic and liberal
perspective assumes consciousness of the convertibility of the rights,
that is to say, that the social and economic rights to health, education,
or work claim to be "converted" forms of property, and this "convertibility" is more than a simple "proprietarization." It also assumes taking
into account the infinite possible combinations of rights, and having in
the forefront the constitutional acts in which their conflicts present
themselves. A new elucidation of the fundamental rights from this
republican point of view that we propose must address the present
problems that are emerging and which are relevant to Chile and to
the world, such as those arising from terrorism and poverty.

When all is said and done, all the Chilean constitutional texts, be it
1811, 1818, 1822, 1823, 1828, 1833, or 1925, including, of course, the
present text, contain an explicit recognition of rights and at least make
references to citizenship or nationality. Additionally, a large part of the
Chilean political debate has referred to the application of rights and
constitutional guarantees. This happens, as was mentioned, with the
recognition of equality as a constitutional right in accessing public
responsibilities and office, and with the controversies in the area of
religious freedom and suffrage in the nineteenth century; with the
political and constitutional debate, and deliberation regarding ownership of land, mines, banks, telecommunications, natural resources, and
industry in the twentieth century; and with the violation of human
rights and the rights of recognition of privacy and honor, and the
guarantee of social and economic rights at the end of the twentieth
and beginning of the twenty-first century.

The constitutional and political notion of citizenship and the priority that should be recognized in relation to the notion of nationality is
also part of a democratic and liberal vision of fundamental rights that
has been absent from Chilean constitutional law since 1990.
Citizenship has been defined as equality of access to public office and
the exercise of the right to suffrage in conditions of political equality;
and nationality as the link between the person and the State. The
Chilean Constitution seems to embody a separation between the fundamental rights of equality and freedom and citizenship, an idea which
formed the base on which the Nazi jurist Carl Schmitt built his non-
democratic conception of rights when he presented his principle of
distribution. The *Schmittian* distribution principle means assigning
a priority to individual rights over other rights, and assumes giving

more importance to such rights as property, religious freedom, and freedom of expression, over political, economic, and social rights. It consists of maintaining that certain fundamental rights outweigh others in absolute terms (Schmitt 1982: 164–185). On the contrary, unlike the Schmittian way of thinking, a democratic liberal vision must postulate that the fundamental rights of citizenship, political rights, and social and economic rights are as important as individual rights, such as property, religious freedom, or the right to life.

Another consequence of the biased way of thinking about the constitutional law from 1990 to date has been to devalue the right to constitutional equality in Chile, to separate doctrinally the right to property from the economic and social rights, and to disassociate Chilean constitutional rights from the substantive and procedural commitments that our country has acquired through international treaties. Table 7.2 is a summary of the catalogs of rights in the main Chilean Constitutions: the 1833 Fundamental Charter (reformed from 1828) and the 1925 Constitution, in its comparison with the main human rights treaties, which include the 1948 Universal Declaration of Human Rights, the Pact of San José, Costa Rica, the International Covenant on Civil and Political Rights, and the International Covenant on Economic, Social and Cultural Rights.

When observing Table 7.2 and studying at first approach and in comparative form the summary of rights contained in the 1925 Constitution, it can be concluded that they are re-formulations or specifications of those already contained in the 1833 Constitution. It is true that during the validity of the 1833 Constitution, the State's official religion, according to the constitutional regulations, was the Catholic faith, but some interpretative statutory laws were adopted, and others of a secular nature related to cemeteries, civil registry, and education, by which these provisions gradually lost their validity. But this change does not allow us to argue that we have to recognize the constitutional regulations adopted at the beginning of the twentieth century as completely original, in their relation to those existing in Chile during the nineteenth century. For example, together with the separation of the Catholic Church from the State, which took place during the 1925 Constitution, a specification of some new rights by way of its form of recognition in Chile was generated. Other rights were added, together with the development of the social issue and the

TABLE 7.2 Fundamental rights in the 1833 and 1925 Constitution and the Declaration of Human Rights and other treaties

1833 Constitution (1828 reform)	1925 Constitution	1948 Universal Declaration of Human Rights	Pact of San José, Costa Rica	International Covenant on Civil and Political Rights	International Covenant on Economic, Social and Cultural Rights
Equality before the law	Equality before the law	Right to life, freedom and security of the person	Right to be recognized as a legal personality	Right of the people to free political, economic, social, and cultural determination	Right of the people to a free political, economic, social, and cultural determination
Admission to all public offices and functions	Freedom of conscience and to exercise any religious cult	Prohibition of slavery	Every person has the right to have his physical, mental, and moral integrity respected	Right to life	Right of men and women to enjoy the same
Equal distribution of taxes and levies	Freedom to declare opinions, without previous censorship	Prohibition of torture	Prohibition of torture	Prohibition of torture	economic, social, and cultural rights of the pact
Freedom to remain in any part of the Republic	Right to assembly without	Right to be recognized as legal personality	Prohibition of slavery	Prohibition of slavery	Prohibition of reducing or restricting in any
Inviolability of property		Right to equality of protection before the law		Right to freedom and personal security	

Right to assembly without previous authorization	previous authorization	Right to effective recourse to the national and competent courts	Right to freedom and personal security	Right to indemnity for legal error	way the fundamental human rights recognized or valid in a country by virtue of the law,
Right to petition	Right to petition	Right to be heard publicly by an independent tribunal	Right to be heard by a competent judge or tribunal	Prohibition of imprisonment for not fulfilling contractual obligations	conventions, regulations, or traditions, with the pretext that the present pact does not
Freedom of education	Freedom of education	Presumption of innocence	Presumption of innocence	Right of movement and to choose residence freely within the territory of a State	recognize them or recognizes them to a lesser degree
Legality of judgment	Equal admissions to all public offices and functions	Right to private life	Right to legal defense	Right to leave a country freely	Right to work
Freedom to publish opinions	Equal distribution of taxes and levies	Inviolability of home and correspondence	Right to appeal against the ruling of a judge	Equality before the tribunals and courts of justice	Right of any person to have an opportunity to earn a living through work
Personal freedom	Inviolability of property	Right to dignity and reputation	Right to indemnity for legal error	Right to be publicly heard by a competent,	
Prohibition of torture	Exclusive ownership of all discovery or production	Right to free movement and to choice of	Right to respect for honor and recognition of dignity		
Inviolability of the home	Inviolability of the home				
Inviolability of epistolary correspondence	Inviolability of correspondence				

TABLE 7.2 (cont.)

1833 Constitution (1828 reform)	1925 Constitution	1948 Universal Declaration of Human Rights	Pact of San José, Costa Rica	International Covenant on Civil and Political Rights	International Covenant on Economic, Social and Cultural Rights
Freedom of work and enterprise Intellectual property	Protection of work, industry, social security, health, and hygiene Freedom to remain in any part of the Republic Legality of judgment	residence in the territory of a State Right to travel to any part of the country Right of asylum Right to nationality, right to get married and to establish a family Right to protection of family Right to individual and	Right to protection of dignity against arbitrary or abusive interference in private life, family, home, or correspondence Right to freedom of conscience and religion Freedom of thought and expression Right to assemble	independent, and impartial tribunal established by law Right to presumption of innocence of any person accused of committing an offense Right to due process Right not to be condemned for acts or omissions that at the moment of	freely chosen or accepted Right to enjoy just and favorable working conditions Right to a fair wage and equal remuneration for work of equal value Right to safe and healthy working conditions Right to rest, leisure, and reasonable

collective property Right to freedom of thought, conscience, and religion Right to free opinion and expression Right to freedom to peaceful assembly and association	peacefully and without arms Right to rectification of inaccurate or injurious information Right to free association Right to contract matrimony and to establish a family Right to your own name	commitment were not an offense according to national or international law Right to be recognized as a legal personality Prohibition of arbitrary or illegal interference in the dignity of people Right to legal protection from such attacks Freedom of thought, conscience, and religion	limitations of working hours and periodic holidays with pay, as well as pay for public holidays Right to found trade unions Right to strike Right to social security and social insurance Right to protection of family Right to protection of the mother during a reasonable time before and after childbirth Right to protective measures for children and young people

importance that work and industry acquired in Chilean society at the beginning of the twentieth century. Ultimately, the rights whose formulation was more innovative, and which were incorporated following the 1925 Fundamental Charter, were as follows:

- Freedom of conscience and the exercise of any religious cult, which already existed since 1865, but which was now linked to the separation between Church and State.
- Protection of work, industry, and social security.

If we concentrate the analysis on the comparison of the present Constitution with those that preceded it, we can see that numerous rights existed that we can catalog as new, in relation to those that were enshrined before:

- Right to life
- Right to legal defense
- Protection of public and private life
- Equal protection of the law in the exercise of rights
- Right not to be judged by special commissions
- Right to due process
- Legal definition of offenses in criminal law
- Right to live in an environment free from contamination
- Right to protection of family
- Freedom of affiliation to any health system
- Right to education
- Political pluralism
- Right to social security
- Right to belong to a trade union
- Right to property in the broad form of Article 19 Nos. 23, 24, 25
- Guarantee of non-assignment of the rights, in their essence, of Article 19 No. 26
- Freedom of association that is restricted in political and trade union matters, and broad in civil affairs.

The rights that appear as new in the present Constitution relative to the 1925 Charter conform, in their majority, to the so-called economic and social rights recognized and embodied in the positive law of post-Second World War constitutionalism. However, these economic and social rights also have a point of contact with the dispositions of the 1925 Constitution, as follows:

212

- The right to life and physical and psychological integrity is linked to the dispositions of the 1925 Constitution that guarantee personal freedom and security.
- The constitutional principles and regulations that give shape to procedural and criminal or penal institutions have a point of contact with the provisions of Article 10 No. 15 and Articles 11–20 inclusive in the 1925 Constitution, which regulate these same matters in a similar way.
- The guarantee to political pluralism is reflected in the 1925 Constitution, with the freedom to express any kind of opinion, freedom of thought, and conscience.
- The right to live in an environment free from contamination is a form of equality.
- The right to education goes in step with academic freedom.
- The guarantee of the non-encumbrance of rights in its essence is new; there are no precedents in Chilean constitutionalism before this.
- The right to social security has a point of contact in the protection of social welfare.
- The right to protection of health is also linked with the protection of public health that was recognized in Article 10 No. 14 of the 1925 Fundamental Charter.
- The right to free initiative in economic terms, Article 19 No. 21, rubs shoulders with the so-called freedom of work in the 1925 Constitution, but not so its special form of guarantee, which is the denominated judicial action or suit for economic protection.
- The right to compensation due to expropriation crosses paths with the previous constitutional regulations, which controlled the subsystem of property law.

Additionally, from analysis of Table 7.2, it can be concluded that a republican conception adapted to Chile has to study the fundamental rights, applying the more integrative notion of a constitutional bloc, an idea that has its origin in France and that can be used to explain the relationship between the Constitutions and the constitutional regulations that are contained in other documents, such as the 1789 Declaration of the Rights of Man and of the Citizen (Ruiz-Tagle 2001b). This notion can be applied in Chile as a true rule of recognition that serves us to identify the constitutional subsystem of fundamental rights. According to the more up-to-date notion of constitutional bloc, the existence of a legal subsystem of fundamental rights can be constructed through a process of interpretation of the Constitution, which is made up of the Chilean constitutional regulations which refer to them. These regulations are found in several chapters of the Fundamental Charter, not only in chapter three on constitutional rights and duties, but also in the international conventions that refer to human rights.

The constitutional regulations constitute a bloc, together with the regulations and principles of human rights contained in the international conventions, such as the Universal Declaration of Human Rights, the International Covenant on Civil and Political Rights, the American Convention on Human Rights, Pact of San José, Costa Rica, the Convention against Torture and Other Cruel, Inhuman or Degrading Treatment or Punishment, the Geneva Conventions regarding the treatment of Prisoners and on Genocide, and the Convention on the Elimination of all Forms of Discrimination against Women, among others. This way of understanding the fundamental rights must also consider its parliamentary and administrative regulation, and its legal application in the context of the jurisprudential and doctrinal development that began in Chile in 1990, in the constitutional government.

If we analyze from this broader perspective the content of the constitutional provisions referring to fundamental rights, we find that the verbs which are most frequently used to refer to them are: to recognize, guarantee, ensure, protect, promote, vindicate, respect, limit, restrict, suspend, violate, and sanction. It is a complex and enormous range of prohibitions and mandates that are contained in constitutional regulations and principles.

To better illustrate this new way of thinking of the fundamental rights in a constitutional bloc, it is also useful to carry out a comparison of the catalogs of rights that have been shaping Chilean law, understood as a combination of constitutional and human rights. There are rights that do not seem to have a point of contact with their predecessors; however, the study of the constitutional doctrine, of practices and national and international jurisprudence leads us to conclude that there are very significant relationships, as can be seen in Table 7.2, which contains the summary of rights.

That is why the analysis proposed allows us to maintain that practically all our constitutional regulations referring to matters linked to fundamental rights have a point of connection that engages with our previous constitutional dogma, which does not mean that there have not been important deviations in the present constitutional text. This is a central idea in the republican conception of rights that, furthermore, is linked to the possibility of having a critical scrutiny of our dogma from a comparative point of view.

For example, in the scrutiny inspired by the comparative constitutional law that is proposed for Chile, the fundamental right to suffrage, access to public office, and equality of citizenship and nationality must be thought of as linked to the other fundamental rights, because a new republican vision of rights must propose to liberate suffrage from most of the limitations of the present Chilean constitutional provisions, such as those of Article 16 No. 2 of the Political Constitution which has already been mentioned, and because suffrage, citizenship, and nationality are not institutions separated from the other fundamental rights. Suffrage must be as important as property in a society like that of Chile, where there is so much inequality.

Furthermore, it is incumbent also to recognize that the catalog of rights in Chile has certain progressive elements, such as the right to the environment and the limit of sovereignty established by virtue of the human rights recognized by international treaties according to Article 5 of the Fundamental Charter. This new vision of fundamental rights must assume the criticism of the confusions that the doctrinaire categories of subsidiarity and economic public order can give rise to, and accept substitution in the light of the primacy of the values of constitutional equality and freedom (Ruiz-Tagle 2000b).

Meanwhile, the ideas of Louis Favoreau can also serve as inspiration: he distinguishes fundamental guarantees, or those related to the content of fundamental rights – which are the direct application of the Constitution, the legal reserve, the guarantee of the essence of the rights and non-retroactivity, the exceptional character of restrictions and strict mechanisms of constitutional reform – from jurisdictional guarantees, which include abstract and concrete control, specialized legal control, and the guarantees assured by ordinary justice (Favoreau et al. 1998: 795–802). All these ideas regarding the different modalities assumed by the guarantees of the fundamental rights can be used to arrange and better understand Chilean public law, and these same explanations can be used by our doctrine and jurisprudence to understand, interpret, and better apply the subsystem of our fundamental rights.

Peces Barba, with respect to the study of the kinds of guarantee of rights, distinguishes general and specific guarantees, and among the latter he lists guarantees of development, control, and inspection, of regulation and interpretation (this, according to Peces Barba, has a universal criterion emanating from the 1948 Universal Declaration), guarantees internal to the right or with respect to its essential content, ordinary and special or constitutional legal guarantees. He also argues that the exclusivity and unity of the jurisdiction gives an efficient condition for the protection of fundamental rights and specifies the guarantees of fundamental rights that can arise in the process. Professor Peces Barba adds international guarantees to the previous analysis, among which he distinguishes those universal in nature that emanate from the 1948 Declaration and the guarantees that have emerged at regional level (Peces Barba 1999: 547–568; Ruiz-Tagle 2003).

Peces Barba's ideas regarding international guarantees of the fundamental rights are also applicable in our country which has integrated progressively with the system of international guarantees of fundamental rights. This is why it should reconfirm its regional links with the Inter-American system, which compared with the European has some of the particular features that we have mentioned, such as its special protection of freedom of expression and of the right to asylum.

Meanwhile, in relation to the interpretation of the fundamental rights, we can say that this process does not consist of a single right answer for each case, because the constitutional investigation must examine more than one pro-democratic general criterion of interpretation, as must be assumed in an open society. It must also contribute to the development and promotion of the values of dignity, equality, and freedom, together with respect for the principle of legality in a broad and inclusive way. In the same way, the constitutional interpretation of fundamental rights is linked to the theme of the defense of the essential content and of the limits to the fundamental rights that can be imposed by the legislature, questions that generate problems of interpretation. For example, the subject of limits includes the study of the actual assumptions about fundamental rights and the legal limits to the same, as Haberle has proposed regarding this issue (Peces Barba 1999: 588).

We must also consider the doctrine of "preferred rights," or "preferred positions," that recognizes the importance for a given case of weighing up a fundamental right, in relation to another, and this way of

216

arguing about rights in a given case must also be considered when thinking about the Chilean legal subsystem, because the conflicts that can appear in relation to the fundamental rights in Chile must be solved by weighing things up. The deliberation consists, in a way, of considering the case and the affected rights in an optimal and proportional way that should be suitable and necessary. Obviously it means the abandonment of any intuitive and absolute conception of hierarchy among these rights. To better understand the Chilean subsystem of fundamental rights, it is also worth keeping in mind, as in North American law, that the solution to conflicts and the interpretation of fundamental rights is linked mainly to the idea of judicial control of lawmaking. So, different criteria have been developed in terms of identifying fundamental rights. These consist of the application of a test of scrutiny, either strict, intermediate, or of rationality that, together with an idea of proportionality, serves to determine if such a description is adequate and compatible with the Constitution (Chemerinsky 2001: 695–701; Garvey et al. 1999: 608–656). This way of thinking about rights might seem, in principle, hard to apply in Chile. However, what seems to be most difficult to accept is that all this kind of reasoning is applied by judges to rights that are not listed in the constitutional text, as happened with the recognition of the right to privacy in the USA.

Additionally, for the purpose of looking at our system of rights from the comparative point of view, it is appropriate to take into account that the social function is conceived and preached as a characteristic of all the rights, and not only of property, as has been stipulated in Chile.

Ultimately, it is important to consider that the legal subsystem of Chilean fundamental rights is part of a greater set, formed by a series of subsystems that coexist in time in each one of the national legal systems, and that get feedback from each other, and also from the development that the regional and international systems of human rights achieve.

7.14   THE CHILEAN DOCTRINES REGARDING THE RIGHT TO PROPERTY

In contrast with the Chilean republican tradition, there is installed in the present Constitution, in a hypertrophied way, a constitutional subsystem of the property right, which to a certain extent alters Chilean republican constitutional law, and which goes back to 1812.

217

The 1980 constitutional text, which emerges from documents that come from the Commission appointed by the military dictatorship, contains an extensive and specific regulation on property that has stayed unaltered until now (Peñailillo 2006: 11–19, 81–92). Article 19 No. 24 section 1 expresses:

> The Constitution guarantees to every person: The right of property in its varied forms over every kind of tangible and intangible assets.

In this regard, the protection of the private property right has been recognized in the constitutional text in its broadest sense, embracing both tangible and intangible assets. In the Constitution, the concept of right of property was embodied as such, not just ownership exclusive of subjective rights. From the history of the aforementioned article, it can be deduced that the authors wanted to give protection to the property right in the broadest possible way. As Professor José Luis Cea Egaña presents it:

> This is therefore a declaration of the recognition of private property acquired as an individual, a family, a cooperative, a community, or in any other form, to all of which an effective protection will be given. This right can benefit any kind of assets: tangible, movable, or immovable; intangibles, whether they are legal or personal interests. It is all the same whether the assets are solely for private use or for production and commerce.
>
> (Cea Egaña 1988: 189)

Despite the details of the Chilean constitutional regulation, the study of ownership adopts a kind of private, minimalistic, and weak dogma, as is expressed in the work by Abraham Kiverstein (1993), *Síntesis del derecho civil* [Synthesis of Civil Law], which was used as study material in the 1980s and 1990s, and which still serves as a guide for law students. Professor Hernán Corral has criticized this idea because, in his opinion, the "minimalistic" doctrine of the private property right cannot be identified with the summary for students produced by Abraham Kiverstein: Corral claims that this identification is not serious because Kiverstein is not recognized as representative of civil doctrine in this area.

However, despite Professor Hernán Corral being right about the lack of recognition attributed to the work of Kiverstein in the latest Chilean civil doctrine, it could be noted that in this last work a minimalistic interpretation of property is used which only refers to the Civil Code in

218

a simplified edition. Therefore, I believe that it is convenient to refer to its importance to teaching, or better still to learning about property in Chile, which contrasts with the importance and complexity of our constitutional regulation on the same topic.

In contrast with this privatist conception of property, the work of Lautaro Ríos can be quoted regarding its social function, which is a serious doctrinal attempt to understand the regulations of the present Constitution and the scope of this particular conception, as a form of limitation of domain in the constitutional sense (Ríos 1987: 57–73). To this work are added the originalist reflections of Enrique Evans regarding the diversity of opinions related to property by the lawyers commissioned during the dictatorship to draft the 1980 constitutional text (Evans 1999: 213–231). Mention should also be made, for their conceptual wealth, to the studies of Alejandro Guzmán and Enrique Brahm regarding the scope of an intangible entity in Article 19 No. 24 of the Fundamental Charter, and the subsequent commentary of Hernán Corral referring to the first of these (Guzmán Brito 1995: 117–256, 235–256; Brahm 1999–2000: 335–349; Corral 1996: 13–18). Also very valuable are the works of Eduardo Aldunate and Eduardo Cordero, in which they argue for the existence of a multiplicity of forms of property in Chile, identify some of the constitutional regulations of ownership, and study the link between social function and its essential content (Aldunate 2008: 256–264; Cordero 2008).

However, in none of these valuable studies, nor in any other Chilean doctrinal work have I found references that are not prejudiced regarding the multiform constitutional subsystem of the public and private property right that exists in the present Constitution in Chile. There are many studies dedicated to describing, in particular, each of the specific regulations of the Chilean Fundamental Charter referring to property. But except for the notable exception of the works of Daniel Peñailillo, I have not found anyone who has visualized Chilean constitutional property as a subsystem of regulations and principles. Here is where the main part of my proposal rests, but before explaining it, we must revise what Daniel Peñailillo has to say about this issue.

Daniel Peñailillo, in his work *Los bienes. La propiedad y otros derechos reales* [Assets: Property and Other Legal Rights], has represented the property right at constitutional level as a subsystem composed of many rules and principles. That is why I believe that he is a true follower of the proposal of Alessandri Rodríguez and Somarriva, which he exposes in an up-to-date and rigorous way.

Peñailillo treats systematically the concept, evolution, and structure of property and, in particular, he declares his guiding principles, among which he includes equity in sharing and development, and in relation to the Chilean constitutional basis, he highlights its essential characteristics of protection; social function, legal reserve, restrictions, deprivations and expropriations; the deprivation or expropriation without compensation and its consequence; natural and cultural preservation; territorial planning, land use, subdivision of property and edification; the so-called forms of ownership and co-ownership. All the above serves as a prior declaratory index of his explanations regarding property right (Peñailillo 2006: 11–19, 81–128). In his work he has stated as a general preface to his conception:

> Taking into account the last decades, maybe only a generalization can be put forward: of a very liberal conception of ownership which gives the most far-reaching faculties to the owner for the exercise of this right, where there has been evolution in the sense of imposing restrictions and charges with the objective that this exercise may benefit, not only the owner, but also the community, a trend that culminates in the decision to reserve for the ownership of the community, represented by the State, certain assets of fundamental importance to the life of the nation. But such a trend has never been free of objections, at least towards the degree of its intensity.
>
> (Peñailillo 2006: 75)

Indeed, Peñailillo has proposed the doctrinal bases of a subsystem of constitutional property that combines in a reasonable way private and public property, a proposal with which we certainly agree. Where we cannot agree with Professor Peñailillo is with his idea of basing his theory on the expanded use of the concept of property in the *Código Civil* [Civil Code] because, in our view, the Constitution does not define a concept of property and, in truth, constitutional concepts outrank concepts of the regulation of private law. In support of his thesis, Peñailillo quotes the work of Juan Andrés Varas: "the reference to the recently mentioned (definition) of the (Civil) Code seems natural, in particular considering its aforementioned flexibility, which accommodates it (without obstacle) to the weighty precepts of the Constitution" (ibid.: 86–87). The idea of completing the constitutional concept of property with the definition of ownership from the Civil Code is, in my opinion, mistaken, because the Fundamental Charter contains principles and regulations that outweigh the private sphere and, indeed, on certain issues they contradict it, as will be shown in this section.

Likewise, Daniel Peñailillo's doctrinal proposal includes Nos. 21–25 of the same Article 19 of the Constitution as part of the most relevant regulations in reference to property. However, this does not explain directly the link between property and the regulations contained in Article 19 Nos. 21 and 22, which Peñailillo himself has included as part of such subsystem (ibid.: 76). At the same time, even if Daniel Peñailillo makes reference to No. 26 in respect of the essential content of the property right, he does not include it when detailing the regulations which make up what he calls the constitutional basis of property.

Unlike Professor Peñailillo's proposal, it is our view that the constitutional subsystem of property in Chile refers to and must embrace, in particular, the regulations of Article 19 Nos. 23–26 inclusive.

Despite these differences, it is true that Professor Peñailillo has expounded with reason on the meaning of the four legal grounds on which the social function may be imposed, which, because they are set down in such general terms, make their restricting character lose all relevance. Also, he explains very precisely the concept of total or partial deprivation of property that is justified only on two constitutional grounds, together with the necessary condition imposed by the constitutional imperative of legal reserve and its resulting compensation (ibid.: 90–91). In terms of the idea of restrictions (limitations) and duties (obligations), Daniel Peñailillo has maintained that these can affect the content of the right of private property as long as it respects the essence of the right; alternatively, they can affect certain attributes or some of the characteristics of ownership. Regarding these complex issues, Peñailillo has stated with great precision regarding the imposition of restrictions and duties: "In a positive way they materialize in regulations on several matters. Among us, they are distributed all over the Civil Code and in countless special laws, both in productive sectors as in residential; both in industrial as in agricultural, mining, and urban sectors" (ibid.: 91–92).

As already mentioned, in the Fundamental Charter of the Chilean Fifth Republic, beginning in 1990 and which continues today, particularly in Article 19 Nos. 23–26 inclusive, are concentrated the main regulations that comprise, in my opinion, the subsystem of property in Chile. It is provided, for example, that access to property will be limited according to the principle of legal reserve and that its affectation must be justified by law. At the same time, the idea that property includes any kind of assets is regulated, and it reaches to all types of tangible and intangible assets. Thus, constitutional property touches on some rights that are intangible assets which are covered by the constitutional concept, but do not easily fit with the civil regulation of property. However, curiously enough, in the present Chilean law, property is still conceived in a way drawn predominantly from the Civil Code, which distorts even more the paradigm of the right of property in the Constitution. For example, it is not noticed that the present doctrinaire formation of property in Chile is different from that of our civil law and that as a result it is considered as an autonomous institution. Even more, there is a doctrinal current that tries to unite them both or even present them as only one (Evans 1999: 213–231). Nor have we found that a republican conception of property has been set out in the doctrinal works available in Chile.

Elsewhere, in the sphere of more radical republican thought, and such as is presented in the work of Jennifer Nedelsky, it has been argued that there are good reasons for not "constitutionalizing" the property right. According to Professor Nedelsky, this "constitutionalization" would imply the validation, perpetuation, and reinforcement of the guarantee of a status quo of those who were owners at a certain moment, affecting in that way the equality of those who do not have property, or even denying the possibility that legislation could affect this right (Nedelsky 1990: 186, 213, 215, 226, 228, 247, 272, 273).

For our part, we assert that the constitutional regulation of property is necessary as an affirmation of personal dignity and as a restraint on government action (Underkuffler 2003: 158–161; Jocelyn-Holt 2014: 223–233). We also believe that constitutional property should be separated from the legal conception of civil law property because it constitutes an autonomous subsystem which in Chilean law must be reconstructed around certain principal features that are treated in the following sections.

Property as a Fundamental Right and Human Right and its Relationship with Dignity (UN Universal Declaration of Human Rights, Articles 5 and 17 and Pact of San José, Article 21)

The regulations and principles of the subsystem of the property right of Article 19 Nos. 23, 24, 25, and 26 of the Political Constitution must be interpreted and integrated in an interface between the rights of the Fundamental Charter and human rights. This is the idea of fundamental right that is raised in virtue of Article 5 of the Chilean Constitution and in which are integrated the regulations on human rights. To understand property in Chile, we must therefore take as current law in this area, Article 17 of the UN Universal Declaration of Human Rights, which says: "1. Everyone has the right to own property alone or in association with others; 2. No one shall be arbitrarily deprived of his property."

The notion of property in the Fundamental Charter also has to be integrated with the dispositions set forth in the Pact of San José that apply in full in law in Chile, and which in Article 21 say:

1. Everyone has the right to the use and enjoyment of his property. The law may subordinate such use and enjoyment to the interest of society.
2. No one shall be deprived of his property except upon payment of just compensation, for reasons of public utility or social interest, and in the cases and according to the forms established by law.
3. Usury and any other form of exploitation of man by man shall be prohibited by law.

According to this notion of property as a human right, we must conceive property as individual and collective, and not only as private property. Professor John Rawls, in *The Law of Peoples*, includes the right to obtain personal property among those freedoms that must be guaranteed in every society that Rawls considers "decent." Rawls defines property as a human right, saying:

Among the human rights there are the right to life (to the means of subsistence and security); of liberty (to freedom from slavery, serfdom, and forced occupation, and to sufficient measure of liberty of conscience to ensure freedom of religion and thought); of property (personal property); and to formal equality as expressed by the rules of natural justice (that is, that similar cases be treated similarly). Human rights, as thus understood this way cannot be rejected as peculiarly liberal or special to the Western tradition. They are not politically parochial.

(Rawls 1999b: 65)

Rawls also highlights at least two ideas linked to property understood as a fundamental right, and these ideas can be considered as concepts or conceptions of property (Ruiz-Tagle and Martí 2014: 110–137; Michelman 1967: 1219–1224). First is the idea of personal property that needs to be determined at constituent or constitutional level, and which is linked to the notion of dignity and moral personality,

223

integrity, or identity of the moral subject, and therefore, to the idea of basic freedom. According to Rawls, this form of personal property stems from the principles of justice and in the international sphere constitutes an indispensable human right. On the one hand, it refers to movable property (or not real estate or rooted or tied to land), and on the other, it is defined by a guarantee of access for all people. This concept of property has a moral connotation that exceeds the typically political and is connected to a conception of the personality of Kantian derivation. Secondly, Rawls conceives the concept or the idea of property, private or social, that should properly be determined by legislation and applied in judicial practice, and this concept of property is a matter for regulation according to the political, historical, and sociological circumstances, and involves decisions over the ways of creating and assigning public assets, choosing a place of work, preventing damage to natural resources, and so on, and its radius of influence can reach as far as the international sphere.

This idea of linking property to the person's dignity and subsistence is also expressed by Robert Reich, Carol Rose, and Margaret Radin, and it can also be incorporated into Chilean constitutional law as a republican idea (Simon 1990: 1361; Ellikson, Rose, and Ackerman 1995: 1–36).

Consistent with this idea of property as a human right and fundamental right, it is also important to take into account that there are also several constitutional texts, even treaties and documents of the United Nations, that consider that property deserves special protection, in what concerns the home, land, water, or other natural resources necessary for human life. Property as a human right, which is necessary as part of the republican conception of property, also supposes a compromise with sharing and recognition of equality in the economic sphere, and a sympathy for smaller-sized businesses that have local connections that allow cooperation and mutual benefit (ibid.: 1338). This conception seeks to set limits on the transfer of property and to give control of these to those participating in one or more communities of owners, and also the imposition of restrictions in terms of the accumulation of property, in order to limit the inequality among the members of a community of owners (ibid.: 1341).

The foregoing implies that, at constitutional level, a distinction must be made between the property right, which should be recognized and guaranteed to every natural individual, and the right to property, which is recognized and guaranteed at constitutional level in relation to legal entities. This distinction does not exist in the present Chilean constitutional regulations, but perhaps it can be deduced and eventually constructed from the necessary interpretation and integration that must take place between these and the regulations of the treaties concerning property.

The Guarantee of Access to Property (Political Constitution, Article 19 No. 23)

The scope of the guarantee of access to property that is contemplated in the constitutional mandate of Article 19 No. 23 has been an object of questioning in the political decisions of the government and Parliament, but only as a prerequisite or foundation of Chilean doctrine and jurisprudence. The Constitutional Tribunal has stated in one of its rulings that the objective and purpose of this regulation is that in relation to the greater number of people, it is understood to refer to natural persons as well as legal entities, and that therefore the legislation must allow access to property in the broadest sense. The principle that the right of ownership must be accessible even for those who are not owners at present, but may become future owners, is part of a republican conception of property, as was expressed in ruling No. 260 of the Constitutional Tribunal when applying the provisions of Article 19 No. 23 of the present Constitution (Pfeffer 1999: 240; Cornejo 2014: 189–222; Ruiz-Tagle 2014: 43–44). In fact, the conception of envisaging the property right, more than a limitation to those ideas about political participation, is a fundamental part of the republican conception and can be introduced into the understanding and interpretation of property in Chilean law (Simon 1990: 1354).

The precept removes from the legal sphere of private ownership, assets common to all, national assets of public use, and the assets that the Constitution itself has expressly excluded. It accepts also that the limitations that can be imposed on access to private property require a statute with a qualified quorum. This regulation recognizes different types of property, and even though it expressly regulates private ownership, in reality it does not give priority or preference to this form of right in relation to the other ownership institutions to which it refers. Neither, from the republican point of view, can it be understood as a constitutional prohibition of nationalization of a universality or set of assets susceptible to private ownership. For that it would be enough to incorporate this method of acquisition in the present constitutional regulation for it to be held to be valid in our law. Also, Article 19

No. 24 section 6 recognizes and maintains the legal effects of the nationalization of mining when it says that the State has exclusive domain, inalienable, imprescriptible of all the mines, without prejudice to these being the object of concessions, a question on which the organic statute for that branch has pronounced. Therefore, to interpret the regulation of Article 19 No. 23 as a prohibition of nationalization is contradictory to these provisions.

The precept of Article 19 No. 23 can also be interpreted as a provision that refers to the controversial question of the three areas of the economy or of property that was raised during the government of President Allende. This question that sought to regulate forms of private, mixed, and State or social property caused a series of conflicts that culminated with the ruling of roll or case docket No. 15 of the Constitutional Tribunal. The regulation of Article 19 No. 23 of the Constitution defines this question when establishing the principle that, as a general rule, things are susceptible to private ownership and that, by exception, there can exist a public domain over things common to all men and over national assets of public use. At the same time, it rules that State or social property can also comprise other assets that are named in the Constitution and the law, and that if it is about excluding something from private ownership, this regulation must have hierarchy of statutory law and be approved by a qualified quorum.

Constitutional Property Comprises all Types of Assets (Political Constitution, Article 19 No. 24)

From a republican point of view, the concept of property is broadly conceived and, therefore, it exceeds that set down in Articles 565, 582 and 583 of the Civil Code. Article 582 rules that ownership covers tangible assets, and Article 583 states that over intangible assets – that is, those that are mere rights, like credits or active obligations – "there is also a kind of ownership."

The constitutional regulations do not describe the right that the Fundamental Charter gives as a "kind of property," but as property or full ownership. This constitutional property is ensured for everyone with respect to all tangible and intangible assets, without making any distinction in terms of the ownership of this right.

Therefore it should not surprise us that as a consequence of this constitutional regulation, new rights find a home in the Fundamental Charter for their protection, in those cases whose structure is not

226

recognized in the civil law on patrimony. This has happened with personality and image rights, publicity rights, the right to position or employment, the names of titles, the right to enrollment, or to a health plan or insurance, and so on, and all assets that have been ensured by way of constitutional protection often generating controversy among those who see in the Constitution a necessary interchange with the regulations of civil law. It is evident that the idea of conceiving work as property is consistent with the republican notion of property, which can even be interpreted as limiting or prohibiting the use of arbitrary forms of dismissal (Simon 1990: 1382).

In Chile, this controversy has been partially addressed in the work of Jessica Fuentes, for her thesis, which was then developed together with Professor Eduardo Aldunate. This work criticizes the inconvenience of having a concept of property exposed to being inflated or deformed by an expansive jurisprudence about new rights that has emanated from actions for protection, in particular the undue inflation of the concept of property (Aldunate and Fuentes 1997).

These new rights, such as ownership of image or of the titles of the domain, position or employment, pension or retirement deserve constitutional legal protection, even though they do not have private domain protection. These rights sometimes acquire more value than real estate or movable assets, which are matters for protection in traditional common law. The breadth of the constitutional regulation serves that way as support for its protection.

In the same way as the regulation of Article 19 No. 23 recently quoted, No. 24 of the same Article can be interpreted as a form of solving the controversial question of the three areas of the economy, to which I have made reference above. Of course, it constitutionalizes, or brings to a constitutional level, the guarantee of all forms of property, whether they are private, mixed, or State-owned. At the same time, it protects ownership over all kinds of things, even the intangibles. It rules on the grounds, obligations, and limitations that can be imposed in the name of social function, and it demands that any form of alienation of property is motivated for legal reasons that are qualified by the legislator. According to this precept, the administrative seizure of property must be founded in law, and thus one of the most controversial issues of the government of President Allende is resolved. It also establishes grounds for limitation and the compensation for any case of deprivation, disturbance, or threat to property, and the regulated procedure of expropriation forces the market price to be paid to the titleholder of the expropriated right. Finally, it recognizes the State's ownership or public domain over mines, hydrocarbons, and other assets, which implies the validation of the process of nationalization of the large-scale mining sector. The above is complemented by a system of private sector concessions for the exploitation of some of these resources, which are regulated by the respective organic statutory laws.

The Social Function of Property (Political Constitution, Article 19 Nos. 24 and 26)

This is perhaps the most controversial of constitutional, doctrinal, and jurisprudential questions, and one that is almost completely in accord with the republican constitutional conception because there is no reference to the social function of property in civil law. Even more, the introduction of the social function means the imposition of a limit to the right of private property. It was Alessandri who introduced the doctrinal status of the social function, influenced by the teachings of León Duguit, and this is incorporated and maintained in the current text (Mirow 2011: 1185–1210).

The social function regulated by Article 19 No. 24 refers, in a general way, to the admissibility of collective interest as a limit on ownership, but it also can be considered as a substantial part of the essential content of property (López y López 1998; López 2014: 52–59). The social function regulates the legislator's action, since it is through a statutory law that limitations and obligations can be set in questions relevant to the general interest of the nation, national security, public interest and health, and the conservation of the environment. Lautaro Ríos has maintained that the social function operates as a general category together with the other justifications that the Constitution recognizes as valid for limiting private property (Ríos 2010; Rajevic 1996).

Additionally, regarding the subject of the social function and its jurisprudential application, it is also necessary to determine if it is appropriate to compensate those cases in which the social function has been invoked in order to impose obligations or limitations on ownership. As a related issue and in cases affected by obligations or limitations proceeding from the social function that affects the essential content of a private property right, it will also be necessary to determine – as was argued in the proceedings of the *Comunidad Galletué* [Galletué Community], and as is now subject to doubt and controversy in the most up-to-date jurisprudence – if any compensation arises in those cases and what is its constitutional basis (López 2014).

The Regulation on Expropriation (Political Constitution, Article 19 Nos. 24 and 25)

The expropriation regulation in Article 19 Nos. 24 and 25 is also a question of constitutional significance that overtakes the private-sector framing of the property right. The expropriation is limited to public use of assets and demands compensation through a regulated legal procedure. That is, a property cannot be expropriated unless the title is to be in the name of the State or to be given, in turn, as a concession to a private individual so that this latter may use it or enjoy it or otherwise dispose of the property in order to obtain a public benefit (Huneeus 1890: 109–116; Evans 1999: 213–231).

The expropriation goes forward for reasons of public use and national interest, and there is in the Constitution a full regulation of this subject, with a procedure established especially for this effect. Thus, for example, a negotiation is always sought with the people involved in the expropriation and only if this is not possible will litigation be initiated. The expropriation procedure is also applicable in relation to exclusive intellectual property rights that are protected in Article 19 No. 25. All this procedure overrules private-sector legal dispositions.

Attributes, Faculties and Deprivation, Privation, Disruption, and/or Threat to Property (Political Constitution, Article 19 No. 24 and Article 20)

The attributes of ownership are free use, enjoyment, and disposal, which of course are regulated by the Civil Code. On the other hand, in the constitutional subsystem of property, Article 19 No. 24 rules that all alienation not directly authorized by law is prohibited, this being understood in broader terms than mere affectation of the attributes of ownership, which certainly can also be included in it because it comprises totally or partially the asset to which the ownership relates.

At the same time, the idea of alienation is tied in to the legal guarantee of the constitutional subsystem of property that comprises the suit for protection of Article 20 of the Constitution and its notions of "disruption" or "threat," which can include other characteristics of the peaceful enjoyment of property that cannot be considered essential attributes. It concerns a topic of great complexity, which, as Daniel Peñailillo has noted in his writing, and, as we have explained before in this work, is linked to a series of regulations and special statutory laws that are not part of the Civil Code and that invoke the constitutional regulations quoted as the legal base and backup.

The Regulation of Intellectual Property and Other Special Properties (Political Constitution, Article 19 Nos. 24 and 25)

The regulation of intellectual property in Article 19 No. 25 is an open mandate of the constituent that must be completed by special statutory laws. This property is built on the idea of protecting valuable information through a repertoire of exclusive rights that resemble and are recognized as property (Ruiz-Tagle 2001c: 133).

In the case of ownership of intellectual property, the constitutional precept is not necessarily about rights over intangible things, because even if its uses can be perceived by the senses, they have a formal definition that allows their use in different formats and material forms. Furthermore, their use has the character of a public good that is not competitive, because the use that a person might make of intangible assets does not reduce the use that other people may have of the same asset, therefore its usage does not generate a relationship of zero-sum among those who take part in its entitlement.

These creations of intellectual property are formed through an act of formal authority that is the decree of concession, and generally, they are of limited duration; once their concession term is over, exclusive ownership comes to an end and these assets move into the sphere of the common or public domain.

It is indeed to do with assets that do not admit a straightforward application of the categories of the Civil Code, and that have a special autonomous institutional character that is only understood as property to the extent of its engagement with the regulations of the Constitution.

Limits, Obligations, and Collective Interests of Property (Political Constitution, Article 19 No. 24)

The same provision of Article 19 No. 24 contains limitations and obligations of the already established property right. It concerns regulations that, where the social function is involved, include the ideas of "general interest of the nation, national security, public use and health, and the conservation of the environmental heritage." Where it refers to the alienation of property, the collective interests that can be invoked to justify such a step, which are subject to the requirement of a legal reserve, are that the expropriation was in the cause of "public use or national interest," qualified by the legislator. Furthermore, in what refers to mining property, the surface areas are obliged and limited by the exploration, exploitation, and benefit of the mines, which also

230

means a collective interest in the subordination of the rights of the first to those of the second, in the cause of a general interest.

These regulations that express collective interests surpass the regulations of the Civil Code and, by appearing in the Constitution, are developed in their application in a complex legislation governing mining, water, and other special assets. They also express collective interests that overrule the exclusive title of the owner. For good reason, part of the doctrine has linked these ideas to the concept of "social function" or "deprivation," but eventually they can acquire certain autonomy in relation to these concepts or even come into conflict with them (López 2014). For example, it is possible to imagine a limitation or obligation imposed for national security reasons, understanding this last doctrine as that which might arise from a war against an internal enemy, which would not be justified from the point of view of republican and democratic constitutionalism because it would come into collision with the "social function" that attaches to any restriction or duty that is imposed on private property and on any right.

The Essential Content of Property (Political Constitution, Article 19 No. 26)

The idea of essential content recognized in Article 19 No. 26, which originates in German doctrine and which has been included in the comparative law, is an important innovation of the present Chilean Constitution, which seeks to impose limits on the legislator and give application to the principle of proportionality in the encumbrance of the right.

It also implies the recognition of private property not only as a fundamental right, but also as a central part of our legal system – that is, as an institution or as part of the institutional character or objective right of the constitutional law and the limitations that the legislature can impose on property, an issue that was not apparently noticed in the origin of the text that from 1990 is part of our Constitution and which has been highlighted by Lautaro Ríos (2010) and Eduardo Cordero (2008).

In relation to this, it is important to ask oneself if, from a republican constitutional conception, the essential content of constitutional property is not identified with its social function, as is maintained by the Sevillian Professor Ángel López y López, and as has been recognized by the most recent of Chilean jurisprudence (López y López 1998).

This regulation is also linked to the debate regarding the three areas of the economy because it imposes requirements of proportionality on the legislator at the time of encumbrance of the property and excludes only the administrative encumbrance of the domain.

Actions, States of Exception, and Transitional Regulations on Property (Political Constitution, Articles 20, 43, and 44, and Second and Third Transitional Regulations)

The influence that the legal recourse of protection has had in the configuration of public and private property in Chile is well-known. The legal recourse of protection is presently regulated in Article 20 of the Chilean Constitution. Some people have suggested that in the absence of administrative contentious tribunals or of a more effective regulation of the possessory injunction in the Civil Code, it has served as a true jurisdictional equivalent, and it has also been criticized for its popularizing character (Jana and Marín 1996). The truth is that it has constituted an efficient way of protecting property, and that its insistence on summoning an illegal or arbitrary action or omission that causes deprivation, disruption, or threat is a constituent element of the doctrinal subsystem of guarantees to property.

To these regulations it is necessary to add also Articles 43 and 44, referring to states of constitutional emergency that, from the republican point of view, are exclusively a regulated method to restrict rights and cannot be considered forms of government. In the case of Articles 43 and 44, they are regulations of the Constitution that admit requisitions and which establish limitations to property in the states of assembly, siege, and catastrophe. Of course, these regulations also integrate the subsystem of constitutional property in Chile.

It is a very different case for the Second and Third Transitional Constitutional Provisions, which establish exceptions in questions of concessions and regulations related to the large-scale copper-mining sector. These regulations should either be part of the permanent text of the Constitution, saving the contradictions that their maintenance means, or should simply be repealed.

Each one of the issues singled out in the foregoing subsections is related directly to the dogma and jurisprudence of property in Chile, and, conceived as part of a republican constitutional idea, they make up a true subsystem that has an autonomous character, different from the private sector conception of ownership predominant in our country.

The republican conception of property that inspires this work, as can be seen, is able to contribute ideas to solve conflicts in Chile – understanding the country as one that can aspire to the political-legal ideal of a Social and Democratic State governed by the rule of law (Aragón 1995: 2–5). By its necessary link to legal and political resolutions and by its *practical* legal connotation, the republican conception of property does not end in a conceptual formulation of the so-called subsystem of property, but must shoulder its doctrinal analysis and criticism of its jurisprudence. Generally, the analysis of jurisprudence around property has been concentrated with reference to one or more court rulings as a sample or manifestation of a particular legal idea. This, however, is an effort of more general jurisprudential analysis and comparison that seeks to criticize the criteria that have been used to organize the indices, repertoires, and compilations of jurisprudence regarding property.

The Jurisprudence of Property: Its Repertoires and Compilations
To summarize this endeavor, I wish to set down a series of commentaries and critical references on two of the best compilations of jurisprudence that have brought together cases related to the regulations of the Political Constitution, Article 19 Nos. 23–26, and these are: the jurisprudential repertoire of Professor Emilio Pfeffer (1999), *Constitución Política de la República de Chile. Concordancia, antecedentes y jurisprudencia* [Political Constitution of the Republic of Chile: Concordance, Precedents, and Jurisprudence], and the repertoire of Enrique Navarro and Carlos Carmona, *Recopilación de jurisprudencia del Tribunal Constitucional (1981–2011)* [Compilation of the Jurisprudence of the Constitutional Tribunal (1981–2011)] (Navarro and Carmona 2011).

In terms of Professor Pfeffer's text, it is important to note that the jurisprudence comprises that coming from the Supreme Court, the Comptroller General of the Republic, and from various courts from 1980 to 1999, including the Constitutional Tribunal. The classification by Professor Emilio Pfeffer relates to the articles in the Fundamental Charter, and therefore we have revised the criteria used and the legal doctrine that emerges in each of the resolutions that have been grouped in this work, in the way of a true jurisprudential constitutional repertoire.

The first thing that stands out when revising the references corresponding to jurisprudential decisions about the Political Constitution, Article 19 Nos. 23–26 in the work of Pfeffer is the absence of references to international treaties that complement the constitutional regulation of Chilean property. In this respect, except for Article 19 Nos. 25 and 26, we do not find any such mention (Pfeffer 1999: 239–247). This implies thinking about property in a way other than as a human and fundamental right, and maybe identifying it completely with the idea of private property in the Civil Code. The second observation is that the criteria for the doctrine that Professor Pfeffer uses to classify the jurisprudence correspond only partially to the issues that are of interest to the constitutional doctrine on property. For example, in respect of the jurisprudence of the Political Constitution, Article 19 No. 23, a series of resolutions are mentioned that explain its objective, sense, and scope, as well as decisions regarding national assets of public use, such as beaches by the sea and water. But later, it treats in great detail the rules on concessions as part of the jurisprudence linked to this part of the Constitution. He groups rulings according to the different types of concession, including rulings on the role of municipalities and their entities, as well as the *Ministerio de Bienes Nacionales* [Ministry of National Assets]. This matter is not dealt with in the constitutional doctrine on property and belongs rather more under administrative law, so its inclusion merits reflection regarding its pertinence and relevance in the subsystem of Chilean constitutional property (ibid.: 239–245). The third observation that emerges from the study of Professor Pfeffer, which is in part coincident with the second, is that the compilation of jurisprudence on which we now comment includes rulings grouped under the constitutional concepts of tangible and intangible objects in their relationship with the Civil Code, relating to the social function and the right to compensation for limitations or deprivations of ownership, which are all classical doctrinal issues of property in the Constitution. However, in the work of Professor Pfeffer, to these are added a subheading and subsequent jurisprudential compilation referring to property in relation to "care" (public), another about image, or good performance bonus and/or social security adjustments, and about student patrimony and other rights that have no direct protection in the sphere of civil law and that are subjects of great constitutional controversy. The fourth observation is that the jurisprudence is classified under the heading of deprivation of property coinciding with the criteria of Article 20 of the Political Constitution, of legal recourse to protection, and not with the doctrinal categories of the civil law on property. These categories include "violations" or "threats," and/or illegal or arbitrary acts which affect the property right, so the relationship of these forms of affectation to the ideas of use, enjoyment, and disposal, and to the limitations or deprivations of ownership recognized in the Fundamental Charter, perhaps needs to be explained or their difference recognized. The fifth observation is that, in the work of Professor Pfeffer, the treatment of the recourse to legal protection and property is open to questions that include the retention of checks and their protestation, the devolution of VAT, mining concessions, and water rights, which shows clearly how Article 19 No. 24 has had broad application in legal matters that surpass Chilean civil law (ibid.: 247–290). The sixth observation refers to the jurisprudence which has been collected in relation to Article 19 No. 25 of the present Constitution, in which are mentioned resolutions of the special justice tribunals in the decisions, in particular, which the Supreme Court resolves by its superintendence and that are in the field of protection, renovation, and cancelation of trademarks; also mentioned is the link between intellectual property and scientific research, and its relationship with industrial property and free competition, with the express quotation of two resolutions on this issue, which, at the time, were handed down by the *Comisión Resolutiva* [Resolution Commission], today called the *Tribunal de Defensa de la Libre Competencia* [Tribunal for the Protection of Free Competition] (ibid.: 289–293). All this jurisprudence shows the wealth of our specialized jurisprudence in terms of property and the broad criteria used by Professor Pfeffer.

Finally, Emilio Pfeffer deals with the legal resolutions that have been based on the Political Constitution, Article 19 No. 26, and gives an account of four court rulings by the Constitutional Tribunal relating to this issue and representing an idea very close to the Chilean conventional doctrine regarding the property right. Of greatest interest in this section is its reference to Article 29 of the UN Declaration of Human Rights and to Article 4 of the International Covenant on Economic, Social and Cultural Rights, regulations that mean an international recognition of the democratic principle and the requirement for general welfare and for legal reserve in the raising of barriers to the exercise of fundamental rights (ibid.: 294–298).

With respect to the jurisprudential compilation of the Constitutional Tribunal by Professors Carlos Carmona and Enrique Navarro, we can say that as in the previously commented work, the rulings are organized according to Articles in the Constitution and, in this case, according to Article 19 Nos. 23–26 inclusive. In the same way, as in the compilation recently commented upon, there are no special references to articles in treaties dealing with the protection of the right of property, and the same observations are applicable to this work as have been made on Professor Pfeffer's work.

It is to be noted that Professors Navarro and Carmona maintain as jurisprudential doctrine that the Constitution, in Article 19 No. 24, made broader the concept of property and that it does not establish a determined type of property. In terms of pensions, it includes a distinction between contribution and pension fund; they add to the forms of property linked to constitutional regulations, rulings on indigenous property, and collect together the jurisprudence of the Constitutional Tribunal governing the distinction between acquired rights and mere expectations, and on the way in which credit rights, or even marriage patrimonial rights, can be the object of the constitutional protection of property (Navarro and Carmona 2011: 225–238).

Also in the work of Professors Navarro and Carmona there are abundant subtle distinctions concerning deprivation and limitation of the domain, the social function, and its relationship with the principle of legal reserve and the regulating authority. They treat these issues with a broad spectrum that comprises urbanistic legislation, fishing, environment, publicity, small real estate, road tolls, stocks and shares, contracts, and the institutions of mining rights, such as easements. Something similar can be said of their treatment of expropriation, which comprises its concept, whether its adjustment and compensation take place, and the idea collected from constitutional jurisprudence of how a severe limitation of property can be considered deprivation (ibid.: 238–253). This jurisprudential compilation, when referring to Article 19 No. 24 of the Political Constitution, concludes with a waiver of the regulations of mining rights and water rights. With respect to Article 19 No. 25, regarding intellectual and industrial property, Navarro and Carmona include the ruling by the Constitutional Tribunal, which said that the compilations have their constitutional guarantee secured (ibid.: 262).

In any case, the greatest novelty in this valuable jurisprudential compilation of Professors Navarro and Carmona refers to the concepts that have been identified in application of Article 19 No. 26 of the Constitution, and in the jurisprudential definition of the principle of the essential content of the fundamental property right. This work contains references to the scope of the principle of legal reserve contained in this regulation; a distinction between encumbrance in its essence and in what constitutes impediment to the free exercise of a right; the idea that the fundamental rights are not absolute and have limits; the criteria for allowing restrictions; and the test of proportionality in the limitation of rights through legal ways, and/or by way of regulation. There are also references to legal security and prescription, and to the exercise of jurisdiction in relation to the essential content that are of great legal value and that are placed in the forefront of the research achieved thus far into the Chilean constitutional doctrine (ibid.: 263–267).

These observations on jurisprudence based on these repertoires have taken their inspiration from a republican conception of property. The idea of conception has been introduced in legal philosophy by Ronald Dworkin, and in the words of Antonio Pérez Luño is understood as follows:

> Whereas the concept refers to the theoretical and general meaning of a term, the conception means the form of putting into practice a concept. When I invoke a concept – Dworkin will say – I state a problem, when I invoke a conception, I am trying to solve it.
>
> (Pérez Luño 1987: 47)

The republican conceptions conceive property as a right-cum-duty for its titleholder and they link it to a set of principles and values, among which the social function is highlighted. It indicates, therefore, in the case of Chile, a revision of our tradition that recognizes the property right as an individual, absolute, and arbitrary right (Article 582 of the Civil Code) because its republican conception conceives property in its relationship with the values of freedom and equality. This idea gives more coherence to the fragmentary overview of ownership in Chile, and implies a re-reading of the civil property right, as a paradigmatic case within the private sphere, but without attributing to it a unique or principal character (López y López 1998). Furthermore, the republican conception of property accepts the principle of constitutional supremacy, its link and direct application, and proposes the repeal of every transitory regulation that limits the application of the Fundamental Charter. For the effects of reinterpretation of the Chilean Constitution, we must redefine the new conception of property post-1990, in the context of the constitutional subsystem described here. This constitutional subsystem of property in the Chilean Fifth Republic is different from those that existed during the history of our country, from its most remote origins until the regime of the 1925 Constitution.

If we move from the sphere of the property right and examine all the fundamental rights of our Fundamental Charter, from the point of view of the law compared with international catalogs which are incorporated in the treaties in force regarding fundamental rights in Chile, and leave aside the hypertrophy of the property right that has been described before and the emphasis on the neoliberal conception of rights, we can conclude that there are practically no rights at international level that are not reflected in the present constitutional text in Chile. The only exceptional case could be the right of asylum in Latin America, which has a specially reinforced form which distinguishes our continent particularly in international *practice*. This should not lead us into complacency regarding the perfect character of our fundamental rights system (Ruiz-Tagle 2002: 66). We should think about how to continue improving the way to recognize, and guarantee more securely, fundamental rights in Chilean jurisprudence. In this task, the subject of the effective guarantee of economic, social, and cultural rights is a major question that we will address in the following section.

7.15 THE STRUCTURE AND FUNCTION OF THE LEGAL GUARANTEES THAT PROTECT FUNDAMENTAL RIGHTS

Finally, in Table 7.3, we can appreciate the present dispersion of subjects of constitutional actions in Chilean constitutional law that needs to be revised, and which, in the terms defined by the work of Mirjan Damaska, also acknowledges the relationship between structure and function of the ways of guaranteeing rights, which has to be considered in every design for control and jurisdiction of the fundamental rights at constitutional level (Damaska 2000: 9–32).

It is to illustrate this issue that we have prepared Table 7.3 on constitutional actions, and a warning is given that this cannot be an exhaustive compilation of all the protection mechanisms of the fundamental rights. The underlying selection criterion is that the Constitution is the direct source from which the action emerges. Therefore, it is essential to take into account that there are many other mechanisms of protection of rights contemplated in several regulations of the legal system, among others, protection before the guarantee judge (Article 95 of the *Código Procesal Penal* [Criminal Procedure Code]), the procedure for the protection of fundamental rights in labor issues (Articles 485–495 of the *Código del Trabajo* [Labor Code]), different administrative procedures before the Comptroller General of the Republic, different Superintendencies, and elements of the administration of the State, State procedures related to electoral justice, procedures contemplated by the *Ley de Acceso a la Información Pública* [Access to Public Information Law] (Statute No. 20.285) before the *Consejo para la Transparencia* [Council for Transparency].

The most evident conclusion that can be extracted from the analysis of Table 7.3 is that there is an enormous dispersion of constitutional actions that guarantee the fundamental rights in Chile and that its rationale is not easily accessible to a common citizen. Thus, the protection of rights is given to a class of specialists with legal training. It is suggested, therefore, to simplify these procedures and to classify them around a pair of criteria which differentiate actions that involve patrimonial issues that should be more strict, formal, and specialized, from those actions that protect the person, their dignity, freedom, or equality, which can be simple, less formal, and with more accessible procedures.

It is necessary also to revise these constitutional actions in their practical application because some have fallen into disuse and are legally archaic, and because others have served to betray the protection of the fundamental right that they were supposed to guarantee. For example, the economic protection action, instead of protecting the free entrepreneurial action, has served to defend the privileges of trade union associations, oligopolies, and marketers' interests (Ruiz-Tagle 2000b). Similarly, constitutional convertibility should be attended to, which affects economic and social rights, health, work, education, or social security, which are protected via property or equality, in order to be able to guarantee them via the legal recourse for protection. The combination of different fundamental rights in case decisions should also be analyzed (Correa and Ruiz-Tagle 2010: 217–219).

7.16 ECONOMIC, SOCIAL, AND CULTURAL RIGHTS AND THE SOCIAL AND DEMOCRATIC STATE GOVERNED BY THE RULE OF LAW

In terms of protection of fundamental rights, the Constitution protects those rights conceived as immune to State interference, but does not

TABLE 7.3 Constitutional actions that protect fundamental rights, and their main characteristics

Action	Reason for proceedings	Plaintiff	Defendant	Competent tribunal	Time limit	Processing
Nullity of Public Law (Political Constitution, Article 7)	Proceeds against any action that contravenes the Political Constitution, Article 7	The entity affected in its rights	State Administration	Civil court	There is controversy. The jurisprudence has estimated that the action of nullity is inalienable, but the patrimonial action prescribes according to general regulations (4 years).	In the absence of a special procedure, an ordinary trial will proceed.
Nationality claim (Political Constitution, Article 12)	Proceeds against acts or resolutions of administrative authority that deprive or do not recognize Chilean nationality	The affected person, by him/herself, or anyone in his/her representation	Act or resolution that deprives or does not recognize the nationality, even against the ignorance of a cause of nationality acquisition	Supreme Court	Thirty days	The Supreme Court hears as jury and plenary tribunal. The doctrine adds that in conscience is appreciated, which implies a healthy criticism.

Compensation for legal error (Political Constitution, Article 19 No. 7 section (i) and General Provision of the Supreme Court of April 10, 1996)	Proceeds in some cases in which it is declared that the submission to trial or conviction has been by Supreme Court resolution, which declares unjustified, mistaken, or arbitrary	Person/entity affected	The State	Civil Court (previous declaration of the Supreme Court)	*Supreme Court:* six months, from the execution of sentence or termination of proceedings *Civil court:* general rule (4 years)	*Supreme Court:* from the request transfer to tax authorities will be conferred; with or without their answer, the writs will be sent to the Prosecutor of the Supreme Court for his decision; once the fiscal authorities have been informed, it will be ordered to report on the request to the Criminal Court Chamber. *Ordinary Courts:* summary trial. Without set forms. The law foresees the same formalities and procedures as for the writ of
Economic protection (Political Constitution, Article 19 No. 21, Statute 18.971)	Proceeds against offenses to Article 19 No. 21 of the Political Constitution	Anyone. It does not require actual interest	Whoever has committed the offense	Court of Appeal	Six months from the time of the offense	

TABLE 7.3 (cont.)

Action	Reason for proceedings	Plaintiff	Defendant	Competent tribunal	Time limit	Processing
Complaint for expropriation (Political Constitution, Article 19 No. 24 and Decree-Law No. 2.186)	(the right to develop any economic activity) Proceeds to complaint about the legality of the expropriatory act	The person who was expropriated	The expropriating entity	Civil court	Thirty days, counted from the publication of the *Official Gazette* of the expropriating writ	protection. The decision can be appealed before the Supreme Court. Summary trial
Protection (Political Constitution, Article 20, writ granted by Supreme Court on June 24, 1992)	Proceeds against any action or omission, illegal or arbitrary, that deprives, disrupts, or threatens the legitimate exercise of certain constitutional rights. It does not proceed against court or	The one who had suffered deprivation, disruption, or threat. (For him/herself or anyone in his representation)	Whoever has violated the constitutional guarantees	Court of Appeal	Thirty days from the execution of the writ or the occurrence of the omission. Exceptionally, it does not have a time limit for permanent acts.	There is an admissibility exam. Once it has been admitted for proceedings, the Court will order that the appellant provides a report. An order of no innovation can be decreed. Court can decree any

Habeas corpus (Political Constitution, Article 21, writ granted by Supreme Court (December 19, 1932), Political Constitution, Article 95, *Código Orgánico de Tribunales* [Statute for the Court Organization], Article 63 No. 2b)	Proceeds against any detention, arrest, or deprivation of freedom that has been verified with an offense to the Constitution or the law	Any person in favor of any individual who was arrested, detained, or imprisoned	Anyone	Court of Appeal	None	... administrative decisions. Without set forms, court can order that the individual be brought to its presence, and can adopt any decisions considered convenient to restore the rule of law. The decision can be appealed before the Supreme Court.

proceedings considered necessary. Recourse is presented "in relation to" time limit to rule: five days. The decision can be appealed before the Supreme Court.

TABLE 7.3 (cont.)

Action	Reason for proceedings	Plaintiff	Defendant	Competent tribunal	Time limit	Processing
Inapplicability requirement (Political Constitution, Article 93 No. 6, Statute for the Organization of the Constitutional Tribunal, Articles 79–92)	Proceeds against legal precepts whose application in a concrete case (any proceeding that is followed in an ordinary or special tribunal) is considered as contrary to the Constitution	Any of the parts or by a writ of warrant by the judge who heard the case	The party or parties to the pending question not having presented the appeal, the Chamber of Deputies, the Senate, and the President of the Republic can present observations.	Constitutional Tribunal	While there are outstanding issues	Admissibility exam: there must be outstanding issues, in which the application of the contested injunction could be decisive and the objection is well-founded. Declared admissible: twenty days to present the cause. Appeal is heard by the plenary. The sentence that declares the inapplicability only will produce effects on the outstanding legal issues.

Requirement of unconstitutionality of precept declared not applicable (Political Constitution, Article 93 No. 7, Statute for the Organization of the Constitutional Tribunal, Articles 93–104)	Proceeds against legal principles that have been declared inapplicable	Anyone – there is public intervention; court can declare it by the powers invested	Chamber of Deputies, Senate, and President of the Republic can *present observations*	Constitutional Tribunal	None	Requirement must be reasonably founded. There is control of admissibility. Once admissibility is declared, notice must be given to the Chamber of Deputies, Senate, and President of the Republic, who have twenty days to record observations. Once the proceedings are finished, there is a time limit of twenty days to pass sentence. The plenary hears the action.

Note: The assistants Javiera Morales and Diego Pérez have worked on Table 7.3 by request of the author.

guarantee with the same force the right to equality or the rights in questions of labor, health, social security, trade unions, and education. It is a Fundamental Charter that does not protect nor guarantee health and education as rights, that does not sufficiently protect the natural resources, and subjects their use to discretional and technocratic systems that are easily turned to arbitrariness and the profit of a privileged few. An economic model based on a naive image of the market has been validated, which is based on extremely high levels of concentration of power and wealth, not on justice or equality. These imperfections of the fundamental rights and the lack of effective guarantees for economic and social rights seem to some politicians a doctrinaire question, but for the vast majority of the population they are true authoritarian enclaves, because they leave them vulnerable to abuse by the private entities that provide health services in Chile, known by the acronym ISAPRES, or by the private institutions that provide social security, known by the acronym AFP, or by private universities and entrepreneurial organizations.

To overcome these problems, media consultants have been hired to draw to a close, as far as possible, the eternal transition to an impossible democracy, at the same time as new transitory articles are being added to the Chilean Constitution (they now number twenty-five, with twenty of them approved since 1990). However, the problem cannot be overcome by simple communicational campaigns, because while there are transitory regulations that limit what the permanent text of our Constitution says, we will not have full democracy. The constitutional organic statutory laws and the abstruse mechanism of constitutional control are also anti-democratic obstructions to our Fundamental Charter. In short, so many and so profound are the issues that require reform in Chile that since the presidential campaign of 2009, all the political forces, including the right, have accepted the possibility of a deep constitutional change in terms of regionalization, the balance of power between President and Congress, and the revision of the constitutional control system, among others.

The need for a new Constitution for Chile does not emerge only after 2005, nor is it a last-minute requirement. On the contrary, this demand was already present in Chile, and was expressed in a more conscious form in the speeches pronounced on August 27, 1980 by Eduardo Frei Montalva and Jorge Millas at the Teatro Caupolicán, calling for a negative vote on the constitutional proposal of the dictatorship. What has been missing in the political establishment is the will to make this demand a reality. In the same way as on human rights issues, it has taken time for an adequate answer with the thesis of *justice as far as possible*; so, on the constitutional issue the intention is to apply a similar axiom, which is *democracy as far as possible*. The leadership of the Coalition of Parties for Democracy seems to have finally accepted the Constitution as if it were fully democratic, calling for the disqualification of the critics of a system that excludes important sectors of the population, such as in the areas of electoral equality, trade union rights, ethnic, and religious minorities.

Our political institutional structures reinforced the centralism and the concentration of power, and gave the leadership of the political parties, with very little representative base, the monopoly of political activity, without establishing as prerequisites internal democracy, transparency in the use of resources, accuracy of the rolls, and so on. To the leadership of these political parties have been given super powers that seem like privileges, to take political actions such as the power to elect judiciary and administrative authorities through parliamentary agreements and to appoint a substitute in case of a vacancy arising in a parliamentary position; and, completing the circle of arbitrariness, secrecy was enshrined over the work of the Members of Parliament when Article 5 of the *Ley Orgánica* [Organizing Statute] of the National Congress was adopted.

For a part of the present leadership, more democratization was reduced to a minimalistic political reform that consists of changing the electoral system, only increasing quotas at the Senate and the Chamber of Deputies, together with removing restrictions on the right to vote of Chilean citizens living overseas and institutionalizing increased public funding of political parties. To this leadership, the political apathy of the young does not matter and they run after the independents and the unruly in order to reinforce the establishment. They have also disowned their campaign commitments of many years, which consisted of broadening the electoral roll to introduce automatic registration, on now discovering that they can take back the reform with a discourse that is presented as being in favor, in rhetorical terms, of compulsory voting. It does not tackle the lack of legitimacy of the political system, arising from the exclusion of 40 percent of the Chileans who could have the right to vote. From 1990, the leadership in Chile has never truly committed itself to elect regional authorities with effective political power, nor to the decentralization of sectoral funds. Neither do they believe in deconcentrating. Until now, those

Members of Parliament who are supporters of the establishment were, for several years, more comfortable with voters who are known and bound by the compulsory voting and binomial system, than with incorporating new voters to their districts and constituencies.

These are some of the issues for the new Constitution and they are not minor issues. The discussion is deep-rooted. The constitutional proposal can provide the drive for the development that Chile needs through a country-wide agreement which calls on all Chileans, citizens, workers, entrepreneurs, and government, to construct a new Social and Democratic State governed by the rule of law. For that, a proposal for constitutional reform is required that is not just idle talk and denomination. What is proposed as the ideal type to follow is the up-to-date model of the Welfare State that European countries developed after the Second World War, which today is known as the Social and Democratic State governed by the rule of law, with the corrections and adaptations that are necessary for the Chilean reality. Even though the ideas of the Welfare State and the Social and Democratic State governed by the rule of law are interlinked concepts, they do not mean the same thing. The Social and Democratic State governed by the rule of law, unlike the Welfare State, and as a perfected model of the same, is based on the recognition of the value of the dignity of all people, in the affirmation of their freedom, equality, and fellowship, and in the idea that democratic policy through the law defines the forms and institutions in which these values have to be made reality (Zapata 2015: 124–125).

About the origin of the establishment of the Welfare State in Europe, from the middle of the twentieth century there have been agitated controversies, some of which have been carried over into our country. For example, Professor Eduardo Aldunate, while explaining some ideas of German constitutional doctrine regarding the Welfare State or the Social State governed by law, has expressed the following:

> Even though the constitutional law can make dispositions on the form and limits of the law, it is not in the position of guaranteeing a certain state of the public finances that permits for ever the satisfaction of those large disbursements that have, over time, been accumulating as defining factors of the German Welfare State. German doctrine could speculate freely over this point due to the spectacular economic development after the war, but later, with the financial difficulties emerging from the unification of the two Germanies in the 1990s, the problem of the constitutional status of the Social State – which implies the right to benefits involved – was questioned, with the basic question: would the

removal or reduction of social benefits constitute a transgression of any constitutional regulation? and, in particular, of any clause of the Social State? This question collided with the conception of a Social State maintained by a part of the doctrine that maintained that the reference to the Social State in Articles 20 and 28 of the *Ley Fundamental* [Fundamental Law] implied a guarantee of status quo in relation to the legal regime of social security and assistance. Thus the concept of the Social State was brought to an absurdity in terms of regulations, for the simple reason that the legal guarantee of the Social State does not produce, in itself, the economic resources to provide what it is supposed to ensure.

(Aldunate 2008: 72–73)

What Eduardo Aldunate, and the German doctrines that he is quoting, criticize is a particular conception of the Social State in its most extreme version, because it does not admit a reduction in the provision of social benefits once provided. However, the defeat of this doctrine does not in any way imply the defeat of the concept of the Social or Welfare State. Additionally, the idea of the Social State does not suppose that the economic resources to finance the provision of the fundamental rights that constitute it are fixed or stable in time – much less that they are necessarily produced by themselves. The resources must come from the State's taxation and income. Incidentally, the most ambitious idea of progressiveness in economic and social rights recognized in the International Covenant in Economic, Social and Cultural Rights, in its Article 2 No. 1 declares:

Each State Party to the present Covenant undertakes to take steps, individually and through international assistance and cooperation, in particular economic and technical, to the maximum of its available resources, with a view to achieving progressively and by all appropriate means the full realization of the rights here recognized, including, in particular, the adoption of legislative measures.

(www.ohchr.org/EN/ProfessionalInterest/Pages/CESCR.aspx)

The Social or Welfare State, by definition, implies recognition of the limitations of public finances in relation to the manner of funding its rights and benefits. The power of discretion in Chile in relation to the execution of social policies is expressed in the power of the Ministry of the Treasury, in particular in the DIPRES, due to a misunderstood role assumed in looking after public funds. The Ministry of the Treasury or the DIPRES distributes the funds on non-essential matters and overlooks basic costs, and, with shameful discretion, pays salaries to the administrators of these funds, which are more than double the salary of their peers in other government departments. Thus is replicated in the public sector the privilege of those who work in the financial sector, compared with other sectors of the economy. This privilege accepts the enjoyment of the unjustified benefits of the finance technocrats, who never go bankrupt, who are insured by the State, who enjoy in exclusivity their profits or those made in relation to other people's funds that they administer, and who are not accountable for losses. Nor do they answer for their mistakes or bad results, because it is the civil servants in charge of policy in the respective ministries or public departments who assume political, legal, and administrative responsibility, and it is not easy to determine the responsibilities of the *sectorialistas* [those in charge of controlling and assessing a sector or ministry] of the Ministry of the Treasury. This model of the Ministry of the Treasury and the DIPRES was imposed on Chile during the military dictatorship by economists who preached the free market, but in the exercise of their power they imitated the discretional methods of command and control of the real socialist countries in the 1950s. Unlike the model of the Treasury and DIPRES, the constitutional requirements of the Social and Democratic State consist of submitting to political deliberation the drafting and application of the legislative programs and/or measures in which social policies are expressed, and leave behind pure technocratic discretion in this respect.

The defeated doctrines mentioned by Professor Eduardo Aldunate to justify the criticisms of the Welfare State or of the Social and Democratic State governed by the rule of law do not, in any way, imply ending or overtaking this political and legal project. Today, the Welfare State or the Social and Democratic State governed by rule of law has enjoyed full application and health in Germany, and despite the controversies that Professor Aldunate has summarized well, and the expenditure generated by the unification of the two Germanies, it has not changed in its essential aspects. It is also of the essence of the Social and Democratic State that there is a continual controversy about it because it has been constructed through negotiation and political agreements that are typical of democracy, and which emerged, in particular, when the Second World War concluded. Tony Judt says:

> The post-1945 European Welfare States varied considerably in the resources they provided and the way they financed them. But certain general points can be made. The provision of social *services* chiefly concerned education, housing and medical care, as well as urban recreation areas, subsidized public transport, publicly funded art and culture and other indirect benefits of the interventionary State. Social *security* consisted chiefly of the State provision of insurance – against illness, unemployment, accident and the perils of old age. Every European State in the post-war years provided or financed most of the resources, some more than others.
>
> (Judt 2005: 120; English translation from http://scienzepolitiche .unical.it/bacheca/archivio/materiale/2467/Materiale%20didattico %20per%20corso%20magistrale%20Storia%20Integrazione%20E uropea/Tony%20Judt-Postwar_%20A%20History%20of%20Euro pe%20Since%201945-Penguin%20Press%20%282005%29.pdf)

Tony Judt explains what has been achieved in terms of social integration with this form of Welfare State because, despite its organizational and funding problems, it has been able to face the most basic contemporary problems and become what is considered normal in the policy of the countries with the best human development indices. Among the achievements of the Welfare State, Judt highlights the following:

> The priorities of the traditional State were defense, public order, prevention of epidemics, and avoidance of discontent among the masses. But after the Second World War, social expenditure did not stop growing until, by approximately 1980, it became the main budgetary responsibility of the modern States. By 1988, with the notable exception of the United States, the principal developed countries dedicated more resources to welfare, in the broad sense, than to anything else. It is understandable that a sharp increase in taxes was also produced at that time. To those who were old enough to remember how things had been before this crescendo of social expenditure and the provision of welfare, it must have seemed almost miraculous. The deceased political scientist, Ralf Dahrendorf, who was well-placed to appreciate the magnitude of changes that he saw in the course of his life, wrote about those optimistic years: "in many ways, the social democratic consensus signals the greatest progress that history has seen so far. Never have there been so many people with so many vital

opportunities." At the beginning of the 1970s it would have been unthinkable to contemplate the dismantling of the social services, welfare provisions, cultural and educational resources funded by the State and many other things that people would have considered natural.

(Judt 2011: 83–84)

This form of the Welfare State that today is called the Social and Democratic State, governed by the rule of law, emerged in Europe in the middle of the twentieth century and proposed to ensure, legally and financially, in a stable way, a network of social protection based on the rights to work, education, health, social security, and unionization, among others. This network guarantees a minimum for each citizen through programs, statutory laws, and even the Constitution, to reduce the degree of discretion that government may exercise in their provision. Also, it must be based on the deliberations of the citizens and a permanent and balanced dialogue between workers and employers. The adaptation of these ideas to Chile requires profound constitutional reforms.

This ideal of the State is defined as democratic because it renounces the centralism which has been of so much service to neoliberal evangelists to control the country without counterbalances, from Teatinos 120 (headquarters of the Ministry for the Treasury and the Budgetary Directorate (DIPRES), from where they actually manage the budgets and public policies of all the ministries), without submitting public issues to deliberation or assuming responsibility before the citizens. Because the Social and Democratic State has resolved to redistribute power in a deeper and more participative way at central, regional, and communal level, and to give more power to the citizens, it assumes also a new spirit of public service in all areas of government. It needs to boost creativity, both public and private engagement, and a culture of republican duties and responsibilities that means a new way of thinking about Chilean citizenship, in its political, social, and also economic aspects. Finally, it proposes to end all kinds of exclusion, such as those who cannot vote because they live overseas, or the lack of recognition of our indigenous people. To carry out this change, constitutional reforms must be approved that ensure a way of distributing the resources of all Chileans, that may have more efficiency, more deliberation, representation, participation, and responsibility, and less command and control in each of these new exercises of power.

7.17 THE LEOPARD CONSTITUTION AND THE CONTRADICTIONS OF THE FIFTH REPUBLIC

We have already explained that in terms of organic aspects, the present Chilean Constitution maintains a feature of authoritarian presidentialism, increasingly exacerbated from 1925 to the present. Additionally, the National Security Council is still present and there is in the Constitution a complete chapter dedicated to the armed forces which is not compatible with republican constitutionalism. More than this, the National Security Council reinforces the authoritarian and military-civic character of the hyper-presidentialism typical of the Constitution. This Constitution does not value but obstructs citizens' participation.

Unfortunately, the 2005 constitutional reform also served to validate and, in some cases, to reinforce, with all the ceremonial of La Moneda Palace, some of the more authoritarian features of our Constitution. At present in the Chilean Constitution there are several provisions that refer to the idea of national security, such as the following: Article 1 (general conception of the State and society); Article 8 (transparency and publicity restrictions); Article 19 No. 11 (freedom for education), No. 16 (freedom to work protection), No. 18 (social security protection), No. 20 (equal taxation), No. 21 (economic freedom), No. 23 (access to property protection), and No. 24 (property protection); Article 22 (flag protection provision); Article 23 (separation of politics and labor organizations); Article 32, No. 17 (presidential power over armed forces), No. 19 (presidential power to declare war), No. 20 (presidential power to impose tax bills); Article 42 (state of emergency declaration); Article 52 (impeachment powers of congressional representatives); Article 60 (expiration of representative mandate in Congress); Article 101 (role of armed forces); Articles 106–107 (National Security Council); Article 109 (Central Bank role in case of war). Article 9 still contains regulations regarding terrorism that contradict the basic principles of criminal law. Some of the regulations regarding nationality and citizenship of chapter 2 of the present Constitution, such as Article 16 No. 2, which suspends citizenship if someone is accused of certain offenses, violate human rights guaranteed in the treaties that are compulsory in Chile. Also, Article 23 of the Chilean Constitution enshrines corporatism at constitutional level when maintaining an archaic separation between politics and the intermediary groups or trade unions. The submission to the rule of law of the President of the Republic and of the titleholders of the executive function, of the para-statal bodies, in particular of the armed forces, has been lenient, despite the gradual advances in these matters.

In the Fifth Republic, a conception of rights has been developed which in its origin was pontifical, and which in its present expression is *jus*-fundamentalist and neoliberal, because it devalues the social and democratic aspects of its application and gives predominance to the judiciary function. The government in its executive function is the great legislator, and it legislates directly or by delegation or by insistence, which, added to its exorbitant and reinforced faculties, implies that it dominates without counterbalance. The laws of the dictatorship, still valid, many times in the form of organic statutory laws and validated by transitory articles still in force, severely limit the possibilities of adopting an economic social legislation that gives relief to the Chilean population that lives with inequality.

From 1990, constitutional legal control has been given in various ways to the Chilean judiciary. The Constitutional Tribunal, the Electoral Tribunals, and specialized Military Tribunals have been organized, and at constitutional level there has been recognition of the autonomous character of the Central Bank, the Comptroller General of the Republic, and the Public Ministry or Public Prosecutor, which was created to give a new guarantee structure to the criminal process. These bodies do not have clear systems of constitutional responsibility, and many times their attributes come into conflict with the titleholders of the executive, legislative, or judicial functions, or between these same autonomous bodies.

In the Fifth Republic, power is concentrated and centralized in Santiago and in the executive function, despite the government rhetoric of decentralization. Political and economic power is mixed with modes of corporatism and with a growing foreign influence, from 1990 expressed in the form of significant foreign investment and an open economy, which has been formalized with an important series of efforts aimed at economic integration.

The Fifth Republic is inspired only partially by republican principles. There persists in it the logic of a transition that still is not complete; forms of domination are maintained that are anti-republican; and the subordination of military power to civil power is not assured. The participation and deliberation of the governed in public issues and the right to dissent are considerably expanded compared to the time of the dictatorship. However, in some areas, the levels of inclusion of the Fourth Republic have still not been reached because suffrage and political representation are still very restricted.

Respect for the law as an expression of civic republicanism has been growing in this period. Severe forms of political exclusion and film censorship have come to an end, but there still persists a high degree of ownership and administrative concentration in the media that is in the control of a few hands, which is an expression of cultural domination. At the same time, political participation is very restricted in the electoral system, and the fight against excessive concentration of power, which is typical of governments with a republican base, has been difficult because the power of the large conglomerates has increased. In a text that assesses the six-year term of Ricardo Lagos, Gabriel Salazar says:

> His government came to an end with Chile still among the countries with the worst income distribution at world level, with high rates of people with work problems, which does not allow an assertion that the growth registered will be used for the benefit of the majority. The concentration of income and wealth continue to be very heavily in the benefit of the usual minorities, as is shown by the exorbitant levels of income of the copper transnational enterprises or of the main economic groups, so the macro-economic policies used were not employed to guide the increases of income originated by economic growth towards redistribution.
>
> (Salazar 2005b: 25–26)

These critical observations are especially paradoxical because they are directed at the government of Ricardo Lagos, who, in his thesis *La concentración del poder económico* [The Concentration of Economic Power], demonstrated an early sensitivity towards these issues. At the beginning of the 1960s, Lagos expressed himself as follows:

> And the truth is that the great concentration that exists in Chile, this true monopoly that affects all activities, cannot be destroyed

with small modifications or with "anti-monopoly" statutory laws such as those that we know at present and that are applied to bakers, owners of vegetable shops, to butchers, and so on. There is not the economic power that abuses the consumer and society: true power is in the financial apparatus (the banks), in the large industrial areas and in the large farms. It is towards them that the regulatory power of the State has to go ... the only and true solution therefore, is the abolition of private property in means of production, which must be the property of the State. As long as such property persists, all the statutes passed will only be palliatives that will never achieve the final elimination of the different forms of concentration.

(Lagos 1961: 171–172)

Ricardo Lagos, who proposed the abolition of private property to avoid economic concentration in Chile, has now passed into history as the President whose government had one of the highest concentrations of income. This is the great paradox of the Fifth Republic. A paradox whose resolution is still outstanding and which is aggravated by the unlimited dominance of the influence and power of the higher and middle class in Santiago, and the lack of any balance with alternative regional authorities. This feature is also the expression of a shortage of republican and democratic citizenship. It is true that the great virtue of the Fifth Republic in Chile is that it has been a very stable political time. It has been very stable despite the fact that the Constitution that rules us was adopted and has been reformed with the participation of very few relevant political actors, and it is a Fundamental Charter in which the convictions of many groups that have political importance in Chile are not reflected (Elkins, Ginsburg, and Melton 2009: 10). This is even more serious because the representatives of Chilean political parties that participate in the system rarely practice an internal democracy.

We have become used to a Constitution that, despite its more than 350 reforms and having been legitimized in a gradual process, has no precedents in Chilean constitutional history. The Fundamental Charter continues to be perceived as a "Leopard" Constitution because, despite all the changes realized, it is still the same in its main doctrinal features, and in its neoliberal and authoritarian principles. This "Leopard" characteristic results in the present Constitution being the most reformed in the history of Chile, and at the same time, a text that urgently requires to progress in terms of its democratic character, in a way that is compatible with the twenty-first century (Cristi and Ruiz-Tagle 2006: 197–217).

In the final sections of this book, we will analyze the substantive and procedural proposals for constitutional change that exist in Chile today, assuming a historical and comparative perspective.

CHAPTER EIGHT

THE MOST RECENT CHILEAN CONSTITUTIONAL MOMENT AND ITS CONTENT

To conclude this analysis of the republican constitutional experience in Chile, we could point out that, despite all the defects found in our political system, from the nineteenth century up to the present, there is significant development in four areas: equality, freedom, affirmation of popular sovereignty, and democracy. There is progress in the creation and implementation of new political institutions, such as Congress, or republican educational institutions, such as the Instituto Nacional José Miguel Carrera and the Universidad de Chile. It is also true that there have been interruptions to this process. Nevertheless, during the Chilean republican periods there have been unprecedented achievements in the construction of modern citizenship, the extension of suffrage, and the broadening of egalitarian access to public office and to education. The fine-tuning of the forms of representative democracy in America and Europe came to an end, and the five Chilean republics were a significant part of that global process. These same changes are reflected in the constitutional mode of organizing the structure of rights and in the distribution of constitutional entities, from an internal point of view and in relationship with citizens.

Today, at the beginning of the twenty-first century, Chile needs a new Constitution for three main reasons. The first concerns the present Constitution's origins under a dictatorship, which affects its legitimacy, and the exercise of the Constitution has failed to legitimize it as the fundamental charter of all Chileans. The second refers to the fact that despite successive reforms, the Constitution's content is still neither democratic nor republican, and its pedigree is authoritarian in the following matters: (a) it does not effectively guarantee the social rights of education, health, work, union organization, and social security, among others; (b) it separates politics from social organization, prohibiting social leaders from being political leaders, a restriction which is not imposed upon business organizations; (c) it reinforces an authoritarian presidentialism; (d) it gives power to non-accountable authorities, such as the Constitutional Tribunal and the Central Bank; (e) it establishes the controversial doctrine of *Seguridad Nacional* [National Security] and the *Consejo de Seguridad Nacional* [National Security Council]. The third reason is that the omissions in the Constitution reveal its present authoritarian conception, in issues such as: (a) not granting recognition to indigenous people; (b) not decentralizing power, nor giving effective power to the regions and municipalities; (c) permitting unlimited re-election to popularly elected positions and nepotism (an absence of restrictions on appointing relatives to public offices in the same local, provincial, or regional government); (d) the absence of inclusion for marginalized groups; (e) the failure to enshrine the principle of the democratic majority, but give the minority an excessive advantage in Congress, which combines high quorum and distortions created by the recently reformed binomial system; and finally (f) not promoting social protection and a social and democratic rule of law.

The new Chilean Constitution should have the following characteristics if it is to stand as a true Fundamental Charter:

- Continuity and stability: the Constitution cannot be changed in accordance with contingent criteria or in a facile manner, because it addresses the most important questions regarding the organization of the State and society and of the legal system.
- Constitutional patriotism: the Constitution should generate attachment and integration, and the collective sense that emerges from internal adhesion to the regulations and institutions of a country when they are just.
- Monitoring of constitutionality: the Constitution should include mechanisms to avoid deviations of power in public or private regulations or decisions.
- Fundamental rights: the Constitution should limit and organize the relationship between citizens and State action, and should be based on respect for the rights of all, majority rule, and the inclusion and participation of minorities.

Furthermore, some of the ideas that must be considered to create a new Chilean Constitution in democracy, which have been expressed recently by different political forces in Chile, include:

1. A constitution must promote more strongly fundamental rights and democracy. There must be a new relationship between the State and society: a social and democratic rule of law.
2. The Constitution should embody new ways of thinking about fundamental rights and duties and their guarantees.
3. A new political regime, which allows for choices among flexible presidentialism, semi-presidentialism, and a parliamentarian system.
4. A new design for legislative and statutory authority.
5. A new system of regional and local government and administration with real political power.
6. A new conception of armed forces and institutions of national security.
7. A new balance between representation and citizen participation.
8. A redesign of the electoral system and electoral districts.
9. A new organization of the judiciary.
10. A new system of electoral justice.
11. A new Constitutional Tribunal.
12. A pro-democratic revision of regional powers and local autonomies.
13. Incorporation of an Ombudsman.
14. New procedures for reform of the form and substantive provisions of the Constitution.
15. A revision of the transitory articles, states of emergency, organic laws, and the associated qualified quorums.

These proposals are not absolute and allow for continual improvement. Any serious proposal of total or partial reform that seeks to be submitted before Parliament and the people for approval should consider the most up-to-date constitutional experience and doctrine that reflects our own tradition, our history, and also knowledge concerning comparative constitutional law and experience.

8.1 THE REASONABLE EXERCISE OF CONSTITUTIONAL CONSTITUENT POWER IN CHILE

Before considering the procedures through which we can arrive at a new Chilean Constitution, we believe it is important to examine three preliminary conditions that we draw as lessons from history and which are present in our previous political experience. The first two conditions, in particular, relate to the projects of profound change, of the center and the left, that were represented by President Eduardo Frei Montalva (1964) and President Salvador Allende Gossens (1970) respectively. The third condition is related to the constitutional political structure that appeared with the inauguration of the Fifth Chilean Republic in March 1990 and continues into the present.

The first condition to carry out deep social transformation in Chile is political and implies that any projects of change must rest upon majority support and be based upon diverse coalitions. Changes cannot be realized by only one political party, as was attempted in 1964 and 1970; nor is it sufficient for a coalition government to pursue substantial reforms if it does not have a majority, as happened between 1970 and 1973. The *Unidad Popular* [Popular Unity Coalition] acceded to power with around 30 percent of the electorate and never had more than a fraction over 40 percent of the vote. The Coalition of Parties for Democracy and the *Nueva Mayoría* [New Majority Coalition] have had the citizens' backing, but have also experienced declines in support, which conspire against the viability of their proposals for change.

The second condition is legal and implies that transformations be brought about following institutional paths in strict compliance with the law. This means using forms of law that are recognized as legal by the majority, and not legal loopholes or twisted interpretations of the meaning of the law. Thus these preconditions for democratic transformation require not only majority support, but also that the transformation should be effected in strict compliance with the principles of the rule of law, in its republican and constitutional version; and, more specifically, during constitutional moments these transformations demand compliance with Bruce Ackerman's normative democratic requirements, which we have noted above.

It is worth pointing out that while this second condition requires respect for the law, under no circumstances am I providing reasons that support the 1973 military coup d'état, which from the constitutional and republican point of view has no justification. Rather, I am saying exactly the opposite. That is, to diverge from the law when seeking profound transformations affects the constitutional validity and the republican base of the reformist effort, and such divergences may undermine the support that reform efforts may have had among the majority of citizens. It is also important to note that from the republican point of view, it is not a question of seeking or preserving majority support just like that. Pinochet, at the end of his dictatorship, still had the support of 43.4 percent of the Chilean people at the polls, and it is possible that his dictatorship had majority support during some periods, like Hitler and other dictators. This type of popular support for dictatorships shows how majorities can go astray, and in no case does this support legitimize their power or modify in the least their anti-republican and anti-democratic character.

The third condition consists of recognizing that the new Constitution is not the 1980 constitutional text originally imposed by General Pinochet, because this authoritarian fundamental charter ceased to exist with the return to democracy. This recognition assumes that we should totally or partially reform the Chilean Constitution which we have had from 1990 to the present day. The 1980 constitutional text approved by Pinochet ceased to rule in Chile from March 1990. The dictatorship came to an end on 11 March 1990. The legislative commissions ended, and the commanders-in-chief ceased to exercise the constituent, legislative, and executive power that they had attributed to themselves in September 1973. From 1990 onwards, the Chilean people, through their elected or appointed representatives, according to the fundamental charter, have exercised constituent, legislative, executive, judicial, and other powers. As Renato Cristi has explained, Andrés Chadwick, and all those who have supported the thesis that we continue to live under the military proclamation that gave validity to the constitutional text of the dictatorship, are mistaken (Cristi and Ruiz-Tagle 2014: 163–166). The Presidents of the Republic, the Members of Parliament, the National Congress, and all the elected or appointed authorities after March 1990 were not authorities of the military dictatorship, but rather of the imperfect democracy of the Fifth Republic that has existed since March 1990.

Chile's post-1990 constitution, which to date nobody has dared to call the 1990 Constitution, is distinguished from the dictatorship's authoritarian constitution by fifty-four reforms and by a referendum that approved the first reforms with electoral registries in force in July 1989. Since 1990, statutes have been enacted twenty times to modify the Constitution and the changes around 257 reformed articles. The charter is by far the most reformed constitution in Chilean history. Yet despite these changes, the text and most of its structure and contents still coincides to a large degree with the 1980 constitutional text of Pinochet. That is why we have called it the *Gatopardo* [Leopard] Constitution (Cristi and Ruiz-Tagle 2006: 197–223): it has the capacity to change and still stay the same, with regard to its fundamental meaning and the Chilean people's sense of not being represented by it. As Ernesto Garzón Valdés says, despite its legitimization or validity, it lacks legality or affinity with the most profound moral convictions of the Chilean people (Garzón Valdés 1993c: 455–471, 573–609).

Strictly speaking, it is a different Constitution from that of Pinochet; it is the Constitution that arises from the negotiations and agreements that the political forces governing since 1990 have accepted. From a political or communications point of view, it is even easier to speak of putting an end to Pinochet's Constitution and of the need to replace it with a new Constitution. In fact, it is a question of doing away with the Constitution of the Fifth Republic, a constitution which was the partial, yet substantive work of the left-wing and center parties that made up the successive coalitions of the Coalition of Parties for Democracy and the New Majority Coalition, and, of course, the political right in the *Alianza por Chile* [Alliance for Chile Coalition]. A sample of the aberrant constituent power exercised from 1990 to the present is found in the transitory articles; although twenty transitory articles have been repealed, twenty-five more have been approved – twenty after 1990. A republican and democratic Constitution cannot have such a high number of transitory articles. We should review which articles ought to be eliminated and which ought to be incorporated into the permanent text, but we cannot continue to maintain that these defects of our Constitution have their origin in the dictatorship.

So the first thing that has to be recognized is that this is a legal and political issue, and not a fantasy or a mystical proposal of political theology, and that it must express, integrate, represent, and give participation to all the political parties and organized political forces, including the independents, who in total are more numerous than the total of active members of political parties, and that generally speaking, all the citizens should be involved. The process of elaborating a new democratic constitution is not done de facto, by decree, or only with the erudite opinion of a group of jurists. Furthermore, it requires an accurate assessment of the political times, its viability, and priorities. Therefore, thought should be given to combining an urgent package of partial reforms of high sensitivity that are perceived as being of consensus and importance for the great majority of the people, together with a wider and more extended process in which the discussion and elaboration of the new Constitution is conceived as a lengthy process that could take several years.

Once the new Constitution is approved, be it by virtue of a total reform presented to the National Congress, or through a Constituent Assembly, it is eventually necessary for the Constitutional Tribunal and/or the Electoral Tribunal (formerly, *Tribunal Calificador de Elecciones* [Elections Qualifier Tribunal]), and the Comptroller General of the Republic to intervene in order to validate the legal terms of a referendum, by which the people and citizens will participate to give their verdict on the projected new Constitution, which can be submitted to their choice in the form of a single question or with alternative texts.

8.2   CONTROL OF CONSTITUENT AND DESTITUENT POWERS, AND CONSTITUTIONAL MUTATION

In Chile today, there is a constituent power that, according to our present constitutional chart, is based on the President and on Parliament. But there is also what we might call a power of constituent constitutional control. Without even considering the existence of these mechanisms of constitutional control, some headstrong advocates of change of our Fundamental Charter have even proposed, in a state of factionist and "Jacobin" mysticism, to change the Constitution, for better or for worse, to impose a Constitution by a decree or through an Assembly of Municipal Advisors, or to call a referendum by *decretazo* [a decree that comes into force by presidential whim without being agreed by a majority], to install a de facto Constituent Assembly, and so it goes on, making all kinds of inflamed proposals of populism, media protagonism, and irresponsible revolutionary infantilism (Zúñiga 2014: 1–49).

Instead of assuming an ethic of responsibility and seeking the agreement of all Chileans for the building of a bicentenary Constitution, the Jacobian spirit has brought them to suggest, influenced by Carl Schmitt, that their political opponents are their enemies who must be faced with *loaded guns*. They certainly ignore what is meant by a democratic constituent process, and also the role of constituent control reposing in the Comptroller General of the Republic, that of the Constitutional Tribunal, should it be needed in order to pronounce on a projected reform, and that of the Electoral Tribunal in case of a referendum. This way of thinking and acting in politics recalls the worst sort of what

James Madison so skillfully describes, in The Federalist No. 10, as the spirit of faction:

> By a faction I understand a number of citizens, whether amounting to a majority or a minority of the whole, who are united and actuated by some common impulse of passion or of interest, adverse to the rights of other citizens, or to the permanent and aggregate interests of the community . . . Liberty is to faction what air is to fire, an aliment without which it instantly expires. But it could not be a lesser folly to abolish liberty, which is essential to political life because it nourishes faction, than it would be to wish for the annihilation of air, which is essential to animal life, because it imparts to fire its destructive agency . . . The latent causes of faction are thus sown in the nature of man; and we see them everywhere brought into different degrees of activity, according to the different circumstances of civil society. A zeal for different opinions concerning religion, government, and many other points, of speculation as well as practice; an attachment to different leaders ambitiously contending for pre-eminence and power, or to persons of other descriptions whose fortunes have been interesting to the human passions, have, in turn, divided mankind into parties, inflamed them with mutual animosity, and rendered them much more disposed to vex and oppress each other than to cooperate for their common good. So strong is this propensity of mankind to fall into mutual animosities that where no substantial occasion presents itself, the most frivolous and fanciful distinctions have been sufficient to kindle their unfriendly passions and excite their most violent conflicts. But the most common and durable source of factions has been the various and unequal distribution of property.
>
> (Hamilton, Madison, and Jay 1982: 35–41)

In Chile, there also exists a responsible civic constituent power that can express itself and has expressed itself before, during, and after the process of constitutional change, and which is brought to bear on proposals of general interest that could become binding through the communications of the President of the Republic or, as the case may be, through parliamentary motions. For example, more recently, and in order to organize the constituent process in Chile in its civic aspect, I proposed this idea of the Commission created by the President of the Republic, in order to use less energy in the process and more in the discussion of the contents, and to give ourselves time and calm. This idea of the Commission, which in order to disqualify it many call the *Comisión de los Expertos* or *Comisión Constituyente* [Commission of

265

Experts or Constituent Commission], was criticized because it is sup-posedly based only on expert advice – which is not necessarily true, because it may include ordinary citizens – because it is formed by decree, and because its resolutions are not binding on constituent issues. As for that, Article 32 No. 6 was used to appoint the Valech and the Rettig Commissions, which prepared a report on human rights violations during the last military dictatorship, and I believe that this same provision could be used to create something that would be a proxy of a constituent assembly, mixing experts with politicians and citizens, in case it were deemed necessary, to give wider representation, order, continuity, and stability to the Chilean constituent process. This proposal is similar to the *Comisión de Observadores* [Observers' Commission], which combined many different citizens and is analyzed in the following section.

It is also important to recognize that the constituent process is influenced by a series of functional and factual powers, such as the press, lawyers, and professionals, businessmen, the Church, the mili-tary, as well as academics. Among these influential powers, I would call attention to the existence of an additional power, which we might call destituent power. There is a constituent power that hopes to change the Constitution partially or totally, and in the opposite direction a destituent power is operating, as described by Giorgio Agamben:

> While a constituent power destroys law only to recreate it in a new form, destituent power, insofar as it deposes once and for all the law, can open a really new historical epoch.

> (Agamben 2013)

In Chile, following the logic of the destituent power that we have exposed, there is a group in operation, or rather two groups of people, on the right and on the left, that do not like the system that we have and want to destroy it because they do not like any constitutional and democratic system and rule out any possibility of rational resolution. Here, there are people who want to have a political organization that in no way has the attributes of a constitutional representative democracy, and who certainly take advantage of this moment – this has to enter the equation – to advance through a destituent process.

All the institutionalized procedures are fully ratified for a total or partial constitutional reform, and there is none that by definition is better than another. From the academic point of view, they ought to be analyzed, but the choice of which ones definitely to use, and with what intensity and in what combination, is mainly an institutional and political decision that falls to those who hold the constituent power in Chile, according to our Fundamental Charter, who are the President of the Republic and the Members of Parliament, which in no way means that it is not subject to control. In a constitutional democracy, this choice falls to the political parties and the political forces, to government, and to the opposition in a conversation in which the citizens obviously can intervene and have their opinion, but the decision is a constitutional political decision, not a theoretical decision.

In this matter there is no equation and no silver bullet which allows us to define the best procedure for constitutional change as the constituent assembly. That is not real. The person who has that belief believes in a constitutional Santa Claus, which does not exist. In fact, the constituent assemblies are of a thousand forms, as can be appreciated by anyone who takes time to study them. The history of constitutionalism reveals very different ways to create constitutions.

In 2015, we celebrated 800 years of the Magna Carta. We continue talking about the Magna Carta, and who knows which method was used to arrive at those constitutional principles that we value today, such as the habeas corpus. Who can explain which were the methods used in the Philadelphia Convention and in the process of ratification in each of the states that were different from that used by the federal government to adopt the Federal Constitution of the USA? It is also known that the process of adoption of the Federal Constitution followed different methods for its approval and that the Philadelphia representatives were selected according to what suited each state. There is no silver bullet. The 1978 Spanish Constitution was made as a by-product of the laws of political reform from the Franco era. The 1957 French Constitution has been criticized for being the expression of General de Gaulle's egotism. The fundamental laws in Bonn, which have governed Germany since 1949 and do not add up to a constitution according to the definition of the Germans themselves in its text, have, as their origin, a memorandum of the Allied forces. We do not have to seek perfection; we humbly seek the best. In this case, as in so many others, "perfect" can be an enemy of "good."

Among the mechanisms of constitutional revision or change, doctrine recognizes total or partial reform, mutation, constitutional interpretation, constituent commissions in each chamber, or bicameral constituent congresses, referenda, and plebiscites, and, of course, the constituent assemblies. Regarding the idea of a referendum to decide if there should be a constituent assembly or an experts' commission or a bicameral commission, it is necessary to bear in mind the doctrine of comparative law regarding referenda of special transcendence, as Professor Francisco Soto has explained (Soto 2016). Furthermore, they are mechanisms much criticized by the constitutional doctrine because they are susceptible to manipulation and because they generate political conditions that allow the recreation of what Bruce Ackerman has called the Juan Linz nightmare, or "Linzeana" (Ackerman 2007: 28–29).

If there is a referendum, the best option from the point of view of the constitutional democratic theory of referendum, which exists today in Europe and other countries, is for it to be called once there are one or more texts in order to decide between one or more options of constitutional projects. To realize a constitutional plebiscite or referendum before having a text or project that is going to be subject to popular approval, means a waste of much political energy, and is also much queried from the point of view of what it means, which leads, in truth, to a kind of constitutional Bonapartism, because it is intervening ahead of the constitutional procedures, and increasing the power of the government compared to that of the people in a disproportionate way.

On the mechanism of the Constituent Assembly, it is important to note that it has several forms and that many people who speak about a Constituent Assembly still have not produced a text that defines how it will be realized, with the sole exception of the proposal by the *Partido por la Democracia* [Party for Democracy], which proposes adding a heading to the Constitution that will allow the use of this mechanism in Chile, which seems to me a valid method to incorporate this mechanism in our Constitution. Furthermore, the Constituent Assembly, from the theoretical point of view, is an instrument of representation, not of participation. The Constituent Assembly seeks to create an alternative representation to Congress or to the usual and ordinary bodies, so that they do not have so much power. That is the rationale underlying its justification. If we accept these reasons as valid, then we have to create a Constituent Assembly. But it is not an institution designed for participation, but to give representation to groups or forces that are not incorporated in the normal institutional framework, or to prevent the constituent Congress from having too much power or to restrict it to work in ordinary legislation. In the democratic constituent assembly, at least, the representatives are elected, and if there are representatives there will be representation. There are assemblies not foreseen in the Constitution, as in the case of Ecuador, and others that are frankly revolutionary, and these last ones operate along the lines of what we might call the "destituent power," about which we have already expressed our criticism.

Together with the possibilities of change that are always available through constitutional interpretation, about which we will not give further details, it is also important to highlight (because it seems to me of the greatest importance) the role performed by constitutional muta‑ tion, a mechanism of constitutional reform that is defined in the work of Karl Loewenstein, as follows:

> in constitutional mutation ... a transformation takes place in the reality of the configuration of political power, of the social structure or in the balance of interests, without such transformation being incorporated in the constitutional document: the text of the Constitution remains untouched.
>
> (Loewenstein 1983: 165)

I believe that the Chilean constitutional text is set at present in a political context in which it is read differently from the ways in which it was originally conceived, which marked the first decade of our Fundamental Charter being in force. And I am going to give one example. (There are many others.) Today, in the clause of the Constitution that says *The family is the fundamental nucleus of society*, when family is read, at least it can be accepted that there are two, three, or four versions of this subsection, considering that there was, until very recently, a unanimous vision that when we were talking about family, it was about a matrimonial family. This idea that a family means a matrimonial family is still valid, it has to be recognized, and it is maintained by a significant group of people, scholars of constitutional law and of Chilean society, but there has emerged – I would say by constitutional mutation – the idea that in Chile a family is much more than a matrimonial notion, that it is a relationship of kinship by affinity, that there can be one‑parent families, in fact all sorts of relationships by a much more open kinship. In its turn, Chilean con‑ stitutional jurisprudence is beginning to recognize this mutation. This is just an example to say that the Constitution, the same Constitution that we have, can be read in a different way, and that is something rather significant when we are embarking on a constituent process.

The constitutional reforms that were promoted in 2005 sought to close the file on the transition to democracy, and to that end, the prestige and power of the presidential figure was used to give impetus and legality to the changes to our Fundamental Charter. However, despite the significant advance that these reforms implied, the progress was partial because they were not enough to establish the idea that they amounted to a democratic new Constitution for Chile. As we have explained, some of the 2005 changes empowered to excess the already unbalanced Chilean presidentialism; they did not address the subject of economic and social rights and maintained the neoliberal logic of the law. Furthermore, even if it was a long-term negotiation, it was carried out behind people's backs, in Congress and behind closed doors, without being validated by a referendum once it was agreed. The most important aspect was that it did not complement the constitutional reform with a change in the electoral system, and this revived the old practices of the cumbersome and deformed binomial electoral system, and the reproduction of that curious form of democracy that has existed in Chile in which the majority governs in a position of equal power with the minority.

The President of the Republic is an actor of the greatest importance in constitutional issues, but certainly is not the only and exclusive entity or individual that should intervene. The Members of Parliament, the political class, the people, and public opinion are there as well, and frankly, I hope that in Chile, a constitutional debate can be generated along the lines proposed by Bruce Ackerman. It is in the respectful words of deliberation, in which we not only accept the existence of political opponents (who are not perceived as an enemy), but invite them to discuss candidly, openly, without duplicity or coercion, the ideas that each one may have, with the hope that a process of mutual persuasion can be produced and that we can convince one another of the best arguments.

8.3   PARTICIPATION AND REPRESENTATION IN THE CHILEAN CONSTITUENT PROCESS

On October 14, 2015, President Michelle Bachelet, in a speech addressed to the Chilean people, called on everyone to begin a gradual constituent process of many stages in order to approve a new democratic Constitution in Chile. This convocation was unprecedented in the history of Chile, both in the way in which it was carried out and in the ambitious purpose that inspired it. The stages set out in Bachelet's proposal began with a period of civic education and information, regarding what is a Constitution, opening with the speech and culminating in March 2016. During this initial period, it was planned that the President of the Republic would appoint a *Consejo de Observadores* [Observers' Council], to be a coordinating and supervising commission of the constituent process, which in March 2016 would begin a process of dialogues and *cabildos* [councils] at provincial level, where the people might express their constitutional ideas, which would finally be collected in a document called *Bases ciudadanas* [Citizens' Foundations], which would be handed over to the President in October 2016. This new stage of President Bachelet's government was dedicated to preparing a proposal for a new fundamental charter that was submitted in a bill to Congress at the end of her mandate. In this same period, the President of the Republic submitted to Congress a proposal with four alternatives relating to the system or procedure for constitutional change, which included the *Comisión Bicameral* [Bicameral Commission], a mixed commission of Members of Parliament and citizens, the Constituent Assembly, and, eventually, the call to a referendum so that the people could choose between the first three alternatives.

Concerning the proposal about the procedure for constitutional change, the government undertook to approve it by two-thirds of the sitting members of Parliament, despite the strict requirement for this quorum being disputed, when it is a case of adding a new constitutional chapter, which could be approved by three-fifths of the Members of Parliament in attendance. As stated in the decree of appointment at the end of 2015, an Observers' Council was appointed in virtue of Article 32 No. 6 of the Constitution, to guide and coordinate the civic process of constitutional debate, composed of people of diverse walks of life and awareness, and with plurality of representation in terms of the political forces that integrate it. The Council also incorporates representatives of the opposition, which entirely coincides with the proposal that, in its time, I had put forward in order to make progress in this important matter. The foregoing certainly does not mean that the composition of this Council has not had criticisms, and of the most diverse kind.

President Bachelet's proposal included questions of procedure and questions of constitutional substance. It was also a proposal that had to be weighed up by the opposition, Members of Parliament, and the people, in order to establish whether they supported or rejected it.

The modification to the electoral system was also enacted and it could have been used to debate the problem of representation of some relevant minorities that exist in Chile, as is the case with the indigenous people: unfortunately, this opportunity did not address this important issue. However, the change in the electoral system has been used to generate a new political scenario and to found the new Chilean constituent process on this reality which is to come. Table 8.1 sets out the stages of the civic participation process which were considered in the Observers' Council, not without criticism and obstruction.

TABLE 8.1 Summary of the citizens' participation process

Phases	Objectives	Actions	Results
1. Preparation of dialogue	Create basic civic knowledge for the constitutional discussion	Educational campaign	National coverage through *El Constitucionario* (www.constitu cionario.cl)
	Generate motivation of citizens to participate in the process	Motivational campaign	Produce desirability and a sense of opportunity
	Prepare citizens for dialogue	Preparation campaign/kit for dialogue	Public report on conversations with citizens; massive pre-registration at communal meetings (ensure your quota)
2. Local	Ensure that all persons have the opportunity to participate	Individual participation	Statistical report of citizens' opinions; patrimonial bank of the constituent process
	Encourage local meetings, where possible, to talk about constitutional topics and set	Local meetings	Reports on local meetings

TABLE 8.1 (*cont.*)

Phases	Objectives	Actions	Results
3. Province	priorities through the agreements reached Participative integration of local citizens' proposals at provincial level (agreements, partial agreements, and disagreements); to integrate, debate, and prioritize again	Provincial councils	54 Provincial Acts
4. Region	Integrate and prioritize provincial proposals at regional level (agreements, partial agreements, disagreements)	Regional plenary proceedings	15 Regional Acts
5. Indigenous dialogue	Fulfill international commitments for indigenous consultation, incorporating their visions and proposals	Indigenous dialogue	Report on dialogues with indigenous people
6. Transversal proposals	Accept proposals of groups with specific interests	Preliminary consultation; audiences for special interest groups (trade unions, academics,	Report on preliminary consultation; draft proposals of transversal group

TABLE 8.1 (cont.)

Phases	Objectives	Actions	Results
7. Country synthesis	Elaborate a synthesis of the participation process	and churches) Task of citizens' council of observers	Citizens' bases for the new Constitution

Source: document from the Observers' Council, *Guía metodológica. Proceso participativo territorial* [Methodological Guide: Territorial Participatory Process], Santiago: General Secretariat to the Presidency, Republic of Chile, January 2016, p. 31

Furthermore, as this is a constituent process that the government has defined as institutional, democratic, and participatory, I believe that it is fitting to give special consideration to Professor James S. Fiskin's work, which helps us to understand what we are trying to say when we speak about improving political participation and deliberation. Fiskin has defined participation as public and large-scale conduct by the people who compose a political system, which has the objective of influencing directly or indirectly the formulation, adoption, or implementation of a political choice by the government. According to Fiskin, to vote is the most accepted form of participating in politics, but to contribute with money, time, effort, or work in relation to political causes, to participate in demonstrations, write letters or send electronic mail to civil servants, or to sign petitions are all activities that can include the participation of a large number of people. Even some passive activities, like keeping informed or watching the news, can be a form of participation, but in general, the term is used to point to active behavior (Fiskin 2009: 44).

Additionally, Fiskin understands deliberation as a process through which individuals consider or ponder the merits of the arguments expressed in the setting of common discussions. This deliberative process can be measured in terms of quality, according to how it fulfills the following five conditions: (a) to give relevant information to each participant; (b) to give a fundamental evaluation to each answer; (c) to value diversity in the representation of the main public opinions; (d) to show sincere cognizance of the arguments; (e) to give equal consideration to all arguments (ibid.: 33–34).

Since March 2018, Chile has been ruled by a right-wing coalition and, not surprisingly, the new government has slowed down the track of constitutional reform. However, in less than six months it proposed two new reform bills for changing the Chilean Constitution.

First, on May 2018, the newly elected government signed a bill for adding a new anti-discrimination mandate to Article 1 of the Chilean Constitution which provides that the State should promote gender equality under the law, and should work to secure equal duties and dignity among men and women, and to avoid any form of violence, abuse, harassment, or arbitrary discrimination. This bill is at present under parliamentary deliberation and means that the government should take an active role in matters pertaining to gender equality, adopting anti-discrimination measures.

Second, in September 2018, the right-wing government announced that it would send to Parliament for its approval a bill for a constitutional reform that would recognize the identity of the indigenous population, as an independent people having Chilean nationality. Most recently, a profound reform of the Constitutional Court has been received by the government that is also part of the proposals that are presently under consideration.

These reforms show that the pace of constitutional reform in Chile will continue, independently of the party or coalition that is in charge of the government. South America, in these years, seems to be moving on a wave of right-wing governments, such as that inaugurated in 2015 by President Mauricio Macri in Argentina, which came to an end in December 2019, and that of Jair Bolsonaro, who became President of Brazil in January 2019. Nevertheless, this move of the region towards the right has not ignored the need to face constitutional reform, a reform that is still very active in Chile, and which gives rise to a constitutional moment that has become a fundamental part of our present political life.

8.4   THE LESSONS WE CAN LEARN FROM PREVIOUS REPUBLICAN EXPERIENCES

Together with analyzing the proposals and procedures of the present constitutional reforms, I would also like to recall previous ones, including the classical, republican experiences, in order to illustrate with historical perspective the Chilean constituent process. In none of these cases is it about a homogeneous and uniform experience. Thus, Athens and Rome present significant contrasts that help to explain the differences that exist among the modern experiences.

Notwithstanding the characteristics explored above, there is a uniform feature that distinguishes republican governments from the other political systems, and it is that they are formed by the experience, political and intellectual capacity, and the participation of many individuals, even different groups of people and generations. Indeed, several generations are required to accumulate a base of shared experiences that are transmitted through time and that can become a tradition. It is pertinent to remember here what Cicero says at the beginning of the second book in *De re publica*. According to the Roman jurist, republics are superior to other forms of government because they have not been established by one man as the sole author of its laws and institutions. Republics have been based on the genius of many individuals and are founded and built not by one generation, but over a period that could extend to several centuries and eras. For Cicero, the republican form is superior, because there has never been one man so brilliant that he could anticipate all the problems, and not even all the faculties of men living at a given time, without the help of experience and the passing of time, could warn of all the precautions that should be taken for the future (Cicero 2000: 111–112).

The Republic of Chile has been built in different versions, which from our independence until now have become five main republics. We should resume, cultivate, and expand this republican tradition to allow the creation of new republics in which future generations might live in peace. It is true that things can be confused. The strategy of those opposed to the republic in its democratic form of government has been to adopt an opportunistic attitude that many times has entailed using it as a facade to cover the authoritarian use of power. Thus, in Chile we have had until recently a Senate with members partially elected by popular vote, armed forces represented in constitutional bodies that appointed some of the judges of the Constitutional Tribunal, and Presidents of the Republic in whom power is concentrated that exceeds by far that of a typical democratic authority. Our present hope is to recognize that by way of mutation, constitutional interpretation, and reform, the peaceful change can take place of one republican regime to another, which in certain substantive ways and procedures could be considered improved.

This situation can be recognized in Chile's case between the Second Authoritarian Republic (1830–1870) and the Third Liberal Republic (1870–1924). These constitutional moments were also times for reflection, criticism, conversation, reading, and deliberation, which inspired patriotism, as the great Benjamín Vicuña Mackenna reminds us in his work, *Los girondinos chilenos* [*The Chilean Girondists*]. In this master work, the author explains the origin of the thinking and action of the Chilean generation that in the middle of the nineteenth century was able to cross over peacefully from an authoritarian republic to a republic that would become liberal and parliamentary, saying:

> One of the favorite observations of those daily sessions was, in virtue of the analogy and similarity of the times, that which the reading suggested, also daily, of *The Girondists* by Lamartine, of the deeds of those illustrious men, their eloquence, their patriotism, their mistakes, their sad and sublime sacrifice, their posthumous glory, a distant radiation of genius, and the scaffold. And it was then, in the intimate scenes of nascent revolution, when there began to appear the figures and names of each of those Chilean Girondists, whose grouping by individualities and schools has been kept intact in our secret annals.
>
> (Vicuña Mackenna 1989: 50–51)

In this possibility of improvement through reflection, persuasion, and pacific political action is founded the strategy of republican constitutionalism to which we can aspire in our present and imperfect Fifth Republic, which is still neoliberal and neo-presidential. Let it be hoped that we could cross over in this peaceful way to a new political form from which may emerge the Sixth Chilean Republic, characterized by a guarantee of economic, social, and cultural rights and by a more democratic and balanced concept of authority – that is, a Sixth Chilean Republic that makes real a moderate and sustainable version of the project of the Welfare State or the Social and Democratic State in Chile. Facing this scenario, the efforts of all the supporters of republican constitutionalism, of the Chilean Girondists of the twenty-first century, acquire still more relevance, and – why not say it? – an additional degree of responsibility.

We hope that this work may make a contribution to the noble purpose of having a new Constitution for the years after the bicentenary of our independence, and that from it will emerge a new legal and political structure that inaugurates the Sixth Chilean Republic.

AFTERWORD

I was working on the final version of this book in English when the great Chilean uprising [*Estallido*] of October 2019 erupted. Students jumped the turnstiles in the subway to evade paying the fare, as a protest against a rate hike. Within hours, several subway stations had been set ablaze. A volatile explosion of massive and peaceful civil disobedience, combined with violent looting and arson, exacerbated by police violations of human rights, came to contaminate the entire Chilean political landscape. The following Friday, at Plaza Italia, two blocks from the Law School where I teach, an unprecedented mass demonstration brought together almost 1.2 million people. Every day since the uprising started, there were anti-government protests a few blocks from my office. Benjamin Vicuña Mackenna said: "Chile sleeps like a groundhog and wakes up like a lion." For many years Chile was asleep; in mid-October 2019, the country awoke.

These never-ending protests express a rejection of the excessive privilege and nepotism that is at the heart of contemporary Chilean society. They shout out that as things stand, the least advantaged people will never make it, and that present-day discrimination against women and the existing urban segregation are unbearable. Furthermore, these same groups are demanding a new structure of social and economic rights, particularly as regards education, social security, discrimination in the workplace, trade union organization, and health, among other things. Angry citizens protested against what they perceived to have been repeated humiliations. "Abuses" is the term used in the protests. Unfortunately, these legitimate claims were followed by violence. Across the country, multitudes of people succumbed to the fatal attraction of violence, with rioting, looting, and burning of super-markets, pharmacies, banks, and public offices. To date, the government has been having a hard time controlling public order in Chile.

Perhaps one of the most distinctive demands that has emerged during the uprising has been the call for a new Chilean Constitution. The circumstances in Chile remind us of the famous letter Thomas Jefferson wrote to his friend, James Madison, from Paris in the midst of the French Revolution. On September 6, 1789 he wrote:

> no society can make a perpetual constitution, or even a perpetual law. The earth belongs always to the living generation. They may manage it then, and what proceeds from it, as they please, during their usufruct. They are masters too of their own persons, and consequently may govern them as they please. But persons and property make the sum of the objects of government. The Constitution and the laws of their predecessors extinguished then in their natural course, with those whose will gave them being. This could preserve that being till it ceased to be itself, and no longer. Every Constitution then, and every law, naturally expires at the end of nineteen years. If it be enforced longer, it is an act of force, and not of right.

(Jefferson 1984: 963)

The Chilean political parties with representation in Congress heard this general call for a new Constitution. At the end of arduous negotiations and debates, the parties adopted an unprecedented political Agreement on November 15, 2019. In response to the demand for a new Constitution, the Agreement sets out a two-year constitutional agenda (see below, Annex, with the text of the Agreement).

This document was signed by ten Chilean political parties that span a broad spectrum of forces, from the left, the center, to right-wing organizations: Democracia Cristiana, Revolución Democrática, Renovación Nacional, Comunes, Partido Socialista, Partido por la Democracia, Partido Liberal, Partido Radical, UDI [Independent Democratic Union], Evópoli, and the Independent Representative Gabriel Boric. The Chilean Communist Party did not sign the agreement, although in a subsequent declaration it announced that it will participate in all stages of the constituent process. A small regional environmental party, the Frente Regionalista Verde Social, which has less than a handful of Deputies in Congress, also refused to sign the agreement.

This Agreement opens a new avenue for the creation of the Chilean Sixth Republic, through a democratic, participatory, and institutional process. This process is complex and still uncertain in some of its parts. However, the Agreement represents a truly republican effort to advance the ideals of self-government, and provides many parties and social actors with the hope that, for the first time, a Chilean Constitution will be established, following and conforming to democratic values, principles, procedures, and rules. This parliamentary Agreement has given rise to new hope for constitutional change.

Still, the possible drafting of a new Constitution is only one of the demands of the October protest movement. The social and economic component of this proposal is still pending, and it may have an impact on the peaceful transition process. It is also important to remember that these constitutional moments are volatile, and there can also emerge serious risks of instability that can precipitate a crisis of democracy. Perhaps the Chilean coup d'état of 1973, the bombing of the presidential palace, and the closure of Congress are the most obvious indicators of the termination of democracy. But democracies may also "die at the hands not of generals but of elected leaders, presidents or prime ministers who subvert the very process that brought them to power" (Levitsky and Ziblatt 2018: 3). These other modes of weakening democracy and eventually causing its demise happen when there is a rejection of (or weak commitment to) democratic rules of the game; a denial of the legitimacy of opposition and particular opponents; toleration or encouragement of violence; and/or a willingness to curtail civil liberties of opponents, including the media (ibid.: 23–24). This is why, at this crucial constitutional moment, Chile needs to secure respect for democratic rules, recognize political differences, reject violence, and guarantee civil liberties for all. As we have seen throughout this book, these rules and practices have long been a part of the best Chilean constitutional, democratic, liberal tradition and could provide solid ground for the construction of the new republic.

ANNEX

AGREEMENT FOR SOCIAL PEACE AND A NEW CONSTITUTION (2019)

In face of the serious political and social crisis in the country, in response to the citizens' movement and the call made by President Sebastián Piñera, the undersigned parties have agreed on an institutional path whose objective is to seek peace and social justice through an unquestionable democratic procedure.

1. The parties that sign this agreement hereby give their guarantee of their commitment to the restoration of peace and public order in Chile and their total respect for human rights, as well as for the democratic rule of law presently in force.
2. A plebiscite will be held in April 2020 that resolves two questions:
   (a) Do you want a new Constitution? Yes or No.
   (b) What kind of body should adopt the new Constitution? A mixed Constitutional Convention or a Constitutional Convention?
3. The mixed Constitutional Convention will be formed for this purpose in equal parts by elected members and Members of Parliament presently in office.
4. In the case of the Constitutional Convention, its members will be entirely elected for this purpose. The election of the members of both instances will be held in October 2020, together with the regional and municipal elections under universal suffrage, with the same electoral system that rules the elections of Deputies in the corresponding proportion.
5. The constituent body ultimately elected by citizens will have the sole purpose of drafting the new Constitution, not affecting the competencies and attributions of the other organs and powers of the State, and it will be dissolved once the task entrusted to it has been completed. Additionally, it may not alter the quorum or procedures for its functions and for adoption of its agreements.

6. The constituent body must approve the norms and regulations for voting by a quorum of two-thirds of its members presently sitting as such and in exercise.
7. The new Constitution will enter into force from the time of its promulgation and publication, repealing organically or entirely the Constitution that is presently in force.
8. Once the new Fundamental Charter has been enacted by the constituent organ it will be submitted to a ratifying plebiscite. This vote will proceed by mandatory universal suffrage.
9. People who currently hold public and popularly elected positions will yield their position by the sole effect of law at the time of their acceptance to become members of the constituent body before the Electoral Service. Members of the constituent body will be disqualified from being candidates for popular election for one year after they cease their term.
10. The parties that sign this agreement will designate a Technical Commission which will focus on the determination of all aspects essential to materialize the aforementioned Agreement. The appointment of members for this Commission shall be equal between the opposition and the ruling party.
11. The term or time limit for complying with the mandate of the constituent body will be nine months, extendable only once for a new term of three additional months. Sixty days after the adoption of the new constitutional text by the constituent body, a ratifying referendum will be held with mandatory universal suffrage. In no case may this referendum take place before sixty days, neither after this term, nor jointly with another popular election.
12. The constitutional and/or legal reform projects that emanate from this Agreement will be submitted for approval by the National Congress as a whole. For this voting, the undersigned parties commit their approval.

Note: New Developments

The date mentioned in point No. 2 of the Annex as fixing the constitutional plebiscite for April 2020 was amended in a constitutional reform bill under Statute No. 21.221, which was published in the Chilean *Official Gazette* on March 24, 2020, establishing that the new date for that plebiscite will be October 20, 2020. Transitory Article 131 finally set the election date for This new provision is presently contained under a transitory constitutional provision of Article 33. Also, under Statute 21.226 published in the Chilean *Official Gazette* on March 24, 2020, several new constitutional procedural regulations concerning "parity" provisions were introduced in order to secure equal representation for women and men, and also to improve the representation of independent or non-partisan candidates in the Constitutional Convention. These rules are controversial and are presently contained in several new constitutional provisions, such as Articles 129–143, and transitory Articles 29–32. These provisions were added to the already existing transitory constitutional provisions of the Chilean Constitution.

BIBLIOGRAPHY

Ackerman, B. 1977. *Private Property and the Constitution.* New Haven and London: Yale University Press.

1991. *We the People. I: Foundations.* Cambridge, MA and London: Harvard University Press.

2007. *La nueva división de poderes.* Mexico City: Fondo de Cultura Económica.

2010. *The Decline and Fall of the American Republic.* Cambridge, MA: Harvard University Press.

Agamben, G. 2013. "For a Theory of Destituent Power." Public lecture in Athens, organized by Nicos Poulantzas Institute and SYRIZA Youth, Athens. Available at: http://criticallegalthinking.com/2014/02/05/theory-destituent-power/ (accessed April 17, 2020).

Agor, W. 1971. *The Chilean Senate: Internal Distribution of Influence.* London and Austin, TX: Institute of Latin American Studies/University of Texas Press.

Alberdi, J. B. 1998. *Bases y puntos de partida para la organización política de la República Argentina.* Buenos Aires: Editorial Universitaria.

Aldunate, E. 2008. *Derechos fundamentales.* Santiago: Legal Publishing.

Aldunate, E. and Fuentes, J. 1997. "El concepto de derecho de propiedad en la jurisprudencia constitucional chilena y la teoría de las garantías del instituto." *Revista de derecho de la Pontificia Universidad Católica de Valparaíso* XVIIII: 195–221.

Alemparte, B. 2016. "Una perspectiva constitucional del presupuesto del sector público en Chile." Unpublished dissertation, Law Faculty, Universidad de Chile.

Alemparte, J. 1963. *Carrera y Freire. Fundadores de la República.* Santiago: Editorial Nascimento.

Alessandri, A., Somarriva, M., and Vodanovic, A. 1974. *Curso de Derecho Civil. De los bienes.* Santiago: Editorial Jurídica de Chile.

1993. *Curso de Derecho Civil. De los bienes,* 3rd ed. Santiago: Editorial Jurídica de Chile.

Amar, A. R. 1998. *The Bill of Rights: Creation and Reconstruction.* New Haven and London: Yale University Press.

2016. *The Constitution Today: Timeless Lessons for the Issues of our Era.* New York: Basic Books.

Amunátegui, G. 1951. *Regímenes políticos*. Santiago: Editorial Jurídica de Chile.
   1953. *Principios generales del Derecho Constitucional*. Santiago: Editorial Jurídica de Chile.
Amunátegui Solar, D. 1933. *Las letras chilenas*. Santiago: Editorial Nascimento.
Andrade, C. 1963. *Elementos de Derecho Constitucional chileno*, 2nd ed. Santiago: Editorial Jurídica de Chile.
Aragón, M. 1995. *Libertades económicas y estado social*. Madrid: McGraw Hill.
Arcos, S. 1989. *Carta a Francisco Bilbao y otros escritos*. Santiago: Editorial Universitaria.
Arteaga Alemparte, J. and Arteaga Alemparte, D. 1910. *Los constituyentes de 1870*. Santiago: Imprenta Barcelona.
Bañados, J. 2005. *Balmaceda, su gobierno y la revolución de 1891*. Santiago: Centro de Estudios Bicentenario.
Barreto, A., Gómez, B., and Magalhães, P. (eds.). 2003. *Portugal. Democracia y sistema político*. Madrid: Editorial Siglo Veintiuno.
Barros, E. 2000. "¿Qué presidencialismo?" in A. Squella and O. Sunkel (eds.). *Democratizar la democracia. Reformas pendientes*. Santiago: Universidad de Chile: 89–98.
Barros, R. J. 2002. *Constitutionalism and Dictatorship: Pinochet, the Junta and the 1980 Constitution*. Cambridge University Press.
Barros Arana, D. 1962. *Historia de América*. Buenos Aires: Editorial Futuro.
   1987. *Páginas escogidas*. Santiago: Editorial Universitaria.
Barros Errazuriz, A. 1921. *Curso de derecho civil*. Santiago: Imprenta Cervantes.
Battista, A. M. 1990. "El poder moral. El modelo clásico de Bolívar," in S. Schipani et al. *Constitucionalismo latino y liberalismo*. Bogota: Universidad Externado de Colombia: 37–68.
Bello, A. 1864. *Principios de derecho internacional*, 3rd ed. Valparaíso: Imprenta de la Patria.
   1979. "Independencia del poder judicial" and "Las Repúblicas Hispanoamericanas," in *Escritos jurídicos, políticos y universitarios*. Valparaíso: Edeval: 49–56, 85–90, 107–116, 125–130.
Bengoa, J. 2003. *Historia de los antiguos mapuches del sur. Desde antes de la llegada de los españoles hasta las paces de Quilín*. Santiago: Editorial Catalonia.
Bernaschina, M. 1958. *Manual de derecho constitucional*, 3rd ed. Santiago: Editorial Jurídica de Chile.
Bloch, M. 2003. *Apología para la historia o el oficio de historiador*, ed. and notes E. Bloch. Mexico City: Fondo de Cultura Económica.
Boas, G. 1969. *The History of Ideas*. New York: Scribner.
Brahm, E. 1999–2000. "La perversión de la cultura jurídica chilena durante el gobierno de la Unidad Popular. Resquicios legales y derecho de propiedad." *Revista chilena de historia del derecho* 18: 335–349.

Bravo, B. 1978. *Régimen de gobierno y partidos políticos en Chile, 1924–1973*. Santiago: Editorial Jurídica de Chile.

2016. *Una historia jamás contada. Chile 1811–2011. Cómo salió dos veces adelante*. Santiago: Origo Ediciones.

Caldera, H. 1979. *Manual de derecho administrativo*. Santiago: Editorial Jurídica de Chile.

Campos Harriet, F. 1956. *Historia constitucional de Chile*. Santiago: Editorial Jurídica de Chile.

Cariola, C. and Sunkel, O. 1983. *Un siglo de historia económica de Chile 1830–1930. Dos ensayos y una bibliografía*. Madrid: Ediciones Cultura Hispánica del Instituto de Cooperación Iberoamericana.

Carmona, C. 2006. "Modificaciones al órgano presidencial que introduce la Ley de Reforma Constitucional No. 20.050." *Revista de derecho público* 68: 85–129.

Carrasco, S. 2002. *Génesis y vigencia de los textos constitucionales chilenos*, 3rd ed. Santiago: Editorial Jurídica de Chile.

Carrasco Albano, M. 1874. *Comentarios sobre la Constitución Política de 1833*. Santiago: Imprenta de la Librería del Mercurio.

Carrillo, J. P. 2014. "Democracia y propiedad en el constitucionalismo radical. Bilbao y Recabarren." *Derecho y humanidades* 24: 93–112.

Castella, J. M. (ed.). 2015. *Derecho constitucional básico*. Barcelona: Huygens Editorial.

Castillo, V. 2003. "La creación de la república. La filosofía pública en Chile 1810–1830." Unpublished doctoral thesis, Faculty of Philosophy and Humanities, Universidad de Chile.

Castillo Sandoval, R. 2007. "Lectura esencial para entrar al siglo XXI." Available at: http://robertocastillosandoval.com/2007/01/19/lectura-esencial-para-entrar-al-siglo-xxi/ (accessed April 17, 2020).

Cea Egaña, J. L. 1988. *Tratado de la Constitución de 1980*. Santiago: Editorial Jurídica de Chile.

1999. *El sistema constitucional de Chile. Síntesis crítica*. Valdivia: Faculty of Legal and Social Sciences, Universidad Austral.

2005. "Contrapunto entre el constitucionalismo de 1925 y el de 1980." *Revista de derecho* 12/2: 87–92.

Chemerinsky, E. 2001. *Constitutional Law*. New York: Aspen Law.

Cicero. 2000. *De re publica. De legibus*. Cambridge, MA and London: Harvard University Press.

Claro Solar, L. 1939. *Explicaciones de derecho civil chileno y comparado. Vol. III: De los bienes y los derechos reales. Vol. IV: De los bienes. Vol. VI: De las obligaciones*. Santiago: Editorial Jurídica de Chile.

Collier, S. 1977. *Ideas y política de la independencia chilena 1808–1833*. Santiago: Andrés Bello.

Comisión de Estudio de la Nueva Constitución Política de la República de Chile. 1978. *Anteproyecto constitucional y sus fundamentos.* Santiago: Editorial Jurídica de Chile.

Consejo de Observadores. 2016. *Guía metodológica proceso participativo territorial.* Santiago: Ministerio Secretaría General de la Presidencia, República de Chile.

Constitución Política de la República de Chile. 2015. Santiago: Editorial Jurídica de Chile.

Cordero, E. 2008. "De la propiedad a las propiedades. La evolución de la concepción liberal de la propiedad." *Revista de derecho* 31/2: 493–525.

Cornejo, C. 2014. "El derecho de propiedad según la interpretación realizada por el Tribunal Constitucional. Dificultades y principios sobre los cuales fundar este derecho." *Derecho y humanidades* 11: 189–222.

Corral, H. 1996. "Propiedad y cosas incorporales. Comentarios a propósito de una reciente obra del profesor Alejandro Guzmán Brito." *Revista chilena de derecho* 23/11: 13–18.

Correa, S. 2000. "La democracia que tuvimos, la democracia que no fue." *Revista de sociología* 14: 117–120.

2004. "El pensamiento en Chile en el siglo XX bajo la sombra de Portales," in Ó. Terán (ed.). *Ideas en el siglo. Intelectuales y cultura en el siglo XX latinoaméricano.* Buenos Aires: Siglo XXI Editores Argentina y Fundación OSDE: 251–265.

Correa, A. and Ruiz-Tagle, P. 2010. *Ciudadanos en democracia. Fundamentos del sistema político chileno.* Santiago: Editorial Random House.

Correa, S., Figueroa, C., Jocelyn-Holt, A., Rolle, C., and Vicuña, M. 2001. *Historia del siglo XX chileno.* Santiago: Sudamericana.

Cristi, R. 2000. *El pensamiento político de Jaime Guzmán. Autoridad y libertad.* Santiago: LOM Ediciones.

Cristi, R. and Ruiz, C. 2015. *El pensamiento conservador en Chile.* Santiago: Editorial Universitaria.

Cristi, R. and Ruiz-Tagle, P. 2006. *La República en Chile. Teoría y práctica del constitucionalismo republicano.* Santiago: LOM Ediciones.

2008. *La República en Chile. Teoría y práctica del constitucionalismo republicano,* 3rd ed. Santiago: LOM Ediciones.

2014. *El constitucionalismo del miedo. Propiedad, bien común y poder constituyente.* Santiago: LOM Ediciones.

Cruz-Coke, R. 1984. *Historia electoral de Chile 1925–1973.* Santiago: Editorial Jurídica de Chile.

Cumplido, F. 1970. *Reforma constitucional de 1970.* Santiago: Editorial Jurídica de Chile.

Damaska, M. 2000. *Las caras de la justicia. Análisis comparado del proceso legal.* Santiago: Editorial Jurídica de Chile.

Diario Oficial. 2005. *Constituciones políticas de la República de Chile 1810–2005*. Santiago: Gráfica Puerto Madero.

Donoso, R. 1967. *Las ideas políticas en Chile*, 2nd ed. Santiago: Editorial Universitaria.

1971. *Breve historia de Chile*, 3rd ed. Buenos Aires: Eudeba.

Duguit, L. 1975. *Las transformaciones del derecho público y privado*, trans. A. G. Posada, R. Jaén, and C. G. Posada. Buenos Aires: Editorial Heliasta.

Durán, C. 2015. "La requisición de la industrial durante la Unidad Popular en relación al concepto republicano de propiedad." Unpublished thesis, Law Faculty, Universidad de Chile.

Duverger, M. 1970. *Institutions politiques et droit constitutionnel*. Paris: Presses universitaires de France.

Edwards, A. 1993. *La fronda aristocrática en Chile*. Santiago: Editorial Universitaria.

Egaña, J. 1830. *Colección de algunos escritos políticos, morales, poéticos y filosóficos*, vol. I. London.

Elkins, Z., Ginsburg, T., and Melton, J. 2009. *The Endurance of National Constitutions*. Cambridge University Press.

Ellikson, R., Rose, C., and Ackerman, B. 1995. *Perspectives on Property Law*. Boston, New York, Toronto, and London: Little, Brown and Company.

Ely, J. W., Jr. 2008. *The Guardian of Every Other Right: A Constitutional History of Property Rights*, 3rd ed. New York: Oxford University Press.

Estévez, C. 1949. *Elementos de derecho constitucional*. Santiago: Editorial Jurídica de Chile.

Etchepare, J. 2006. *Surgimiento y evolución de los partidos políticos en Chile 1857–2003*. Concepción: Editorial Universidad Católica de la Santísima Concepción.

Evans, E. 1973. *Chile. Hacia una Constitución contemporánea. Tres reformas constitucionales*. Santiago: Editorial Jurídica de Chile.

1999. *Los derechos constitucionales*, vol. III. Santiago: Editorial Jurídica de Chile.

Eyzaguirre, J. 1948. *Fisonomía histórica de Chile*. Mexico City: Fondo de Cultura Económica.

1957. *Ideario y ruta de la emancipación chilena*. Santiago: Editorial Universitaria.

1962. *Historia constitucional de Chile*. Santiago: Editorial Universitaria.

Faúndez, J. 2011. *Democratización, desarrollo y legalidad. Chile 1831–1973*. Santiago: Universidad Diego Portales.

Favoreau, L., Gaïa, P., Ghevontian, R., Mestre, J.-L., Roux, A., Pfersmann, O., and Scoffoni, G. 1998. *Droit constitutionnel*. Paris: Dalloz-Sirey.

Fernández Concha, R. 1966. *Filosofía del derecho o derecho natural*, vols. I and II, 3rd ed. Santiago: Editorial Jurídica de Chile.

Figueroa, M. A. 1967. "Apuntes sobre el origen de las garantías a los derechos humanos en la legislación hispano-chilena." *Estudios de Historia de las*

Instituciones Políticas y Sociales, vol. 2: Santiago: Editorial Jurídica de Chile: 33–101.

Fiskin, J. S. 2009. *When the People Speak: Deliberative Democracy and Public Consultation*. Oxford University Press.

Fontaine, J. A. 1993. "Transición económica y política en Chile." *Estudios públicos* 50: 229–275.

Furet, F. 1983. *Penser la Révolution Française*. Paris: Gallimard.

Gargarella, R. 2005. *Los fundamentos legales de la desigualdad. El constitucionalismo en América, 1776–1860*. Madrid: Siglo XXI.

2014. *La sala de máquinas de la Constitución. Dos siglos de constitucionalismo en America Latina 1810–2010*. Buenos Aires/Madrid: Katz Editores.

Garvey, J. H., Aleinikoff, T. A., and Farber, D. A. 1999. *Modern Constitutional Theory: A Reader*, 4th ed. Saint Paul, MN: West Publishing Co.

Garzón Valdés, E. 1993a. "El concepto de estabilidad de los sistemas políticos," in *Derecho, ética y política* (1993). Madrid: Centro de Estudios Constitucionales: 201–234.

1993b. "Consenso, racionalidad y legitimidad," in *Derecho, ética y política* (1993). Madrid: Centro de Estudios Constitucionales: 455–471.

1993c. *Derecho, ética y política*. Madrid: Centro de Estudios Constitucionales.

1993d. "Las funciones del derecho en Latinoamérica," in *Derecho, ética y política* (1993). Madrid: Centro de Estudios Constitucionales: 573–609.

Gil, F. 1969. *El sistema político chileno*. Santiago: Editorial Jurídica de Chile.

Gill, L. 2005. *Escuela de las Américas. Entrenamiento militar, violencia política e impunidad en las Américas*. Santiago: LOM Ediciones/Cuatro Vientos.

Góngora, M. 1981. *Ensayo histórico sobre la noción de Estado en Chile en los siglos XIX y XX*. Santiago: Editorial Universitaria.

1986. *Ensayo histórico sobre la noción de Estado en Chile en los siglos XIX y XX*. Santiago: Editorial Universitaria.

González, M. 2011. *De empresarios a empleados. Clase media y estado docente en Chile, 1810–1920*. Santiago: LOM Ediciones.

Goytisolo, J. 2010. *Blanco White. El español y la independencia de Hispanoamérica*. Madrid: Taurus.

Guzmán Brito, A. 1995. *Las cosas incorporales en la doctrina y el derecho positivo*. Santiago: Editorial Jurídica de Chile.

Hamilton, A., Madison, J. and Jay, J. 1980. *El federalista*, 3rd ed. Mexico City: Fondo de Cultura Económica.

Hayek, F. A. 1975. *Los fundamentos de la libertad*, 3rd ed. Madrid: Unión Editorial S.A.

Heise, J. 1974. *Historia de Chile. El periodo parlamentario 1861–1925*. Santiago: Andrés Bello.

1996. *150 años de evolución institucional*, 9th ed. Santiago: Andrés Bello.

Huneeus, J. 1890. *Obras de Don Jorge Huneeus. La Constitución ante el Congreso*, vol. I, 2nd ed. Santiago: Imprenta Cervantes.

1891. *Obras de Don Jorge Huneeus. La Constitución ante el Congreso*, vol. II, 2nd ed. Santiago: Imprenta Cervantes.

Informe Ortega. 1990. *Pre-Informe de la Comisión de Estudio del Régimen Político chileno*. Created in Chile by agreement of the Chamber of Deputies, adopted on May 9, 1990.

Irisarri, A. 1946. *Historia crítica del asesinato del gran mariscal de Ayacucho*. Buenos Aires: W. M. Jackson Editores.

Izquierdo Araya, G. 1934. *La racionalización de la democracia. Un estudio de las nuevas tendencias constitucionales*. Santiago: Editorial Universitaria.

Jaksic, I. 2001. *Andrés Bello. La pasión por el orden*. Santiago: Editorial Universitaria.

Jana, A. and Marín, J. C. 1996. *Recurso de protección y contratos*. Santiago: Editorial Jurídica de Chile.

Jefferson, T. 1984. *Writings*, vol. 17. New York: Library of America.

Jocelyn-Holt, A. 1992. *La independencia de Chile. Tradición, modernización y mito*. Santiago: Planeta/Ariel.

1997. *El peso de la noche. Nuestra frágil fortaleza histórica*. Santiago: Planeta/Ariel.

1998. "El liberalismo moderado chileno. Siglo XIX." *Estudios públicos* 69/ summer: 439–485.

1999. *La independencia de Chile. Tradición, modernización y mito*, 2nd ed. Santiago: Planeta.

Jocelyn-Holt, E. 2014. "Lear: de rey y propietario a súbdito y vagabundo. La relación entre propiedad, poder y dignidad en El Rey Lear." *Derecho y Humanidades* 24: 223–227.

Judt, T. 2011. *Postguerra. Una historia de Europa desde 1945*. Madrid and Pensamiento: Taurus/Santillana.

2010. *Algo va mal*. Madrid: Santillana.

Kartal, F. 2001–2002. "Liberal and Republican conceptualizations of citizenship: A theoretical inquiry." *Turkish Public Administration Annual* 27–28: 101–130.

Keen, B. and Wasserman, M. 1984. *A Short History of Latin America*. Boston, MA: Houghton Mifflin.

Kelsen, H. 1995. *Teoría pura del derecho*, trans. R. J. Vernengo. Mexico City: Editorial Porrua S.A.

2003. "Observaciones sobre la Constitución Chilena." *Anuario de filosofía jurídica y social* 21: 643–647. (Trans. J. García-Huidobro from original German, 1926.)

Kiverstein, A. 1993. *Síntesis del derecho civil. De los objetos del derecho*. Santiago: Editorial La Ley.

Lagos, R. 1961. *La concentración del poder económico*. Santiago: Editorial del Pacífico.

Lamartine, A. 1847. *Historia de los girondinos*. Madrid: Imprenta de la Ilustración.

Lastarria, J. V. 1865. *Elementos de derecho público constitucional*. Santiago: Imprenta Chilena.

2001. *Recuerdos literarios*. Santiago: LOM Ediciones.

Latcham, R. 1924. *Organización y creencias de los Araucanos*. Santiago: Editorial Cervantes.

Letelier, V. 1917. *Génesis del Estado y de sus instituciones fundamentales*. Buenos Aires: Cabaut y Cía.

Levitsky, S. and Ziblatt, D. 2018. *How Democracies Die*. New York: Crown Publishing.

Linz, J. 1990. "Democracia. Presidencialismo o parlamentarismo ¿hace alguna diferencia?" in O. Godoy (ed.). *Hacia una democracia moderna. La opción parlamentaria*. Santiago: Ediciones Universidad Católica: 41–108.

Lira Urquieta, P. 1944. *El Código Civil y el nuevo derecho*. Santiago: Editorial Nascimento.

Loewenstein, K. 1983. *Teoría de la Constitución*, trans. A. Gallego Anabitarte. Barcelona: Ariel.

López, J. J. 2014. "Derecho constitucional chileno y función social de la propiedad." *Derecho y humanidades* 24: 59–89.

López y López, Á. 1998. "El derecho de propiedad. Una relectio." *Anuario de derecho civil* LI/IV: 1639–1691.

Loveman, B. 1988. *Chile: The Legacy of Hispanic Capitalism*. Oxford University Press.

MacIntyre, A. 1990. *Three Rival Versions of Moral Inquiry: Encylopaedia, Genealogy, and Tradition* (Gifford Lectures). Indiana: University of Notre Dame Press.

Madison, J., Hamilton, A., and Jay, J. 1961. *The Federalist Papers*, ed. C. Rossiter. New York: Mentor Books.

Matteucci, N. 2010. *Organización del poder y libertad. Historia del constitucionalismo moderno*. Madrid: Editorial Trotta.

Merryman, J. H. 1971. *La tradición jurídica romano canónica*. Mexico City: Fondo de Cultura Económica.

Michelman, F. I. 1967. "Property, Utility and Fairness: Comments on the Ethical Foundations of 'Just Compensation' Law." *Harvard Law Review* 80: 1165–1258.

Mirow, M. C. 2011. "Origins of the Social Function of Property in Chile." *Fordham Law Review* 80: 1183–1217.

Molina, H. 1993. *Derecho constitucional*. Concepción: Universidad de Concepción.

Mora, J. J. de. 1830. *Curso de Leyes del Liceo de Chile*. Santiago: Imprenta Republicana.

Morris, J. 1966. *Elites, Intellectuals and Consensus: A Study of the Social Question and the Industrial Relations System in Chile.* Ithaca, NY: New York State School of Industrial Relations, Cornell University.

Muñoz, P. 2015. *Elementos para una concepción republicana de la propiedad en el Chile actual. La propiedad y el proceso de reforma agraria.* Unpublished dissertation, Law Faculty, Universidad de Chile.

Navarro, E. and Carmona, C. (eds.). 2011. "Recopilación de jurisprudencia del Tribunal Constitucional (1981–2011)." *Cuadernos del Tribunal Constitucional* 45: 15–17, 225–238, 238–252, 262, 263–267.

Nedelsky, J. 1990. *Private Property and the Limits of American Constitutionalism.* University of Chicago Press.

Novoa, E. 2006. *Nacionalización, derecho y propiedad. Textos escogidos* (ed. and prologue C. Margota). Santiago: Universidad Arcis.

Paz, O. 1994. *El laberinto de la soledad.* Mexico City: Fondo de Cultura Económica.

Peces Barba, G. 1999. *Curso de derechos fundamentales. Teoría general.* Madrid: Universidad Carlos III.

Peñailillo, D. 2006. *Los bienes. La propiedad y otros derechos reales.* Santiago: Editorial Jurídica de Chile.

Pérez Luño, A. 1987. "Concepto y concepción de los derechos humanos, acotaciones a la ponencia de Francisco Laporta." *DOXA* 4: 47–66.

Pescio, V. 1978. *Manual de derecho civil, de las personas, de los bienes y de la propiedad.* Santiago: Editorial Jurídica de Chile.

Pfeffer, E. 1999. *Constitución política de la República de Chile. Concordancia, antecedentes y jurisprudencia.* Santiago: Editorial Cono Sur.

Pinto, J. and Valdivia, V. 2009. *¿Chilenos todos? La construcción social de la nación 1810–1840.* Santiago: LOM Ediciones.

Pizzorusso, A. 1984. *Lecciones de derecho constitucional,* vols. I and II. Madrid: Centro de Estudios Constitucionales.

Post, R. 2014. *Citizens Divided: Campaign Finance Reform and the Constitution.* Cambridge, MA and London: Harvard University Press.

Purdy, J. 2014. "Neoliberal Constitutionalism: Lochnerism for a New Economy." *Law and Contemporary Problems* 77: 195–213.

Rajevic, E. 1996. "Limitaciones, reserva legal y contenido esencial de la propiedad privada." *Revista chilena de derecho* 23/1: 62–77.

Ramírez, A. 2014. "La ciudadanía en los primeros años de la República. ¿Una comunidad política de propietarios? Republicanismo y sufragio en Chile 1810–1833." *Derecho y humanidades* 24: 133–157.

Rawls, J. 1999a. *A Theory of Justice.* Cambridge, MA: Harvard University Press.

1999b. *The Laws of Peoples.* Cambridge, MA: Harvard University Press.

Recabal, P. 2015. "Historia de la ciudadanía y la representación. La construcción de un sistema electoral deliberativo y su destrucción por la imposición de un sistema político electoral instrumental en Chile 1810–1860." Unpublished dissertation, Law Faculty, Universidad de Chile.

Ríos, L. 1987. "El principio constitucional de la función social de la propiedad." *Revista de derecho y jurisprudencia* LXXXIV/2: 57–73.

2010. "El principio constitucional de la función social de la propiedad." *Revista de derecho y jurisprudencia*. Bicentenary edition: Derecho civil, bienes, ed. R. Tavolari: 116–136.

Rojas, R. 2009. *Las Repúblicas de Aire. Utopía y desencanto en la revolución de Hispanoamérica*. Mexico City: Taurus.

Roldán, A. 1913. *Elementos del derecho constitucional*. Santiago: Imprenta Barcelona.

Rosanvallon, P. 2007. *El modelo político francés. La sociedad contra el jacobinismo, de 1789 a nuestros días*. Buenos Aires: Siglo XXI Editores Argentina.

2009. *La legitimidad democrática. Imparcialidad, reflexividad, proximidad*. Buenos Aires: Ediciones Manantial.

Ruiz Schneider, C. and Castillo Rojas, V. 2001. "El pensamiento republicano en Chile durante el siglo XIX. Notas de investigación." *Revista jurídica de la Universidad de Puerto Rico* 70: 1063–1096.

Ruiz-Tagle, P. 1985. "Las definiciones legales." *Revista de ciencias sociales* 26–27: 55–60.

1989. "Debate público restringido en Chile 1980–1988." *Revista chilena de derecho* 16: 189–211.

2000a. "Apuntes sobre la igualdad constitucional en Chile." *Revista jurídica de la Universidad de Palermo*: 19–48.

2000b. "Principios constitucionales y estado empresario." *Revista de derecho público* 62: 48–65.

2001a. "Constitucionalidad de los tratados internacionales en Chile," in *Los tratados internacionales en la jurisprudencia constitucional*. Santiago: Fundación Facultad de Derecho, Universidad de Chile: 48–65.

2001b. "Una dogmática general para los derechos fundamentales en Chile." *Revista de derecho público* 63/1: 179–199.

2001c. *Propiedad intelectual y contratos*. Santiago: Editorial Jurídica de Chile.

2002. *Derecho, justicia y libertad*. Mexico City: Fontamara.

2003. "Los derechos fundamentales en el siglo XXI y la disminución de su efecto mariposa." *Revista de derecho* 15/2: 181–190.

2006. "Una visión democrática y liberal de los derechos fundamentales para la Constitución chilena del bicentenario," in A. Bordalí (ed.). *Justicia constitucional y derechos fundamentales*. Santiago: Lexis Nexis: 69–128.

2008. "Una Contraloría General de la República que sirva a todos los chilenos." *Revista de derecho público* 70/1: 241–250.

2009. "Un proyecto constitucional para la generación del bicentenario. Igualdad y derechos económicos y sociales en Chile." *Derecho y humanidades* 15: 17–35.

2010. "La propuesta de reforma constitucional del Senador Eduardo Frei". Summary of presentation given at the Centro de Estudios Públicos, March 10, 2009. Available at: www.cepchile.cl/cep/site/docs/20160304/20160304094803/sem_pruiztagle.pdf (accessed April 17, 2020).

2012. "El presidencialismo chileno. Evolución de sus atribuciones constitucionales y propuestas de reforma." *Revista de derecho público* 76: 229–247.

2014. "Dogmática sobre la propiedad civil y constitucional en Chile." *Derecho y humanidades* 24: 21–58.

Ruiz-Tagle, P. and Martí, J. L. 2014. *Una concepción republicana de la propiedad.* Madrid: Fundación Coloquio Jurídico Europeo.

Salazar, G. 2003. *Historia de la acumulación capitalista en Chile. Apuntes de clase.* Santiago: LOM Ediciones.

2005a. *Construcción de estado en Chile 1800–1837. Democracia de "los pueblos". Militarismo ciudadano. Golpismo oligárquico.* Santiago: Sudamericana.

2005b. *El gobierno de Lagos. Balance crítico.* Santiago: LOM Ediciones.

2009. *Del poder constituyente de asalariados e intelectuales. Chile, siglos XX y XXI.* Santiago: LOM Ediciones.

Salazar, G. and Pinto, J. 2010. *Historia contemporánea de Chile. Vol. III: La economía. Mercados, empresarios y trabajadores.* Santiago: LOM Ediciones.

Salvat, M. 1982. "155 años de la Constitución de 1828." *Revista de derecho público* 31–32: 223–226.

Sartori, G. 1996. *Ingeniería constitucional comparada.* Mexico City: Fondo de Cultura Económica.

Schama, S. 1989. *Citizens: A Chronicle of the French Revolution.* New York: Alfred A. Knopf.

Schlesinger, R. 1980. *Comparative Law: Cases, Text, Materials*, 4th ed. Mineola, NY: Foundation Press.

Schmidt-Assmann, E. 2003. *Teoría general del derecho administrativo como sistema.* Madrid: Marcial Pons.

Schmitt, C. 1982. *Teoría de la Constitución.* Madrid: Alianza Editorial.

1991. *El concepto de lo político.* Madrid: Alianza Editorial.

Silva Bascuñán, A. 1963. *Tratado de derecho constitucional.* Santiago: Editorial Jurídica de Chile.

1997. *Tratado de derecho constitucional. La Constitución de 1980.* Santiago: Editorial Jurídica de Chile.

Simon, W. H. 1990. "Social-Republican Property." *UCLA Law Review* 38: 1335–1413.

Soto, F. 2016. "La regulación del referéndum de especial trascendencia en perspectiva comparada y su eventual reconocimiento en la Constitución chilena." *Estudios constitucionales* 14/1: 291–306.

Soto, S. 2015. *Congreso Nacional y proceso legislativo*. Santiago: Legal Publishing Chile.

Soto Kloss, E. 1996. *Derecho administrativo. Bases fundamentales*, vol. II. Santiago: Editorial Jurídica de Chile.

Stolleis, M. 1998. *The Law under the Swastika: Studies on Legal History in Nazi Germany*. University of Chicago Press.

Sunstein, C. 1993. *After the Rights Revolution: Reconceiving the Regulatory State*. Cambridge, MA: Harvard University Press.

Tocqueville, A. de. 1981. *Democracy in America*. New York: McGraw-Hill.

Underkuffler, L. 2003. *The Idea of Property: Its Meaning and Power*. Oxford and New York: Oxford University Press.

Uribe, A. and Opazo, C. 2001. *Intervención norteamericana en Chile. Dos textos claves: El libro negro de la intervención norteamericana en Chile y Acciones encubiertas en Chile 1963–1973, "Informe Church."* Santiago: Editorial Sudamericana.

Urzúa, R. 1969. *La demanda campesina*. Santiago: Ediciones Nueva Universidad.

Valdés, D. and Soto, S. 2009. "¿Cómo fortalecer la labor legislativa del Congreso? Propuestas para un nuevo sistema de asesoría parlamentaria." *Estudios públicos* 114: 53–88.

Valencia Avaria, L. 1951. *Anales de la República*, vol. I. Santiago: Imprenta Universitaria.

Véliz, C. 1980. *The Centralist Tradition*. New Jersey: Princeton University Press.

Verdugo, M., Pfeffer, E., and Nogueira, H. 1994. *Derecho constitucional*, vol. I. Santiago: Editorial Jurídica de Chile.

Vial, G. 1987. *Historia de Chile 1891–1973*, vol. I, part II. Santiago: Editorial Santillana.

Vicuña Mackenna, B. 1976. *Vida del capitán general don Bernardo O'Higgins*. Santiago: Editorial del Pacífico.

1989. *Los girondinos chilenos*. Santiago: Editorial Universitaria.

Vicuña, C. 1938. *La tiranía en Chile. Libro escrito en el destierro en 1938*. Santiago: Universo.

Villalobos, S., Silva, O., Silva, F., and Estelle, P. 2000. *Historia de Chile*. Santiago: Editorial Universitaria.

Villey, M. 1976. *Estudios en torno a la noción de derechos subjetivos*. Valparaíso: Ediciones Universitarias de Valparaíso.

Weber, M. 1964. *Economía y sociedad. Esbozo de sociología comprensiva*, vol. II, 2nd ed. Mexico City: Fondo de Cultura Económica.

Wood, G. 1969. *The Creation of the American Republic, 1776–1787*. New York and London: W. W. Norton.

Young, I. M. 1989. "Polity and Group Difference: A Critique of the Ideal of Universal Citizenship." *Ethics* 99/2: 250–274.

Zapata, P. 2015. *La casa de todos. La nueva Constitución que Chile merece y necesita*. Santiago: Ediciones Universidad Católica de Chile.

Zavala, S. 1971. *Las instituciones jurídicas en la conquista de América*. Mexico City: Editorial Porrua.

Zeitlin, M. 1984. *The Civil Wars in Chile or the Bourgeois Revolutions that Never Were*. New Jersey: Princeton University Press.

Zovatto, D. and Orozco, J. J. (eds.). 2008. *Reforma política y electoral en América Latina*. Mexico City: Universidad Nacional Autónoma de México/IDEA Internacional.

Zúñiga, F. (ed.). 2014. *Nueva Constitución y momento constitucional*. Santiago: Legal Publishing.

Zweig, S. 1998. *Momentos estelares de la humanidad*. Barcelona: Editorial Juventud S.A. [1999. *Decisive Moments in History*, trans. L. A. Bangerter. Riverside, CA: Ariadne Press.]

INDEX

absolutism, 31, 61, 96
Ackerman, Bruce, 5, 51, 156, 157, 160, 190, 261, 268, 270
Acta del Cabildo Abierto (Open Cabildo Act) 1810, 45
administrative disputes, 131
Agamben, Giorgo, 266
Agor, Weston H., 112
Agreement of the Chamber of Deputies (*Acuerdo de la Cámara de Diputados*), 138
agricultural property reform, 122–126
Alberdi, Juan Bautista, 90
Aldunate, Eduardo, 219, 227, 248, 250
Alemparte, Benjamín, 55, 182–183
Alemparte, Domingo Arteaga. *See* Arteaga Alemparte, Domingo
Alemparte, Justo Arteaga. *See* Arteaga Alemparte, Justo
Alessandri Palma, Arturo, 105, 106, 108, 114, 119, 121, 127, 219, 228
Alessandri Rodríguez, Arturo, 50
Alessandri Rodríguez, Jorge, 126, 128–129, 133, 219
Alianza Liberal (Liberal Alliance), 105
Allende, Salvador, 121, 125, 126, 132, 133–139, 140, 182, 197, 202, 226, 227, 261
Alliance for Chile (*Alianza por Chile*), 263
Alliance for Progress (*Alianza para el Progreso*), 122
Amar, Akhil, 15
Amunátegui, Gabriel, 12, 27–28, 45, 60, 73, 95, 98, 108, 110–111, 114, 115
Amunátegui, Gregorio, 22
Amunátegui, Miguel Luis, 22
Amunátegui Solar, Domingo, 22, 61
anarchy, political, 60
Andrade, Carlos, 99
anti-liberalism, 39, 100, 166
anti-republican, anti-democratic, anti-liberal movement, 39, 262
anti-republicanism, 16–18, 39, 41, 69, 108, 132, 144, 151, 255, 262
Aragón, Manuel, 233
Arcos, Santiago, 40, 68

armed forces, 18, 31, 42, 57–60, 74, 96, 97, 133, 138, 139, 140, 150, 153, 154, 168, 253, 254, 260, 276
Arteaga Alemparte, Domingo, 93
Arteaga Alemparte, Justo, 93
asylum, right to, 216, 238
Austria, House of, 25
authoritarianism, 16, 37, 42, 70, 71, 72, 99, 103
   in Chile, 13, 31
   conservative, 38
   constitutional, 32
   in Latin-American governments, 74–80
   personal, 58, 74

Bachelet, Michelle, 179, 270, 271
Balmaceda, José Manuel, 16, 17, 96–98, 103, 138
Bañados, Julio, 97
Barros, Robert, 10, 13, 15, 16
Barros, Enrique, 79, 98
Barros Arana, Diego, 22, 44, 70
Barros Borgoño, Luis, 122
Barros Errázuriz, Alfredo, 130
Battista, Ana María, 59
Beauchef, Jorge, 68, 69
Bello, Andrés, 12, 30, 74–80, 84, 87
Bengoa, José, 49
Bernaschina, Mario, 109, 111, 114, 115
Biblioteca del Congreso Nacional (National Library of Congress), 9, 180
Bilbao, Francisco, 40, 73
Blanco Encalada, Manuel, 66
Blanco White, José María, 44
Bloch, Marc, 13
Boas, George, 4
Bolívar, Simón, 16, 59
Bordalí, Andrés, 9
Bourbon, House of, 25
Brahm, Enrique, 136, 219
Bravo, Bernardino, 29–32, 136, 139
Bush, George H. W., 152

Caldera, Hugo, 158
Campos Harriet, Fernando, 22, 25–27, 98
Carmona, Carlos, 167, 171, 173, 233, 235, 236

CAMBRIDGE STUDIES IN LAW AND SOCIETY

Institutional Inequality and the Mobilization of the Family and Medical Leave Act: Rights on Leave
Catherine R. Albiston

Authoritarian Rule of Law: Legislation, Discourse and Legitimacy in Singapore
Jothie Rajah

Law and Development and the Global Discourses of Legal Transfers
John Gillespie and Pip Nicholson (eds.)

Law against the State: Ethnographic Forays into Law's Transformations
Julia Eckert, Brian Donahoe, Christian Strümpell, and Zerrin Özlem Biner (eds.)

Transnational Legal Ordering and State Change
Gregory C. Shaffer (ed.)

Legal Mobilization under Authoritarianism: The Case of Post-Colonial Hong Kong
Waikeung Tam

Complementarity in the Line of Fire: The Catalysing Effect of the International Criminal Court in Uganda and Sudan
Sarah M. H. Nouwen

Political and Legal Transformations of an Indonesian Polity: The Nagari from Colonisation to Decentralisation
Franz von Benda-Beckmann and Keebet von Benda-Beckmann

Pakistan's Experience with Formal Law: An Alien Justice
Osama Siddique

Human Rights under State-Enforced Religious Family Laws in Israel, Egypt, and India
Yüksel Sezgin

Why Prison?
David Scott (ed.)

Law's Fragile State: Colonial, Authoritarian, and Humanitarian Legacies in Sudan
Mark Fathi Massoud

Rights for Others: The Slow Home-Coming of Human Rights in the Netherlands
Barbara Oomen

European States and their Muslim Citizens: The Impact of Institutions on Perceptions and Boundaries
John R. Bowen, Christophe Bertossi, Jan Willem Duyvendak, and Mona Lena Krook (eds.)

Environmental Litigation in China: A Study in Political Ambivalence
Rachel E. Stern

Indigeneity and Legal Pluralism in India: Claims, Histories, Meanings
Pooja Parmar

Paper Tiger: Law, Bureaucracy and the Developmental State in Himalayan India
Nayanika Mathur

Religion, Law and Society
Russell Sandberg

The Experiences of Face Veil Wearers in Europe and the Law
Eva Brems (ed.)

The Contentious History of the International Bill of Human Rights
Christopher N. J. Roberts

Transnational Legal Orders
Terence C. Halliday and Gregory Shaffer (eds.)

Lost in China? Law, Culture and Society in Post-1997 Hong Kong
Carol A. G. Jones

Security Theology, Surveillance and the Politics of Fear
Nadera Shalhoub-Kevorkian

Opposing the Rule of Law: How Myanmar's Courts Make Law and Order
Nick Cheesman

The Ironies of Colonial Governance: Law, Custom and Justice in Colonial India
James Jaffe

The Clinic and the Court: Law, Medicine and Anthropology
Ian Harper, Tobias Kelly, and Akshay Khanna (eds.)

A World of Indicators: The Making of Government Knowledge through Quantification
Richard Rottenburg, Sally Engle Merry, Sung-Joon Park, and Johanna Mugler (eds.)

Contesting Immigration Policy in Court: Legal Activism and its Radiating Effects in the United States and France
Leila Kawar

The Quiet Power of Indicators: Measuring Governance, Corruption, and Rule of Law
Sally Engle Merry, Kevin Davis, and Benedict Kingsbury (eds.)

Revisiting the Law and Governance of Trafficking, Forced Labor and Modern Slavery
Prabha Kotiswaran (ed.)

Incitement on Trial: Prosecuting International Speech Crimes
Richard Ashby Wilson

Criminalizing Children: Welfare and the State in Australia
David McCallum

Global Lawmakers: International Organizations in the Crafting of World Markets
Susan Block-Lieb and Terence C. Halliday

Duties to Care: Dementia, Relationality and Law
Rosie Harding

Insiders, Outsiders, Injuries, and Law: Revisiting "The Oven Bird's Song"
Mary Nell Trautner (ed.)

Hunting Justice: Displacement, Law, and Activism in the Kalahari
Maria Sapignoli

Injury and Injustice: The Cultural Politics of Harm and Redress
Anne Bloom, David M. Engel, and Michael McCann (eds.)

Ruling Before the Law: The Politics of Legal Regimes in China and Indonesia
William Hurst

The Powers of Law: A Comparative Analysis of Sociopolitical Legal Studies
Mauricio García-Villegas

A Sociology of Justice in Russia
Marina Kurkchiyan and Agnieszka Kubal (eds.)

Constituting Religion: Islam, Liberal Rights, and the Malaysian State
Tamir Moustafa

The Invention of the Passport: Surveillance, Citizenship and the State, Second Edition
John C. Torpey

Law's Trials: The Performance of Legal Institutions in the US "War on Terror"
Richard L. Abel

Law's Wars: The Fate of the Rule of Law in the US "War on Terror"
Richard L. Abel

Transforming Gender Citizenship: The Irresistible Rise of Gender Quotas in Europe
Eléonore Lépinard and Ruth Rubio-Marín (eds.)

Muslim Women's Quest for Justice: Gender, Law and Activism in India
Mengia Hong Tschalaer

Children as "Risk": Sexual Exploitation and Abuse by Children and Young People
Anne-Marie McAlinden

The Legal Process and the Promise of Justice: Studies Inspired by the Work of Malcolm Feeley
Jonathan Simon, Rosann Greenspan, and Hadar Aviram

Sovereign Exchanges: Gifts, Trusts, Reparations, and Other Fetishes of International Solidarity
Grégoire Mallard

Measuring Justice: Quantitative Accountability and the National Prosecuting Authority in South Africa
Johanna Mugler

Negotiating the Power of NGOs: Women's Legal Rights in South Africa
Reem Wael

Indigenous Water Rights in Law and Regulation: Lessons from Comparative Experience
Elizabeth Jane Macpherson

The Edge of Law: Legal Geographies of a War Crimes Court
Alex Jeffrey

Everyday Justice: Law, Ethnography, and Injustice
Sandra Brunnegger

The Uncounted: Politics of Data in Global Health
Sara L. M. Davis

Transnational Legal Ordering of Criminal Justice
Gregory Shaffer and Ely Aaronson

Five Republics and One Tradition
Pablo Ruiz-Tagle

Lightning Source UK Ltd.
Milton Keynes UK
UKHW022353290922
409682UK00004B/21